Edward Whelan

The Union of the British Provinces

1864

Edward Whelan

The Union of the British Provinces
1864

ISBN/EAN: 9783337178611

Printed in Europe, USA, Canada, Australia, Japan

Cover: Foto ©ninafisch / pixelio.de

More available books at **www.hansebooks.com**

INDEX.

	Page.
INTRODUCTION.	
THE CONFERENCE OF DELEGATES AT CHARLOTTETOWN,	1
Preliminary Observations — Resolutions of the Maritime Legislatures,	1—4
NAMES OF THE DELEGATES,	5
BANQUET IN CHARLOTTETOWN,	6
Speeches of Lieut. Governor Dundas, of Honorables Colonel Gray, J. A. McDonald, George E. Cartier, (Canada); Dr. Tupper, Adams G. Archibald, (Nova Scotia); John M. Johnson, Col. Hamilton Gray, (New Brunswick,); William McDougall, (Provincial Secretary, Canada,) Hons. J. Longworth and T. Heath Haviland, and F. Brecken, Esqr., (P. E. I.)	7—17
THE DELEGATION CONFERENCE IN NOVA SCOTIA,	17
BANQUET IN HALIFAX,	18
Speeches of Lieut. Governor McDonnell, of Sir James Hope, Vice Admiral—of the Hon. Dr. Tupper, (Nova Scotia); Hon. G. E. Cartier, Hon. G. Brown, (Canada;)—Hon. S. L. Tilley, (New Brunswick)—Hon. Col. Gray, (P. E. I.)—Hon. J. A. McDonald (Canada)—Hon. A. T. Galt, (Canada),	18—49
THE DELEGATES IN NEW BRUNSWICK,	49
PUBLIC DINNER AT ST. JOHN, N. B.,	50
Speeches of the Hon. G. E. Cartier—Hon. George Brown—Hon. Charles Tupper—Hon. Col. J. H. Gray—Hon. George Coles—Hon. A. T. Galt,	50—57
THE VOYAGE TO QUEBEC,	57—59
THE CONFERENCE AT QUEBEC,	60
Names of the Delegates from Canada, and from all the Maritime Provinces—Preliminary Arrangements of the Conference,	60—61
"DRAWING ROOM" AND RECEPTION OF THE DELEGATES,	62
INVITATIONS TO FESTIVITIES,	ib.
Ball in the Parliament Buildings,	ib.

PUBLIC DINNER BY BOARD OF TRADE, ... 63
　　Speeches of Delegates — Speech of Chairman of Board of
　　Trade — Speeches of Hon. Dr. Tupper—Hon. S. L. Tilley—
　　Hon. Mr. Carter, (Newfoundland)—Hon. Col. Gray, (P. E.
　　Island)—Chairman of Board of Trade—Hon. Sir E. P. Tache
　　—Mr. Forsyth—Hon. Mr. Galt, ... 65—80
Continued Meetings of the Conference — Ball at Madame
　　Tessier's, ... 80

VISIT TO, AND ADDRESS FROM, LAVAL UNIVERSITY, ... 81

THE BACHELORS' BALL, ... 83

DEPARTURE FROM QUEBEC, ... 84

ARRIVAL IN MONTREAL .... ib.
　　Visit to Public Institutions—Conference—Ball, ... 84—85

PUBLIC BANQUET, (Montreal) .... 85—86
　　Speeches of Delegates and others — Speeches of Sir William
　　Fenwick Williams — Col. Dyde — Sir Richard MacDonnell—
　　Hon. Dr. Tupper — Hon. Mr. Archibald — Hon. Col. Gray,
　　(New Brunswick)—Hon. J. A. Shea, (Newfoundland)—Hon.
　　Col. Gray, (P. E I.)—Hon. E. Whelan — Hon. T. Heath
　　Haviland—Hon. G. E. Cartier—Hon. Mr. McGee—Hon. Mr.
　　Galt, ... 85—126

DEPARTURE FOR, AND ARRIVAL AT, OTTAWA, ... 126
　　River Scenery—Reception of the Delegates by the Mayor and
　　Corporation of Ottawa—Torchlight Procession—Speeches by
　　Honorable Messrs. J. A. McDonald and Charles Tupper—
　　Drive through the City—Visit to the Rideau Falls—Trip on
　　the Ottawa River—Visit to the Parliament Buildings, ... 126—129

THE DEJEUNER (at Ottawa,) 129
　　Description of Dejeuner—Speeches, by Hon. J. A. McDonald
　　—Mr. T. C. Clarke—Hon. W. A. Henry, (Nova Scotia,)—Hon.
　　J. M. Johnson, (New Brunswick)—Hon. George Coles, (P. E.
　　Island)—Hon. A. T. Galt, (Canada)—Mayor Dickinson—Col.
　　Gray, (P. E. Island,) .... 129—146

BALL AT OTTAWA, ... 146

DEPARTURE FOR TORONTO, ... ib.
　　Reception at Kingston, Belleville and Coburg—Dinner at
　　Kingston, by Mr. Brydges—Complimentary Remarks by Dr.
　　Tupper—Mr. Brydges' Speech in acknowledgment .... 147—148
　　Address from Mayor and Corporation of Belleville—Col. Gray's
　　Reply, ... 149—151

INDEX.

Address from Mayor and Corporation of Coburg—Col. Gray's Reply,..151—153
Torchlight Procession at Coburg—Hospitalities at the Residence of the Hon. Solicitor General,.........................153

ARRIVAL AT TORONTO,......................................*ib.*
Brilliant Reception—Torchlight Procession—Address from the Mayor and Corporation—Reply—Addresses at the Queen's Hotel,..153—155
Visit to the College of Upper Canada—Address from the Principal and Alumni—Col. Gray's Reply ;—Visit to Osgood Hall ;—Visit to the University—Eloquent Address from the Rev. Dr. McCaul, and Reply by Dr. Tupper—View of the Institution ;—Visit to the Normal School—Its great attractions,........156—161

THE BANQUET AT TORONTO,....................................161
Speeches by Mayor Medcalf, General Napier, Colonel Denison, Hon. Mr. Allan—by Hon. Mr. McCully, (Nova Scotia)—Hon. Charles Fisher, (New Brunswick)—Hon. Mr. Carter, (Newfoundland)—Hon. Edward Palmer, (P. E. Island)—Mr. Ross, (Red River)—Hon. George Brown, (Canada)—Hon. A.T.Galt, (Canada)..161—206

INSPECTION OF THE VOLUNTEERS,..............................206
Speches by General Napier and Colonel Gray,............207—209

THE PUBLIC BALL, (at Toronto)..............................209

DEPARTURE FROM TORONTO,....................................210
Reception of the Delegates at Hamilton, St. Catherine's and Clifton, and Visit to Niagara Falls,.......................210
Address at Hamilton — Reply by Hon. Mr. Tilley ; — Address from Board of Trade (Hamilton)—Reply by Hon. Mr. Shea ;—Address at St. Catherine's—Speech by Mr. McGiverin—Reply by Hon. Mr. Pope ;—Dinner at Clifton—Complimentary toast to Mr. Swinyard (Manager of the Great Western)—Mr. Swinyard's Reply ; — Visit to the Falls ;—Return to Toronto and Montreal ;—Concluding Remarks,........................210—217

APPENDIX—
Report of the Quebec Conference,........................219—231

INTRODUCTION.

The compilation of the following pages was commenced, during the past winter, at the request of several gentlemen who have taken a deep interest in the question of a Confederation of the British American Colonies. The Conferences held in the Maritime Provinces and in Canada, in connection with that question, in the autumn of 1864, have excited a great deal of public attention in Great Britain and America; and it has been considered, that—notwithstanding the confidential manner in which the proceedings of the Conferences were conducted—there should be some connected account of their meetings—of the times and places when and where they met—and of some of the leading incidents connected with the great business entrusted to them. The most important of these incidents were the utterances of the Delegates on important public occasions.

It has been the object of the Compiler to collect all the principal speeches delivered on those occasions. They contain valuable information bearing upon the interests of the Colonies; and nearly all abound with high-toned patriotic sentiments which entitle them to a more lasting record than could be allotted to them in the newspapers of the passing hour.

The speeches herein presented have been revised with much care. The Compiler has availed himself, in all cases where he could do so conveniently, of the polite attention of the speakers residing in the several Provinces, in assisting him to correct the errors that were necessarily attendant upon hastily prepared newspaper reports. This has certainly delayed the issuing of the present little work, but it is to be hoped that it may be all the more useful from the delay, as being more correct than otherwise it would be.

This little book makes no pretension to the dignity of authorship, and on that account it may not be supposed to be within the range of criticism. The Compiler cannot, however, but expect that those who look with an unfavorable eye on Confederation will find something to cavil at in these pages. It is the fashion of some persons—wise in their own conceit—to sneer at "after-dinner speeches" as altogether unworthy of consideration. Such speeches would, indeed, be entitled to the most contemptuous rejection if it were the practice amongst gentlemen to utter one thing at the festive board and mean another; but every intelligent reader knows that all public men of character and standing, in Europe and America, frequently make use of festive occasions for the utterance of their most sincere and honest convictions in reference to important public affairs. The best and most eloquent speeches known to the British Parliament are those which are delivered "after dinner;" and no one out of Bedlam would be mad enough to disparage them simply because the speakers "fared sumptuously" during the day. There is reason to apprehend that ere long we shall be infested with a brood of philosophers and physiologists who will be prepared to determine the value of a man's eloquence by the exact quantity he eats and drinks; the less of both, the more valuable his eloquence will be considered. A school of philosophers, who regard themselves as Financiers, have lately arisen, and are prepared to shew to the world what the expenditure and income of any given country will be, even to the fraction of a dollar, for a hundred years in advance of their age. Those ingenious Financiers appear to work their calculations with empty stomachs, as they are loudest in their complaints against those who make *their* deductions in a more comfortable condition at the festive board.

The progress of Confederation has, no doubt, been checked by the decision pronounced in New Brunswick at the late elections in that province. The cause is not, however, abandoned, nor are its advocates discouraged. The elections referred to, were influenced more by local interests and personal feeling than by a calm and intelligent consideration of the great Question. The people of New Brunswick will yet see it in its true light; and will not, it is to be hoped, continue as an obstacle to the accomplishment of a measure which affects the interests of half a continent—which has certainly met with the warm approval of an overwhelming majority of British Americans, when taken altogether—and which has received the liveliest encouragement from the press, the people, and the Government of Great Britain, who can have no other desire than to see the Colonies in that condition which would give assurance of their permanence and prosperity.

Charlottetown, P. E. Island, May, 1865. E. W.

UNION OF THE BRITISH PROVINCES.

THE CONFERENCE OF DELEGATES AT CHARLOTTETOWN.

The question of uniting the British American Colonies under one Legislature and one Government, or the greater question of forming them into a Confederation, somewhat after the model of the United States Government, but preserving the connection with the British Crown—has for more than ten years engaged the close attention of leading statesmen in all the Colonies—the chiefs of rival parties merging sectional considerations in the advocacy of the measure. The late Lord Durham had advocated it many years before in his celebrated Report on the affairs of British America; and there is no doubt that that Report was the incentive to an enquiry by Colonial Statesmen into the merits of a Legislative or Federal Union. In the Parliament of Nova Scotia the question of Union was discussed with singular ability in 1854, the Hon. Mr. Howe and the Hon. Mr. Johnston, leaders of the rival parties, although differing widely on questions of local policy, manifested a cordial agreement in their advocacy of a measure which they felt assured would be the means of constituting a great nation, by combining the elements of strength and wealth which all the British American Provinces possess. Since 1854, the great directors of public opinion in England, have, through their press, strenuously advocated the question of Union—statesmen occupying the highest places in the Imperial Cabinet, have, on public occasions, frequently done the same; and within the last three years it seems to have become the unalterable policy of the Crown towards the Colonies, to insist upon their uniting, in order to relieve Great Britain from the *whole* burthen of defending them in the event of any hostilities that might arise between the Mother Country and any Foreign Power. The subordinate question of Defence is, indeed, the one which may be said to have brought the primary question of Union to the position which it now occupies in the eyes of the world; and there is no doubt that if the Union be accomplished, it will be owing to the sentiment of self-preservation against the perils which now threaten the Colonies from abroad, more than to a belief in the pecuniary advantages which new commercial regulations would confer.

The first official action on the Union Question arose out of a resolution adopted unanimously by the Parliament of Nova Scotia on the 15th April, 1861. It was moved by the Provincial Secretary, and is as follows:—

"WHEREAS the subject of a Union of the North American Provinces, or of the Maritime Provinces of British America, has been from time to time mooted and discussed in all the Colonies;

"And whereas, while many advantages may be secured by such a Union, either of all these Provinces, or of a portion of them, many and serious obstacles are presented which can only be overcome by mutual consultation of the leading men of the Colonies, and by free communication with the Imperial Government: therefore *Resolved*, That His Excellency the Lieutenant Governor be respectfully requested to put himself in communication with His Grace the Colonial Secretary, and His Excellency the Governor General, and the Lieutenant Governors of the other North American Provinces, in order to ascertain the policy of Her Majesty's Government and the opinions of the other Colonies, with a view to an enlightened consideration of a question involving the highest interest, and upon which the public mind in all the Provinces ought to be set at rest.

"Which Resolution being seconded and put, was agreed to by the House."

This resolution, having been forwarded to the Colonial Office, was transmitted by the Duke of Newcastle in a despatch of the 6th July, 1862, to the Governor General, and to the Lieutenant Governors of the several Provinces; and in a separate despatch to the Lieutenant Governor of Nova Scotia, his Grace expressed his unqualified approval of the matter referred to in the resolution above quoted, whether the Union referred to should include amalgamation with Canada, or merely a Union of the Lower Provinces. Referring to both topics, "I am far from considering," said His Grace, "that they do not form a very proper subject for calm deliberation." Then cautiously saying that Her Majesty's Government was not prepared to announce any definite course of policy, on a question which seemed to originate with only one Province, the noble Duke expressed his own opinion on the question in the following words:—

"If a union, either partial or complete, should hereafter be proposed with the concurrence of all the Provinces to be united, I am sure that the matter would be weighed in this country both by the public, by Parliament, and by Her Majesty's Government with no other feeling than an anxiety to discern and to promote any course which might be the most conducive to the prosperity, the strength, and the harmony of all the British communities in North America."

Thus prompted to consider the question of Union, the Lieut. Governors of the several Provinces brought it under the notice of their respective Legislatures, at the commencement of their Sessions of 1864, with the view to the appointment of Delegates to confer upon the practicability of establishing a Legislative Union between the Maritime Provinces. The question was discussed in the several Legislatures, with calmness and ability, by the leading men of the contending parties, and without reference to local party issues. The discussion elicited, however—and more particularly in the Prince Edward Island Legislature—a strong feeling of dissatisfaction at the proposal for a *Legislative* Union; but still the Legislature of the Island felt that they could not honourably keep aloof from the proposed Conference, and on the 18th of April passed, but not without a division, the following resolution, which is identical with the resolutions, aiming at the same object, passed in the Legislatures of Nova Scotia and New Brunswick:—

"RESOLVED, That His Excellency the Lieutenant Governor be authorized to appoint Delegates (not to exceed five), to confer with Delegates who may be appointed by the Governments of Nova Scotia and New Brunswick, for the purpose of discussing the expediency of a Union of the three Provinces of Nova Scotia, New Brunswick and Prince Edward Island, under one Government and Legislature, the report of the said Delegates to be laid before the Legislature of this Colony, before any further action shall be taken in regard to the proposed question."

In conformity with the resolutions referred to, Delegates were appointed by the Governments of Nova Scotia, New Brunswick and Prince Edward Island. Canada was at this time, without previous concert with the Maritime Provinces, engaged in considering the necessity of a change in its constitution, so as to reconcile, if possible, the conflicting interests of the Eastern and Western Divisions of the Province; and it was deemed an appropriate time to bring the question of Colonial Union generally, which would embrace Canada, under the notice of the proposed Conference. With this view the Canadian Government solicited permission to be present by Delegation at the Conference. Their request was most cordially complied with; and on the 1st September, the whole of the Delegates met according to previous arrangement, at Charlottetown.

THE DELEGATES.

NOVA SCOTIA was represented by—
— The Hon. Charles Tupper, M.P.P., Provincial Secretary.
" Wm. A. Henry, M.P.P., Attorney General.
" Robert Barry Dickie, M.L.C.
" Jonathan McCully, M.L.C.
" Adams G. Archibald, M.P.P.

NEW BRUNSWICK was represented by—
The Hon. S. L. Tilley, M.P.P., Provincial Secretary.
" John M. Johnston, M.P.P., Attorney General.
" John Hamilton Gray, M.P.P.
" Edward B. Chandler, M.L.C.
" W. H. Steeves, M.L.C.

PRINCE EDWARD ISLAND was represented by—
The Hon. Col. Gray, M.P.P., President of the Executive Council.
" Edward Palmer, M.L.C., Attorney General.
" W. H. Pope, M.P.P., Colonial Secretary.
" George Coles, M.P.P.
" A. A. Macdonald, M.L.C.

NEWFOUNDLAND sent no Delegates to this Conference.

CANADA was represented by—
The Hon. John A. McDonald, M.P.P., Attorney General, Upper Canada.
" George Brown, M.P.P., President of Executive Council.
— " Alexander T. Galt, M.P.P., Minister of Finance.
— " George E. Cartier, M.P.P., Attorney General, Lower Canada,
" Hector L. Langevin, M.P.P., Solicitor General, of Lower Canada.
" William McDougall, Provincial Secretary.
" Thomas D'Arcy McGee, M.P.P., Minister of Agriculture.

The Canadian Ministers—not having been delegated to consider the question of a *Legislative* Union, to which the attention of the other Delegates was specially directed by a resolution of their respective Assemblies—were informally present at the Conference.

Although no report of the Charlottetown Conference has yet been given to the public, it is well understood that the proposal to unite the Maritime Provinces under one Government and one Legislature was deemed impracticable; but the opinion of the Delegates was unanimous that a Union upon a larger basis might be effected; and with the view of considering the feasibilty of such a Union in all its details, it was proposed by the Canadian Ministers to hold a further Conference at Quebec, with the consent of the Governments of the Lower Provinces, and at such time as might be named by His Excellency the Governor General. This arrangement was agreed to, and the Conference at Charlottetown suspended its deliberations.

BANQUET IN CHARLOTTETOWN—SPEECHES OF DELEGATES AND OTHERS.

Before leaving Charlottetown, a Committee composed of members of the Executive Council of Prince Edward Island, and some of the most prominent citizens of the capital, had made arrangement for entertaining at a Ball and Banquet the distinguished Delegates from the other Provinces, together with the Lady friends and others who had accompanied them. The entertainment was given in the Provincial Building at Charlottetown on the evening of the 8th September. The members of both branches of the Legislature, as well as the principal office-holders in the Colony, were invited as the guests of the Committee; and no expense or trouble was spared to make the entertainment worthy of the occasion, creditable to the Colony, and acceptable to its guests, who were unanimous in expressing their appreciation of the generous spirit which prompted and characterized the festivity. At the Banquet several of the Delegates gave utterance to their sentiments on the great question of Union—all declaring their adhesion to that measure, pointing out its advantages, and urging its adoption. The speeches were not reported as fully as could be desired, owing to the inexperience of the Reporter; but they were considered accurate in so far as they conveyed the spirit of the remarks of the different speakers.

The main object of this unpretending Compilation is to preserve the sentiments of the Delegates and other prominent public men, uttered on public occasions, while the former were employed in the duties of their mission in the Lower Provinces and in Canada; and Charlottetown being the first place where an occasion of this kind presented itself, such a report of the speeches there delivered as can now be obtained, should, of course, appear first. After the usual loyal toasts were honoured in the customary way, the health of the Governor General and that of the Governors of the Maritime Provinces, were mentioned in the complimentary style which time-honored usage has prescribed.

George Dundas, Esquire, Lieutenant Governor of Prince Edward Island, returned thanks for the toast, on behalf of His Excellency the Governor General, and likewise on his own behalf and that of his brother Governors in the other Provinces. He expressed great satisfaction at the auspicious meeting of so many distinguished gentlemen from the neighbouring Provinces, whose Convention would, he trusted, be conducive to the best interests of Her Majesty's subjects on this side of the Atlantic—enabling them to form, as it would, a more extensive acquaintance with our people and their resources than could be acquired in our present isolated condition, and thus greatly enlarge the commercial and social intercourse between the several Provinces.

The next toast was that of " Our distinguished Guests, the Delegates from Canada, Nova Scotia, and New Brunswick."

Colonel Gray, the leader of the Government of Prince Edward Island, who was Chairman on this occasion, said, in proposing the above toast, he had no doubt but that he was giving utterance to the sentiments of all the people of this Colony, in expressing pleasure and entire gratification at this visit to our Island home of some of the ablest statesmen of Canada and the adjoining Provinces. He would not, he said, attempt to make a speech, as he was proud to know that those who had honorably assembled to welcome their distinguished visitors would now be addressed by some of the representatives of two of the greatest nations of the world, whom he had the honor and extreme pleasure of seeing around him. One remark, however, he would make, and it was this, that he sincerely and confidently believed that this visit would be productive of much good, and serve as the happy harbinger of such a union of sentiment and interests among the three and a half millions of freemen, who now inhabit British America, as neither time nor change could forever destroy.

The Hon. JOHN A. McDONALD, Attorney General for Upper Canada, on rising to respond to the toast, was loudly applauded. He said the people of these lower Provinces and of Canada were separated too long. Our hearts were one, our loyalty and attachment to the throne of England one, and we were one ancestry—except a portion of Canada—and yet, we were unfortunately severed from each other by the present construction of our respective constitutions and governments. He had, however, every reason to believe that the result of the Convention which held its sittings in Charlottetown for the past week, would lead to the formation and establishment of such a Federation of all the British North American Provinces as would tend very materially to enhance their individual and collective prosperity, politically, commercially, and socially ; and also give them, in their united manhood, that national prowess and strength which would make them at least the fourth nation on the face of the globe. He then alluded to the uninterrupted pleasure and happiness which he, in common with all the Delegates, felt at their visit to this lovely Island. He said he appreciated the hospitality and kindness which they all received at the hands of their co-Delegates and others in this place; and he felt assured that the very favorable impressions made on the hearts and minds of all the Canadian gentlemen, whether married or unmarried, would lead to other, and if possible, more happy visits to this charming place.

The Hon. GEORGE ETIENNE CARTIER, Attorney General for Lower Canada, rose also to return thanks for the toast, and was loudly cheered. He felt reluctance, he said, in following his able colleague, the learned Attorney General for Upper Canada, and after some playful badinage on the remarks of the latter in reference to the ladies, he said, it was a gratifying fact for the British American Provinces that they could claim, as their ancestry, two of the greatest nations of the world. He, in common with his countrymen in Canada East, claimed to be the descendants of the inhabitants of old France. He said we are Frenchmen as to race, but Frenchmen of the old *regime*. He spoke of a recent visit to France, and said when present at a meeting of the French Academy of Paris, a few years ago, he was asked how had the French in Lower Canada managed to maintain their nationality? His reply was, that it was because they separated from France before the French Revolution. Had it not been for that fact their nationality would have been lost in the convulsions which followed that period of their country's history. They owed the preservation of their nationality to the free institutions which they had received from England. It was a happy day, in his opinion, when England and France fought side by side as brothers in the Crimean war. That was the first time since the 12th century that they did battle together in one common cause; and he was proud to say that the French Canadians to-day rejoice as much at the prosperity of England as that of France. As to the question of Colonial Union, he said, though the Convention held its meetings with closed doors, and he was not at liberty to state all that transpired, yet this much he would say, that he hoped and believed the result of their deliberations would end in a grand Confederation of the British Provinces, such as must prove beneficial to all, and an injury to none. They (the Delegates) met to enquire whether it were possible for the Provinces, from their present fragmentary and isolated materials, to form a Nation or Kingdom; Canada of herself, though she was a large Country, with a vast and extensive interior, could not make a nation; neither could the Maritime Provinces of themselves become a kingdom. It was, therefore, essentially necessary that those national fragments and resources of all the Provinces should be concentrated and combined, in order that they, in their trade, intelligence, and national power and prosperity, might be rated as at least the fourth nation of the world. He concluded his address by complimenting the ladies, and referred to Francis the First, King of France, who was a chivalrous and brave King—for, said he, chivalry and bravery always accompany each other—who had said that festivities like those we had now the honor and pleasure to enjoy, without the ladies, was like a year without a Spring, and Spring without flowers. This, remarked the hon. and learned gentleman, cannot be said of the present assembly, for charming flowers were in their blooming beauty all around us, and he would fain wish that the flowers of Canada had the advantage of a contrast. After repeating his thanks for the honour conveyed by the toast, the learned gentleman resumed his seat amidst great cheering.

The Hon. Dr TUPPER, Provincial Secretary of Nova Scotia, said he felt that he would not do justice to the people of P. E. Island did he not render, on his own behalf as well as for all the Delegates present, his sincere and heartfelt thanks to the Government of this Colony and all classes of the community, for the generous hospitality and goodwill manifested by them towards their brethren from the other Provinces, who were now assembled at Charlottetown, on a mission, the momentous character of which he would not then attempt to describe. The deliberations of the Convention, he said, were conducted apart from the public, not because there was any desire to conceal its proceedings, but in order that the confidential character of the Delegation might lead to speedier results. He felt assured that all would endorse the sentiment that it was our duty and interest to cement the Colonies together by every tie that can add to their greatness. A Union of the North American Provinces would elevate their position, consolidate their influence, and advance their interests; and at the same time continue their fealty to their Mother Country and their Queen, which fealty is the glory of us all. The British American statesman who does not feel it his duty to do all in his power to unite, politically, socially, and commercially, the British Provinces, is unworthy of his position, and is unequal to the task committed to him. We know full well that the strong arm of England is ever ready to be outstretched in our defence, should the Colonies ever have the misfortune to require its powerful aid in defensive operations. He was fully convinced that the great question of Colonial Union did not depend on the fluctuations incident to political parties. He believed this question would be safe if the political wheel in any of the Colonies were turned to-morrow. There were those in the ranks of the Opposition in all the Colonies who, he had no doubt, would lend their abilities to the advocacy of every measure calculated to unite the energies or elevate the status of the British North American Provinces. If we would preserve the constitution under which we have the happiness to live, and that British connection so highly appreciated by us all, we should lend our aid for the consummation of that important event, the Union of the Provinces.

The Hon. ADAMS G. ARCHIBALD, Leader of Her Majesty's Opposition in Nova Scotia, followed Dr. Tupper, and said he would assure all, that in regard to this question they in Nova Scotia had no Government—no Opposition; they were all one on this important subject. They want, as the Hon. Mr. Cartier very properly observed, to bind the Colonies together, and make of them one nation. Nova Scotia and New Brunswick feel that by joining together they can become what in their present separated condition they never can be. Who but will admit that the man who five years ago would predict the present condition of the American States, would be called a false prophet—hence the necessity of their joining together. It would be the proudest day in the history of British America, when they would unite hand in hand, and form a nation, which, in all the elements that constitute real greatness, might be ranked as the third or fourth on the face of the globe. Well, then, said he, may we be proud of the inauguration of a movement, which at no very distant day, will be looked upon as one of the greatest and most important events of the present age. He then alluded to the harmony and good-will which prevailed during all the deliberations of the Convention—in proof of which he adduced the fact that the Conference was about to adjourn to Halifax, lest Nova Scotia and New Brunswick should, without further notice, become annexed to P. E. Island.

The Hon. JOHN M. JOHNSON, Attorney General of New Brunswick, returned thanks on behalf of that Province which he was appointed to represent in the Conference Chamber. He said he would like to make the Union one of the heart as well as of the understanding. We have the happiness to belong to a country second to none for the beneficence of her rule, the bravery of her sons, and the extent of her power—a country which differs materially from that across the border. The constitution under which we have the honor and happiness to be governed keeps constantly expanding with the wants of the people. Its elastic qualities can be adapted to the growing requirements of its people. Hence the superiority over that of the States of America. The defects of their constitution have led to the present lamentable state of civil war into which they have been plunged. Well may we boast of the glorious constitution of old England. He concluded his remarks by expressing his gratification at the progress which had marked this Colony since his last visit some twenty years ago. It had been said, that when you see one scene on the Island you see all, such being the sameness of its scenery, and its characteristic slowness. This, from his own personal knowledge, he could contradict; for that which twenty years ago might be considered as barely attractive was now extremely captivating—that which was then undeveloped and unimproved, has grown in beautiful proportions, rendering Prince Edward Island a place of no mean importance in British America, and one also which would be very materially benefitted in all its relations by its union with the other Provinces.

The Hon. Col. JOHN HAMILTON GRAY, M.P.P., for St.

John, New Brunswick, and one also of the New Brunswick Delegates, then rose and expressed in chaste and eloquent terms his high appreciation of the hospitality of the people of Prince Edward Island, which, he said, "would not be readily effaced from the memories of the Delegates." Alluding to the influence of Union on the affairs of Prince Edward Island, Mr. Gray observed that one of the leading features of a Colonial Union would be an adjustment of the Land Question, which had for upwards of half a century retarded the progress of this Island. He was confident that whatever the nature of the Union might be, the difficulties under which the people of this Island had laboured relative to that long vexed question, would be forever settled. When, said the learned gentleman, the people of all British North America, should, with one voice, proclaim the Colonies united, and when their united talent and influence shall be exercised for the maintenance and advancement of their common interests, prosperity, and happiness, every barrier to their advancement would be removed. The greatest drawback to this Island was its land tenures; the removal of this grievance would certainly follow as the result of Colonial Union. The agriculturists of Prince Edward Island should, therefore be amongst the first to hail the day when British Colonial interests would be united against the continuation, any longer, of that system of Landlordism which has retarded and paralysed the energies of the farming population of the Colony.

Hon. WILLIAM McDOUGALL, Provincial Secretary of Canada, said the main object of this Convention was to secure unanimity of sentiment on the important question of a Federation of all British America. He spoke of the differences existing between Upper and Lower Canada, but said they had common aspirations in connection with this subject. They all considered the absolute necessity of uniting the Provinces into one grand Confederation. They had no desire to sever their connection with the Mother Country. Their rights and liberties would remain untouched. Their attachment to the throne and person of our beloved Sovereign the Queen would continue as unsullied as ever. All they wanted was a concentration of the wealth, talent, resources, and all the inherent elements which British Americans possess, and which, when blended in one common country, would be capable of forming a Nation possessing no ordinary capabilities. He then said that, being an agriculturist, and feeling interested in that important branch of Colonial industry, he, in company with some friends, had taken a drive through a portion of [th]is Island since his arrival here, and was much pleased, [an]d he might add agreeably disappointed at the agricul[tu]ral prosperity which met his view. The fertility of the [so]il, the salubrity of the climate, and the healthful appear[an]ce of the inhabitants, are indeed unsurpassed in any [p]ortion of Her Majesty's Colonial possessions. And he was free to admit that he would return to his Canadian home considerably subdued from what he had witnessed of agricultural science and skill on this lovely Island.

The toasts which followed that in compliment to the Delegates, elicited speeches of a somewhat general character, and it is unnecessary to reproduce them here even in the limited proportions which they occupy in the local journals. But in all cases they made some reference to the Union Question; and it will not be out of place, to give short extracts from some of the speeches made by the leading public men on this occasion, who, though not Delegates, fully coincided in opinion with those who were.

The Hon. JOHN LONGWORTH, M.P.P., and Member of the Executive Council, in his capacity as Vice Chairman, proposed the toast of the "Army and Navy," and in doing so, made some appropriate preliminary remarks, and then observed: It is not necessary, that I should, dilate upon the prowess of our country's arms, or upon her military or naval achievements of past days, or to show that those branches of the service are entitled to our highest considerations. We know that our country stands high in the scale of nations, that under her banners freedom is secured and the blessings of peace maintained and preserved to her people; and when we recognize the fact so forcibly referred to by our distinguished guest, Mr. Cartier, that Great Britain (including in the term Ireland, of course) and Imperial France, from one or other of which the distinguished statesmen whom we have the honor to entertain to-night derive their ancestry—countries which after long years of rivalry, were now happily united together in the bonds of what we hope may prove a lasting peace, and were now marching forward together in the foremost rank of civilization; and when we also reflect that the power and greatness to which our common country has attained is in a large measure due to the chivalrous bearing and indomitable courage of her sons, which have earned for them the respect of other nations—we could not but appreciate the merits of the military and naval power of Great Britain. He observed that we as Colonists, enjoying the rights and immunities of British subjects, could not but feel a just pride in forming a part of so great an empire; and, whatever the future destiny of these North American Colonies may be, whether linked together in a Federal Union or not, he felt assured that he spoke the sentiments of the inhabitants of this little Island, in common with those of the larger and more important sister Colonies, when he expressed the hope, that the tie which now so happily bound them to the parent country would long be preserved, and that they, her children, while endeavouring to emulate her in her moral and intellectual attributes, might continue to grow in national prosperity, and in loyal attachment to the Throne and Constitution of that Country.

Hon. T. H. HAVILAND, M.P.P., responded to this toast. He said that his profession was that of the pen, and not the sword, but if his country required it, he hoped that he would be found, like Hampden, ready to take up arms for the defence of his country. Slaves, said he, can never be made of the three and a-half millions of British North Americans, who are as brave and as loyal a people as the sun ever shone upon. A people, too, who, if they go together as their forefathers did in the days of Hampden, have nothing to fear from any foe. He alluded to the glorious constitution of old England as being the basis of our liberties—the revolution of Democracy—the current of which must be stemmed by the monarchial institutions of our common country. He spoke of the important character of the Convention—the momentous nature of its deliberations—and its effects upon the future destinies of the Colonies. He alluded to the superior knowledge and practical experience of the distinguished Delegates from Canada and the lower Provinces. He believed, from all that he could learn, that the Provinces would, ere long, be one great country or nation, from the Pacific to the Atlantic. Never, said he, was there such an important meeting as this held before in the history of British America; and it may yet be said that here, in little Prince Edward Island, was that Union formed which has produced one of the greatest nations on the face of God's earth.

The next toast, which enunciated the noble sentiment of " Fraternal Feeling " between all British Americans, having been proposed, was responded to by FREDERICK DE ST. CROIX BRECKEN, Esquire, M.P.P., for Charlottetown, who said that after hearing some of the most talented and experienced statesmen of Canada, Nova Scotia and New Brunswick, on the grave question which engaged their attention for the past week, he felt that it would be presumptuous on his part to attempt a speech on the subject. He could not, however, refrain from expressing the gratification he experienced at hearing from their distinguished visitors how favourably they were impressed with what they had seen of the Island, and that they would return to their homes with new and enlarged ideas of our capabilities. It would appear from the remarks of some of the gentlemen that they were under the impression that some wooing and courting was necessary to induce us to join hands with the other Provinces. He would, however, assure them that we had no prejudices to overcome. We viewed the British North American Provinces as a portion of one great family, who owed and were bound to pay common allegiance to our Noble Queen. This was not a question for bringing foreign elements together; he regarded it rather in the light of a family arrangement, in which the Island, as the youngest and smallest member, naturally looked after its own interest. He believed that at present public opinion in this Colony was adverse to a Union, but this might arise from a misapprehension of the question.

What is required is to convince the people that their real and substantial interests will be advanced by the change ; they will then lend a willing ear to the proposition. Much as the people of Prince Edward Island value the privilege of having the entire control of their own affairs, and highly as they esteem the present Representative of their Sovereign, they would, if once satisfied that their condition would be improved, willingly yield up the little paraphernalia of a very little Government for the more respectable and powerful *status* of being part of Confederated British North America. He concluded his remarks by observing that whether a Union of the Colonies be effected or not, by the present Conference, he felt confident that beneficial results must flow from the interchange of sentiments and opinions that had taken place in the Conference Chamber, as well as at the festive board.

Several other speeches were delivered at the Banquet, but they were not of sufficient importance, as connected with the Union Question, to require a place here.

THE DELEGATION CONFERENCE IN NOVA SCOTIA.

The Canadian and the other Provincial Delegates having left Charlottetown on Friday morning, the 9th September, in the beautiful steamship *Victoria*, belonging to the Canadian Government, which was specially detailed and appointed for the service of the Delegates—they arrived in Halifax on the following day, where the Delegates again met in Council on Saturday the 10th September. The meeting being a *pro forma* one, no business was done to change, in the least degree, the character of the Charlottetown Conference. Every consideration was reserved for the then projected scheme of Confederation, which the Ministers of Canada proposed to submit in all its details at Quebec.

BANQUET IN HALIFAX—SPEECHES.

In order to afford, however, to some of the statesmen of Canada, New Brunswick, and Prince Edward Island, a further opportunity of explaining their views on the Union question, in a City of greater importance, size and wealth than Charlottetown, where the explanation could reach a larger number of the whole community, the Delegates of Nova Scotia entertained them at a sumptuous Banquet, in the Dining Hall of the Halifax Hotel, on Monday evening, the 12th September. The Hon. Charles Tupper, Provincial Secretary of Nova Scotia, acted as Chairman, and the Hon. W. A. Henry as Vice Chairman. His Excellency the Lieut. Governor of the Province, and His Excellency the Vice Admiral of the North American and West Indian station, graced the occasion by their presence. There were in attendance also, the Chief Justice, the President of the Legislative Council, several members of both branches of the Legislature, and many prominent persons connected with the public and learned institutions of the Province.

After disposing of the usual loyal toasts in reference to the Royal Family, the Chairman proposed, in a few eloquent and well chosen sentences the health of—

The Lieutenant Governor, Sir RICHARD GRAVES MCDONNELL, C.B., who, after expressing his thanks for the honor thus conferred, and for the complimentary remarks of the Chairman, proceeded to say:—It would give me very great satisfaction were I to realize in the future course of my administration one half of what the Provincial Secretary has ventured to anticipate; but whatever I might wish to effect, or whatever any individual might hope to accomplish, is nothing in comparison to that which a free and intelligent people have it in their own power to accomplish for themselves. (Cheers.) I have had some experience, gentlemen, in the administration of public affairs, and have at all events been able to learn this during my term of office—that there is no greater mistake in governing than governing too much. In a country like this, whose institutions have grown up under the auspices of the British throne and constitution—the freest ever known in history—a Governor must rely on his Ministry and on the people whose representatives they are, if he hopes to effect any real public benefit. Yet whilst he looks to the Ministry and to the people for assistance, it is his duty to aid by every means in his power the development of the intellect and education of the country, so that if power be given to the masses they may so use it as to promote the general happiness and prosperity of the country. Therefore I feel that I am here in the discharge particularly of that duty, and I should be very sorry indeed if I had been absent on this occasion, which is so calculated to be pre-eminently serviceable, by leading the people of Nova Scotia to look beyond the limited horizon of every day life and take a survey of the general interests of all British America. As I stated when I had the great pleasure of meeting several representative men from the sister Provinces, on a recent occasion, it is the special duty of the Governor of the Colony which they visit to countenance re-unions such as this, and to be present with you. I cannot hope and certainly have no wish to divest myself altogether of that representative capacity which, whether I will or not, attaches to me, within the limits of Nova Scotia; and I now prize it the more as giving me the privilege of expressing to your guests this evening, though feebly, on the part of the community at large of which for the time being I am the head, the pleasure which I know the whole Province experiences at our having with us, and under such special circumstances, such distinguished men as we have to-night. (Loud cheers.) I feel, Mr. Chairman, that it is impossible for us to entertain in this room, or to meet in social intercourse, those who are so decidedly representative men of the British Colonies—and some of whose names before I expected to be among you had been familiar to me as historical names on this continent—without deriving from the mutual interchange of thought and experience some considerable advantage. It is impossible that such men should come here to discuss the questions on which they have been deliberating without disseminating among us larger views, which must in due time—sooner or later— bear their appropriate, and I hope fortunate, fruits. Nevertheless in my position you may expect that I should feel some reserve in speaking on that subject. There is, however, one great pleasure which any representative of the British Crown must feel—and very unlike what he must have often felt in the old days of our colonial history—viz., that no man is now really a representative of that crown, or of the feelings which animate Her Majesty's government, unless he has at heart the interests of the people among whom he is placed, and unless he be determined to promote these interests by all the means in his power. Therefore, gentlemen, I feel in that capacity there is very little reserve necessary on my part when I say in bidding you welcome that whatever may be the result of the deliberations of the delegates of the British Provinces, the Crown of England and the British Government have but one object in view, namely; to give the most indulgent consideration to whatever plan you yourselves may devise with a reasonable hope and prospect of promoting the social welfare and material progress of Her Majesty's subjects here. I have already alluded to the change which has come over the colonial administration in late years—how very different it is from the days when we lost one of the finest portions of the earth, the neighboring States, through what would now be considered very great ignorance of the first principles of government, and very culpable mismanagement. Any gentleman serving Her Majesty in the capacity that I do, must feel very differently from what one would in former days. He is not sent out to build up or maintain any monopoly here for the benefit of parties in England. He has no such mission now; and I have no hesitation in saying that Her Majesty's Government, though for obvious reasons unlikely to initiate any scheme of union amongst you, yet looks with an affectionate and parental interest on the proceedings which you have initiated. Though there may be a difference of opinion as to the measures which you are considering, Her Majesty's Government, equally with yourselves, is desirous that you should agree upon some unity of action, as to many matters in which you have a community of interest. Her Majesty's Government have not forbidden me to say this much; and I believe it is its intention to give the most

UNION OF THE BRITISH PROVINCES. 21

favourable consideration to the result of the deliberations of the gentlemen who are now around this Board. I cannot help adding, as being personally more or less identified with Nova Scotia, that I trust whatever project may hereafter be submitted to the united wisdom of the Legislatures of the different Provinces, in case these deliberations ever ripen so far as to bear the fruit of a distinct proposition—that it will be such as will give the maritime provinces a worthy and adequate position. (Cheers.) At all events, their geographical position and their identity of interest point to some more intimate union amongst themselves at least. Should that be accomplished in the first instance, I am sure our Canadian fellow-countrymen would not less willingly receive us when representing larger revenues, and larger territories, and larger populations— all of which are matters which could not but have an effect even with a people so disinterested as those of Canada are. (Cheers and laughter.)

The toast of the "Army and Navy" having been proposed by the Chairman, who referred, in a few felicitous remarks to the vast importance of these Services in maintaining, as they would do, when the hour of peril came, the connection between England and her Colonies—and the toast having been honoured with the usual enthusiasm, it was responded to, on behalf of the Army, by Commissary General ROUTH; and on behalf of the Navy, by—

His Excellency SIR JAMES HOPE, K.C.B., Vice Admiral on the North American and West Indian Station. After expressing his thanks for the toast, His Excellency said: I am glad I have been able to be present, not simply on account of the personal gratification which is afforded me of making the acquaintance of so many gentlemen with whom I could hardly have hoped to meet under ordinary circumstances, but because not long from England I think that I may venture to say to you that the feelings of jealousy with which a project such as you now entertain might have been regarded not many years ago, are now entirely outgrown. We are now well assured of the strength of the ties by which you are bound to us—the tie of loyalty to a common Sovereign—the tie of a common kindred—the tie of many a name common to us all, and last, though not least, the tie of "Auld Lang Syne." Rest well assured that your aspirations for nationality will find nothing else than a cordial response among us. I know that there are some who have now begun to tell us that the colonies and the mother-country will cease to be united when common interests cease, but I don't believe one word of that, and I am sure you don't believe it. Rest well assured that there are feelings which lie far deeper than that, and which are far nobler too, and those who tell us this have either never read history, or if they have read it, have never read it aright. (Cheers.) Only look back to the history of the best men in the War of Independence, what a severe wrench it was to sever them from their allegiance to the mother-country, and you can tell better than I how many descendants still live among you of those who sacrificed their all for loyalty to England. Can you forget when that young Queen presented herself to her Hungarian nobles—when she supposed that she was to be crushed by all the forces of Europe united—and held up her babe before them—can you forget the answer that they made? "We will die for our Queen Maria Theresa." Now are there those who will tell us that England, who sent her best blood to the Crimea, would give a deaf ear to the cry of Canada in the time of peril, or do you doubt that if a son of our common Sovereign presented himself in British America, feelings deeper than those of self-interest would be stirred to their inmost depths? Therefore it is, that I, looking to the glory and interest of my country, am able to say to you, in this project as in any other which is for your advantage and welfare, go on and prosper: (cheers).

The next toast was: "The Provincial Delegates." In introducing it, the Hon. CHARLES TUPPER, (Chairman), said: It is no secret to any person in this assemblage that a number of public men of Canada, New Brunswick, Prince Edward Island and Nova Scotia, have been engaged for some time at Charlottetown in deliberating upon questions of the deepest importance to British America. I have had the pride and the satisfaction on the present occasion of asking my fellow citizens in Halifax to testify their appreciation of the visit of so many distinguished public men from all these provinces. I am, perhaps, safe in saying, that no more momentous gathering of public men has ever taken place in these provinces—whether regarded as comprising the ablest and best men, not only of one party, but of both the great parties into which all these Colonies have been divided—the 'Ins,' and the 'Outs.' When I speak of Canada, it is true that on the present occasion only the Executive Government is represented; but I need not tell this assembly that which is no news to them, that on the great question which has engaged our deliberations, two parties who have stood in the most determined political antagonism to each other have been brought together. All minor considerations of questions of party have been merged into one common sentiment—to unite, in order to elevate their country, and provide it with a stable and efficient Government. I feel, therefore, on the present occasion, that both of the great parties in these provinces are represented as fully as they could be. I may say, that engaged as we have been with these deliberations during the past week, I have the proud satisfaction of being able to state to this Assembly to-night that a more harmonious, or more united, or more cordial body of men, without a single exception, never were brought together in an endeavour to benefit their common country. I will go further, and say that I believe, and I have reason for believing so, that the great question in which they are engaged will receive at no distant day a satisfactory solution at their hands. But, even if that were not the case, if at present we should fail in devising such a system of Government in these Colonies as would be calculated to unite us and consolidate our influence, and place us in a position not only to aid each other, but in the hour of danger and need to give that united co-operation to the Parent State which is due to her at our hands—even if our deliberations should fail, I say, still I am confident they will not have been lost upon us, but will exercise a most salutary influence. I believe the discussion of these questions would enable public men to co-operate on other matters as they have on this.

The toast having being drunk—

The Honorable GEORGE ETIENNE CARTIER, Attorney

General of Lower Canada, rose to return thanks on behalf of the Canadian Delegates. After a few preliminary remarks, he said:—True it is that the deliberations of that Conference to which allusion has been made, have been to a certain extent carried on with closed doors; but at the same time it must be known that the great object and the great question submitted to that Conference is nothing else than this: If there could not be any means devised by which the great national fragments comprised in each of the British American Provinces could be brought together and made into a great nation? Now here is the question: Shall we continue to remain separate Provinces, presided over, it is true, by a common Sovereign, our worthy and gracious Queen, but at the same time politically divided? We know very well that there must be attached to that separation a certain amount of weakness, and it must be obvious to every one of us that if these Provinces can be brought together in one government they would be more powerful and more worthy of being an appendage to the British Crown. (Cheers.) The question, as I have submitted it to you, is of very great importance, but is it a presumption on the part of those who have sent us together to deliberate on this matter? I don't think so. I think there was good cause for this Conference, and that this is a most propitious time for holding it. When we consider that Canada has a population of 3,000,000, Nova Scotia 350,000, New Brunswick nearly 300,000, Prince Edward Island very nearly 100,000, or a total population of over three million and a half, we see there is a sufficient personal element in these Provinces to make a nation. When we come to the territory occupied by these Provinces, we see again another great element requisite for the foundation of a great State. I need hardly bring to your notice, gentlemen, that we in Canada have those two great elements of nationality—the personal and territorial elements; but we know our short comings—that though great in territory and population, we want the other element which is absolutely necessary to make a nation, that is the maritime element. What nation on earth has obtained any amount of greatness unless it has been united with a maritime element? We know that for a long time it was thought that the sea was a barrier to the progress of a people. I remember when the people of Great Britain were called the *insulaires*; yet this nation has managed to become the greatest power in Europe. Take again Austria, great in territory and population,—take Prussia, even Russia, or any of the great territorial powers—they have had a certain amount of power, but it is limited, for they have not had the sea to enable them to expand it *ad infinitum*. Knowing as we do in Canada, that we possess so large a personal element—that we have cleared so much of our territory as would secure to us as respectable a position as many of the European Powers, we want to be something greater yet; but that cannot be unless you unite with us. Nor must you lose sight of this fact, that though the Maritime Provinces occupy a sea board position, yet if they do not unite with us, they must be for all time to come only a mere strip of sea-shore. (Laughter.) We have too much love for you, I can assure you, and at the same time consideration for ourselves, to allow any such thing. (Renewed laughter.) Is it not within our power to form a vigorous Confederation, leaving to the local governments the power of dealing with their own local matters? There are difficulties in the way, but they are susceptible of solution if managed with wisdom. All that is requisite to overcome difficulties is a strong will and a good heart. When I think of the nationality which can be formed if we can but bring the Provinces under one Federal Government, it seems to me I see before me— and I am now speaking by a sort of metaphor—a great British American nation, with the fair Provinces of New Brunswick and Nova Scotia as the arms of the national body to embrace the trade of the Atlantic. None could make so fair a head as Prince Edward Island. This national body will then want a trunk, and we in Canada having the "Grand Trunk," can afford to be the trunk to the nation. The two Canadas will stretch with their toes far out to the West, and bring as much as possible of the Western territory into the Confederation. When we are united in a system of Federal Government, one of the most important questions that will be submitted to us will be the defence of the country. As it is now, we have each of us the will and determination to defend ourselves if attacked,—but can we do so at present with efficiency?

Take for instance, Prince Edward Island, or Nova Scotia, or New Brunswick, or the Canadas—can they defend themselves or help England in their defence, whilst separated as they are? No, but united, one of the questions with which the General Government must deal will be that of Defence. We know very well that united the Militia of the Provinces could turn out to the number of at least 200,000, and then, with the 60,000 sailors that the Canadas and the Maritime Provinces could provide, to help the army and navy of England, what power would be crazy enough to attack us? I have heard since I have been in Halifax, the objection thrown out that there is much danger that you would be absorbed. It will be very easy for me to dispel such fears. I answer them by a question: Have you any objection to be absorbed by commerce? Halifax through the Intercolonial Railroad will be the recipient of trade which now benefits Portland, Boston and New York. If you are unwilling to do all in your power to bring to a satisfactory consummation this great question, you will force us to send all this trade which you ought to have through American channels. Will the people of Nova Scotia or New Brunswick be better off because they are not absorbed by commerce or prosperity? It is as evident as the sun shines at noon that when the Intercolonial Railway is built—and it must necessarily be built if that confederation takes place—the consequence will be that between Halifax and Liverpool there will be steamers almost daily leaving and arriving at the former—in fact it will be a ferry between Halifax and Liverpool. (Cheers.) We know very well too, that very many travellers would come to visit you at the sea side. When I am addressing myself to you on this question I must also dispel a certain amount of fear which I see exists in certain minds, that if this union takes place the tie which connects us with England will be weakened. Now I believe the contrary will be the case. I am living in a Province in which the inhabitants are monarchical by religion, by habit and by the rememberance of past history. Our great desire and our great object in making efforts to obtain the federation of the Provinces is not to weaken monarchical institutions, but on the contrary to increase their influence. We know very well that, as soon as confederation is obtained, the Confederacy will have to be erected into a Vice-Royalty, and we may expect that a member of the Royal Family will be sent here as the head. With regard to the feeling in England, I am sure they understand the question very well. Any one conversing with Englishmen, or reading the English papers, will see that the question which prevails there is the defence of the country. I may say at once that I dislike that school of Bright, Cobden & Co. I was glad to hear a little while ago, the brave and noble Admiral tell us that there is an under-current which is deeper than all that school. We know that all this utter indifference to colonial dependency only exists among a certain number of politicians; but at all events it behoves us to be wise and take away from that school every cause of complaint which they may have against the colonial system. If we can organize our militia in such a way as to assure England that in any case of emergency we can help her, you may depend upon it that school will have no very long existence. Gentlemen, you must not be afraid of us who come from Canada because we represent a country greater in respect to population and territory. Don't be afraid of us,—don't tell us to go back with all our offers of no avail—don't tell us as it was said formerly of others:—

Timeo Danaos, et dona ferentes.

Let me assure you that the promises we make are made in all sincerity and good faith—in urging union upon you we believe we are doing that which will be for your happiness and prosperity. (Cheers.)

The Hon. GEORGE BROWN, President of the Executive Council of Canada, followed the Attorney General of Lower Canada, in a speech replete with statistical and other information. After a few introductory remarks, complimentary to the people of Halifax for their large and generous hospitality, the honorable gentleman said:—It may be expected that I should say a few words as to the object of our present mission; and perhaps I cannot begin better than by noticing certain statements that have appeared in the public press, and which have received some credence in reference to our visit. It has been said that we have had the opportunity before now of entering into closer union with Nova Scotia and New Brunswick, but we did not avail ourselves of it—that we were offered an Intercolonial railway, but refused to undertake it—and that we only come now seeking union with these Provinces to escape from our own sectional difficulties at home. Now, Sir, I am a member of the party in Canada, which up to this moment has been most strenuous in its resistance to the Intercolonial Railway; and I am persuaded there is not one man in this assembly who, under similar circumstances, would not have acted precisely as we did. In these Lower Provinces you have all had your political troubles, but we in Canada have had sectional difficulties to distract and embitter us vastly more serious than any you have had to contend with. Our Constitution of 1840 brought together under one government two countries peopled by two races, with different languages, different creeds, and different laws and customs; and unfortunately, while making us nominally one people, it retained the line of demarcation between Upper and Lower Canada, and gave the same number of representatives in Parliament to each section, without regard to their respective populations, their contributions to the general revenue, or any other consideration. The disproportion between the two sections gradually increased, until Upper Canada has 400,000 people more than Lower Canada, and pays full three-fourths of the whole national taxation,—but all the while the Lower Canadians had equal representation with us in both Houses of Parliament. A systematic agitation for the redress of the great wrong was commenced in Upper Canada—and as the only means of enforcing justice, we resisted all large schemes of improvement, we refused to enter into any new undertakings involving an increase of our public debt until a reform of our constitutional system was obtained, and we knew what our future position as a people was to be. We regarded the apparently far-off scheme of Federation of the whole Provinces as no remedy for our present wrongs, and we scouted the idea of building more railroads from the public chest until the taxpayers who were to bear the burden of their construction, had their just share of control over the public purse. Long and earnestly did we fight for the justice we demanded, but at last light broke in upon us. Parties were nearly equally balanced, the wheels of government had nearly ceased to move, a dead lock was almost inevitable, when Mr. Cartier, who wields great power in Lower Canada boldly and manfully took the ground that this evil must be met, and he would meet it. On this basis, I and two political friends, * joined the Administration, and the existing coalition was formed expressly for the purpose of settling justly and permanently the constitutional relations between Upper and Lower Canada. We have agreed to a principle of settlement acceptable to a large majority of the representatives in Parliament, and, I am also persuaded, to the great mass of our people in both sections of the Province. We are pledged as a Government to place before Parliament, at its next session a Bill giving effect to the conditions of our compact,—and should the union of the whole Provinces not be proceeded with, our Canadian Reform Bill will go on and our grievances be redressed. You will therefore clearly perceive that we have not come here to seek relief from our troubles—for the remedy of our grievances is already agreed upon, and come what may of the larger scheme now before us, our smaller scheme will certainly be accomplished. Our sole object in coming here is to say to you—" We are about to amend our constitution, and before finally doing so, we invite you to enter with us frankly and earnestly into the inquiry whether it would or would not be for the advantage of all the British American Colonies to be embraced under one political system. Let us look the whole question steadily in the face—if we find it advantageous let us act upon it, but if not, let the whole thing drop. This is the whole story of our being here—this is the full scope and intention of our present visit. But, sir, there is another objection raised. It is said that the debt of Canada is very great, our taxation is heavy, and that we seek to throw a portion of our burdens on the shoulders of our neighbors. Now, I belong to the party of economy in Canada—the party that has resisted the increase of the public debt and taxation, and

---

* The Honorable William McDougall, Provincial Secretary, and Member of Parliament for North Lanark, Upper Canada, and the Honorable Oliver Mowatt, lately Postmaster General, and now Lord Chancellor for Canada.

has loudly complained of their rapid advance—but large as our debt and taxation undoubtedly are for a young country, the people of Canada are abundantly able to bear it all and much more without assistance from any quarter whatever. (Cheers.) Were our burdens much greater than they are, we would but have to stand still in our extraordinary expenditures for a few years, and the rapid increase of our population, industrial energy and wealth would easily enable us to overcome it all. And if gentlemen who make this suggestion would look narrowly into the finances of their own Provinces—and having regard to the populations of their respective countries, will compare them with ours, I fancy they will find no great disparity between our respective burdens. Sir, it ought not excite any surprise that the Federation of all the British North American Provinces is at last presented to us as a practical question. The subject has often and again been discussed in the press and in Parliament, but at no time has any Provincial Statesman ever expressed a doubt that the fitting future of these Colonies was to be united under one Government and Legislature under the sovereignty of Great Britain. But two questions ever sprang up at once in considering so great a movement—Have the Colonies yet gained such a strength as to warrant their undertaking such a charge?—and could such terms be agreed upon and such a constitution be framed as would be acceptable to the whole of the Provinces? These questions are as serious and needful to be met at this hour, as they ever were in the past. It is no light matter to change the whole political and commercial relations of any country. In these Colonies, as heretofore governed, we have enjoyed great advantages under the protecting shield of the mother country. We have had no army or navy to sustain, no foreign diplomacy to maintain—our whole resources have gone to our internal improvement—and notwithstanding our occasional strifes with the Colonial Office, we have enjoyed a degree of self-government and generous consideration such as no colonies in ancient or modern history ever enjoyed at the hands of a parent state. Is it any wonder that thoughtful men should hesitate to countenance a step that might change the happy and advantageous relations we have occupied towards the mother country? I am persuaded there never was a moment in the history of these Colonies when the hearts of our people were so firmly attached to the parent state by the ties of gratitude and affection as at this moment; and for one I hesitate not to say, that did this movement for colonial union endanger the connection that has so long and so happily existed, it would have my firm opposition. (Cheers.) But far from fearing such a result, a due consideration of the matter must satisfy every one that the more united we are, the stronger will we be—and the stronger we are, the less trouble we will give the Imperial Government, the more advantageous will be our commerce, and the more proud they will be of us as a portion of the Empire. Our relation to the Mother Country does not, therefore, enter into the question. Whether the right time for a general union has arrived, must be determined by a close examination into the present position of all the Provinces, and the possibility of such an arrangement being matured as will be satisfactory to all concerned. And that, Sir, has been the work in which the Conference has been engaged for two week's past. We have gone earnestly into the consideration of the question in all its bearings, and our unanimous conclusion is, that if terms of union fair to all and acceptable to all could be devised, a union of all the British American Provinces would be highly advantageous to every one of the Provinces. (Loud cheers.) In the first place, sir, from the attitude of half a dozen inconsiderable colonies, we would rise at once to the position of a great and powerful state. At the census taken on 12th January, 1861, the population of the Provinces was as follows:—

Upper Canada	1,396,091
Lower Canada	1,111,566
Nova Scotia	330,857
New Brunswick	252,047
Newfoundland	122,635
Prince Edward Island	80,857
Total in 1861	3,294,056

But since then nearly four years have elapsed, and the average increase meanwhile, calculated at fifteen per cent. makes the population of the six Provinces at this moment

3,787,750. And if to this we add the large numbers necessarily omitted in countries so vast and sparsely settled, we will find that our total population, in the event of a union, would from the start be not much less than four millions of souls. (Cheers.) And there is perhaps a better way of measuring our strength than by mere numbers—and that is, by comparing ourselves with other countries. Now there are in Europe forty-eight Sovereign States. Of these there are no fewer than than thirty-seven containing less population than would the united British North American Provinces—and among them are no less prominent countries than Portugal, Holland, Denmark, Switzerland, Saxony, Hanover and Greece (cheers)—all of which are inferior to us in population. There are but eleven states in Europe superior to us in population; and three of these are so little in advance of us that a very few years would undoubtedly send us far ahead of them. The three are Sweden and Norway, containing 6,349,775 people — Belgium, containing 4,782,255—and Bavaria, with 4,689,837. These three once passed, and but eight European States would be in advance of us. (Cheers.) And let us see how we would stand in regard to the question of defence. I find by the Census returns of 1861, that the male persons then in the provinces were as follows :—

```
UPPER CANADA——From 20 to 30—128,740
                     30 to 40— 84,178
                     40 to 50— 59,660
                     50 to 60— 36,377
                                        ......308,955
LOWER CANADA——From 20 to 30— 93,302
                     30 to 40— 59,507
                     40 to 50— 42,682
                     50 to 60— 30,129
                                        ......225,620
NOVA SCOTIA———From 20 to 60..................67,367

NEW BRUNSWICK-—From 21 to 40— 33,574
                     40 to 50— 10,739
                     50 to 60—  7,312
                                        ......51,625
NEWFOUNDLAND——From 20 to 60..................25,532
```

PRINCE E. ISLAND—From 21 to 45— 11,144
..... 45 to 60— 3,675.......14,819

Total Males from 20 to 60.....................693,918

Of this enormous body of men, about 150,000 were between the years of 45 and 60—but striking them all off, and throwing off fifty thousand for the lame and the halt, we would have still left half a million of able bodied men ready and willing to defend their country. (Cheers.) But let us look at the aspect we should present to the world in an industrial and commercial point of view. And first let us examine the agricultural interest. From the Census Returns it appears that there were in 1861 no fewer than 333,604 farmers in the six British American Provinces, and 160,702 laborers, of which doubtless a very large proportion are farm laborers. It also appears that the land granted by government and now held by private parties in the Provinces is not less than 45,638,854 acres—of which 13,128,229 are under cultivation, and the balance has yet to be brought into use. These lands are thus distributed:—

	Held.	Cultivated.
Upper Canada	17,708,232	6,051,619
Lower Canada	13,680,000	4,804,235
Nova Scotia	5,748,893	1,028,032
New Brunswick	6,636,329	835,108
Newfoundland, about	100,000	41,108
Prince Edward Island	1,365,400	368,127
	45,638,854	13,128,229

And mark the enormous amount of produce obtained from these cultivated lands. I compile from the Census Returns of the several Colonies the following results as our united crop in the year 1860:—

Wheat	bushels	28,212,760
Barley	"	5,692,991
Rye	"	1,934,583
Peas	"	12,302,183
Oats	"	45,634,472

Buckwheat............bushels....................3,648,450
Indian Corn.............. " 2,624,163
Beans................... " 75,755
Potatoes................ " 39,485,246
Other Roots............. " 23,730,706
Grass Seed.............. " 115,345
Hay.................tons....................2,242,596
Hops.................lbs....................300,439
Maple Sugar............ " 16,782,872
Wool.................. " 7,010,914
Flax and Hemp......... " 2,183,759
Butter................. " 52,570,886
Cheese................ " 4,602,005
Beef.............bbls, 200 lbs...............134,562
Pork................. " 581,802

At a fair valuation, these crops will be found to sum up to the enormous amount of nearly one hundred and twenty millions of dollars—and if to this we add the increase on the number and value of the farm stock during the year, and the value of garden and orchard produce during the year, and the improvements in clearing and fencing and buildings during the year—we will come safely to the conclusion that the products of our fields and gardens in 1860, was not less than $150,000,000. (Cheers.) The assessed value of our farm lands in 1860 was upwards of $550,000,-000. And then, if we consider that our agriculture is yet in its infancy—that only a small portion of the thirteen millions of acres in pasture and under the plough is yet in high cultivation and much of it almost in a state of nature —that thirty millions of good lands over which the plough has not passed are yet in private hands—and that vast quantities still remain with government for disposal—some slight conception may be gained of the future agricultural capabilities of the united British American Provinces. (Cheers.) But, Mr. Chairman, if our position would be so remarkable as an agricultural people, our union would give us almost as high an attitude before the world as a great Maritime State. By the census of 1861 it appears that four years ago the sailors and fishermen of the six Colonies summed up no fewer than 69,256. (Cheers.) There were

In Upper Canada............................808
In Lower Canada..........................5,150
In Nova Scotia............................19,637
In New Brunswick........................2,765
In Newfoundland..........................38,578
In Prince Edward Island................2,318

Total sailors and fishermen...........69,256

Setting aside the unspeakable value of such a body of men in defence of the country, the commercial returns from their industry must be very great. The exports of fish alone from the united provinces amounted to no less a sum than nearly ten millions of dollars. I have been unable to ascertain with accuracy the number and tonnage of the shipping owned and sailed in British America—but this we do know, that last year no fewer than 628 vessels were built within our borders, having an aggregate tonnage of 230,312 tons. (Cheers.) These vessels were distributed thus :—

Built in Canada..................158 vesssels   67209 tons.
  "   Nova Scotia............207   "   46,862 "
  "   New Brunswick......137   "   85,250 "
  "   Newfoundland......... 26   " about   6,000 "
  "   P. E. Island.......... 100 "   24,991 "

Total...............628 vessels   230,312 tons

And highly gratifying as are these results, they are the product of two branches but yet in their infancy and both capable of great extension. I might continue this analysis through our whole industrial pursuits and show you one and all of them in the same high state of efficiency—I might tell you how we exported last year $15,000,000 in timber alone—I might expose to you the rapidly increasing importance of our Coal Mines, our Gold Fields, our Copper Mines, our Iron Works and our Petroleum Wells —I might enlarge on the fast rising importance of our manufactures—but already I have detained you far longer than I intended and must come to a close. Let me, however, wind up with this, that were the Provinces all united to-morrow, they would have an annual Export trade of no less than $65,000,000, and an Import traffic to an equal amount—they would have two thousand five hundred miles of railway; telegraph wires extending to every city and town throughout the country, and an annual government revenue of nearly thirteen millions of dollars. (Cheers) Mr. Chairman, it needs no special wisdom to perceive that a state presenting such resources and offering such varied and lucrative employment to the immigrant and the capitalist, would at once occupy a high position and attract to it the marked attention of other countries. It would be something to be a citizen of such a state. Heretofore we have been known as separate colonies, and the merits and disadvantages of each compared and set off against the other —but with union the advantages of each would pertain to the whole,—a citizen of one would be a citizen of all—and the foreign emigrant would come with very different feelings of confidence to our shores. In England we should occupy a very different position from what we have ever done as separate and feeble colonies. I cannot agree with my hon. friend, Mr. Cartier, in his opinion as to the great political party in Great Britain that has done so much to break the fetters of trade and raise the commerce of England to its present unexampled point of high prosperity. But regretting, as all must do, the extreme colonial views of Messrs. Bright and Cobden and their political friends, who cannot fail to see that a union of the whole Provinces would have the effect of inspiring respect even with that school of public men, and commanding confidence in our commercial future. The doubt and uncertainty as to the future of these Colonies that have hung so long and so injuriously over us, would be greatly modified by the union; and our securities would sensibly feel the effect in the money market of the world. How different a position, too, would we occupy in the eyes of our American neighbors. Instead of appearing in their commercial returns as separate buyers, we would stand out unitedly as their very best customer— and we would be able to deal with them for a permanent renewal of the Reciprocity Treaty, under advantages that we have not enjoyed before. But far in advance of all other advantages would be this, that union of all the Provinces would break down all trade barriers between us, and throw open at once to all a combined market of four millions of people. You in the east would send us your fish and your coals and your West India produce, while we would send you in return the flour and the grain and the meats you now buy in Boston and New York. Our merchants and manufacturers would have a new field before them—the barrister in the smallest provinces would have the judicial honors of all of them before him to stimulate his ambition—a patentee could secure his right over all British America—and in short all the advantages of free intercourse which has done so much for the United States, would at once be open to us all. One other argument there is in favor of the Union that ought with all of us to weigh most seriously, and that argument is, that it would elevate the politics and the politicians of our country (cheers)—it would lift us above the petty strifes of small communities, and give to our public affairs a degree of importance and to our leading public men a status very different from that they have heretofore occupied. On a survey of the whole case, I do think that there is no doubt as to the high advantages that would result from a union of all the Colonies—provided that terms of union could be found just to all the contracting parties, and so framed as to secure harmony in the future administration of affairs. That is the unanimous conclusion of the Conference, and I am persuaded that when the facts are before the country it is a conclusion that will be cordially endorsed by the people of all the Provinces. But it were wrong to conceal for a moment that the whole merit of the scheme of union may be completely marred by the character of its details. The consideration of the details has already received in an informal manner the earnest attention of the Convention. I commit no indiscretion in saying that as yet we have arrived at no formal conclusion as to any of those details— and I am sure you will feel we are right in studiously refraining at present from all discussions of our views in regard to them. A formal meeting for their earnest and mature consideration will be held at an early day—and when difficulties have been removed and our plans matured, the whole scheme will be placed fully and frankly before our constituents in all the Provinces. The hon. gentleman resumed his seat amid applause.

The Honorable S. L. TILLEY, Provincial Secretary and Leader of the Government of New Brunswick, in replying to the toast on behalf of that Province, said :—I must confess that I rise under no ordinary degree of embarrassment to-night. We are summoned here by the representatives of royalty, and surrounded by the ablest men that Canada has produced at the present day; and I am quite sure that the feelings which embarrass me at the present moment will be, to a certain extent, participated in by my friends of New Brunswick and Prince Edward Island, when they reflect on the insignificance of our position in comparison with that of the great country so ably represented by the men who have already spoken. I may say with regard to the question which we have been considering during the past week, that I do not intend to keep my mouth quite as close as my friend Mr. Brown. I don't hesitate to declare my own sentiments upon one or two matters which I consider are of some importance. I may state here emphatically as one of those delegates constitutionally appointed for the purpose of considering the Union of the Maritime Provinces, that I am decidedly in favor of that proposition ; but I am prepared, at the same time, if an arrangement equitable to these Provinces, can be made, to expand this union and have a general confederation. I have been in favor of a Union of the Maritime Provinces because it has been my good fortune to represent my government in delegations in England, in Canada, and in Nova Scotia, either for the purpose of increasing or improving our inter-colonial communication, or extending our trade ; and I don't hesitate to say that in every step we have made we have been frustrated by the existence of these separate Legislatures and Governments. Mr. Chairman, I made a visit to Nova Scotia some years ago, in order to extend, if possible, our trade relations, but when we sat down to consider this, what did we find ? We found that any manufacture sent over to New Brunswick from Nova Scotia, was met by a duty of fifteen per cent., and any from my own province to this one had to pay ten per cent. It is just the same as if a man going from Cumberland into Colchester was met by a duty on his products. We have tried our best to remedy the evil and to remove these absurdities, but we found difficulties presenting themselves at almost every step. The expenditure in some of the Provinces requires a large revenue, and therefore the imposition of large duties. The raw material in some pays two per cent., in another it is free; and so you will perceive that where that article is free, that province would have a great advantage over the other. Then, again, when we were discussing the subject of an Intercolonial Railway, what did we find? We found at once a difference in the interests of the respective Provinces. In Upper Canada, we found that the people were opposed to the project because it was so far from them, and would not create an expenditure in Canada. And then, as my friend, Mr. Brown, has told you, they have had their constitutional difficulties to settle before this railway could be built; and I am glad to hear that these difficulties have been settled. When we go to Lower Canada we find objections also meeting us there. We go to Nova Scotia, and we hear you say: You have large territories to be opened up, and the road is of greater advantage to you than to Nova Scotia. In New Brunswick, they say: all the trade is to be carried away from that Province to Halifax. Now suppose we were all drawn together into one confederation, you would not be met with these difficulties in any of your negotiations. If you wanted to secure intercolonial free trade or an inter-colonial railway, then there would be no trouble. How much more effectually could measures of self-defence be arranged if we were all united; and I don't hesitate to say that the time is not far distant when we must do more than we have done heretofore. It is shewn that we have a population of nearly four millions; that our exports reach $130,000,000; that the value of our agricultural property amounts to $150,000,000; that our assessed property is put down at $550,000,000; under these circumstances, knowing, as I believe I do, something of the spirit and intelligence of the people of these Colonies, they are prepared to say, that in view of the privileges we enjoy, and the responsibilities which we ought to assume, we are ready to pay our share for the defence and the maintenance of the liberties of our country. When it is said that those who are engaged in securing the confederation of the Maritime, or of the whole of the Provinces, do so because the Imperial Government desires it, I say that those who are acting in common with me, and I think I have had abundant opportunities of knowing it, are actuated by higher motives. I believe there are no feelings on the part of the Imperial Government that are antagonistic to these Colonies. We have had it from the lips of those distinguished gentlemen sitting by you, sir, that they are ready to assent to any proposition in reference to the provinces which is likely to advance their happiness and promote their prosperity. (If arrangements can be satisfactorily completed, so that the interests of each province will be maintained, I can see no objection to a confederation of the whole.) We are in the Lower Provinces a manufacturing people to a large extent, and we would, to the whole of British America, occupy the same position that Massachusetts does to the United States. Reference has been made to our proceedings having been carried on secretly. I think any man who reflects upon the delicacy of our mission—and knows that we have been discussing it in a merely conversational matter—must see that it was absolutely necessary that such informal discussions should be carried on with closed doors; but when we have come to some conclusion, then it will be submitted to our respective Legislatures. We have only one common object in view—the promotion of the prosperity of these Provinces, their advancement, socially and politically; and I can assure you that all of us fully feel the importance and responsibility of the trust that has been placed in our hands. (Cheers.)

The Honorable Colonel GRAY, Premier of Prince Edward Island, and President of the Convention of Maritime Delegates, spoke, also, on behalf of his Colony, in the following terms:—If an old practised politician like Mr. Cartier approaches this subject with diffidence and hesitation, how much more must I feel who am the youngest politician, if indeed one at all. Perhaps it would display a far greater amount of wisdom if I would observe a complete reticence; but, Mr. Chairman, there are points with regard to which I feel called upon to deal shortly—the one being that which involves my giving thanks to the people of this city for their reception of myself and colleagues, and the other being my firm resolve upon all public occasions to raise my voice in order to disabuse the public mind on a subject on which considerable misapprehension exists—I allude to our public defences. The people of the Colony in which my lot is at present cast, have been so long intimately connected with Nova Scotia—so much unity has ever existed between them in all their relations, that I consider no union is necessary between them further than that which already exists. I have always entertained great prognostics as to the future of this city; I look upon it as certain to be the London of the Western Confederation; but throwing aside the politician let me speak individually. I have had some little acquaintance with many countries in the four quarters of the globe, and I have come to the conclusion that in the city of Halifax hospitality has taken her seat.— (Cheers.) I thank you cordially on behalf of the Colony I represent, for myself and colleagues, for the high honor you have conferred upon us in the toast which has been proposed. But there is a question which I think deeply upon, and that is one on which I may offer an opinion. I consider that a considerable amount of misapprehension has arisen in reference to the question of self-defence, both on the part of the profession in which I passed so many years of my life, and of those of our fellow-colonists who appear to me to underrate themselves, and to forget from whom they are descended. It has been asserted that in case of an invasion—and I suppose that in any war that might arise, it would be one of self-defence on our side simply—that our frontiers cannot be maintained, but that the regular soldiery would have to withdraw and concentrate behind fortifications, and that the militia of the Confederation would be scattered like a flock of sheep. I take issue with those that assert this. To my old comrades I would say, that when that day arrives I hope I may not live to see them taking positions behind stonewalls. Their place has ever been in the front, and there they must ever be. To my fellow colonists, I would say, why underrate your capabilities? Consider what was the conduct of the Militia of Britain during the Crimean war. I remember, during that period, when serving on the Staff of a General Officer in the Mediterranean, we had two Regiments of the Lancashire farmers counted worthy to hold the all important fortress of Gibraltar;—at Malta the glistening bayonets of the brave men of Kent lined the ramparts, and at Corfu that important post washeld by the stout yeomen of Norfolk ; and need I remind the men of a Province which has lately sent forth a Williams, an Inglis, the saviour of India, a Welsford and a Parker to add imperishable lustre to the arms of Britain, that they have plenty such, quite as capable of holding Quebec, Montreal, St. John or Halifax. (Cheers.) Only let a wise and vigorous policy be adopted, let our Militia be armed and organized as they will be proud to be, and standing shoulder to shoulder with their brethren of the Royal Army, should the day of trial arrive when our gallant neighbors forget that, descended from the same stock and lineage, we ought to live in peace and amity as brothers, then we will be prepared to shew them that, profitting by their own example in days gone by, there are four millions of free men in these provinces not unworthy descendants of their sires. (Cheers.) I have now but to say that whatever may be the result of our deliberations, the people we represent may rest assured that we approach the consideration of this grave and momentous question in all its bearings with a full sense of our solemn responsibilities.

Hon. Dr. TUPPER then proposed as the next toast, "Colonial Union," coupling with it the name of Hon. J. A. McDonald, Attorney General for Canada West.

Hon. J. A. MACDONALD then rose amid loud cheers, and spoke as follows: My friends and colleagues, Messrs. Cartier and Brown, have returned their thanks on behalf of the Canadians for the kindness bestowed upon us, and I shall therefore not say one word on that subject, but shall approach the question more immediately before us. I must confess to you, sir, and to you, gentlemen, that I approach it with the deepest emotion. The question of "Colonial Union" is one of such magnitude that it dwarfs every other question on this portion of the continent. It absorbs every idea as far as I am concerned. For twenty long years I have been dragging myself through the dreary waste of Colonial politics. I thought there was no end, nothing worthy of ambition, but now I see something which is well worthy of all I have suffered in the cause of my little country. This question has now assumed a position that demands and commands the attention of all the Colonies of British America. There may be obstructions, local difficulties may arise, disputes may occur, local jealousies may intervene, but it matters not—the wheel is now revolving, and we are only the fly on the wheel, we cannot delay it—the union of the colonies of British America, under one sovereign, is a fixed fact. (Cheers.) Sir, this meeting in Halifax will be ever remembered in the history of British America, for here the delegates from the several provinces had the first opportunity of expressing their sentiments. We have been unable to announce them before, but now let me say that we have arrived unanimously at the opinion that the union of the provinces is for the advantage of all, and that the only question that remains to be settled is, whether that union can be arranged with a due regard to sectional and local interests. I have no doubt that such an arrangement can be effected, that every difficulty will be found susceptible of solution, and that the great project will be successfully and happily realized. What were we before this question was brought before the public mind? Here we were in the neighborhood of a large nation—of one that has developed its military power in a most marvellous degree—here we were connected by one tie only, that of common allegiance. True it was we were states of one Sovereign, we all paid allegiance to the great central authority, but as far as ourselves were concerned there was no political connection, and we were as wide apart as British America is from Australia. We had only the mere sentiment of a common allegiance, and we were liable, in case England and the United States were pleased to differ, to be cut off, one by one, not having any common means of defence. I believe we shall have at length an organization that will enable us to be a nation and protect ourselves as we should. Look at the gallant defence that is being made by the Southern Republic—at this moment they have not much more than four millions of men—not much exceeding our own numbers—yet what a brave fight they have made, notwithstanding the stern bravery of the New Englander, or the fierce *elan* of the Irishman.— (Cheers.) We are now nearly four millions of inhabitants, and in the next decennial period of taking the census, perhaps we shall have eight millions of people, able to defend their country against all comers. (Cheers.) But we must have one common organization—one political government. It has been said that the United States Government is a failure. I don't go so far. On the contrary I consider it a marvellous exhibition of human wisdom. It was as perfect as human wisdom could make it, and under it the American States greatly prospered until very recently; but being the work of men it had its defects, and it is for us to take advantage by experience, and endeavor to see if we cannot arrive by careful study at such a plan as will avoid the mistakes of our neighbors. In the first place we know that every individual state was an individual sovereignty —that each had its own army and navy and political organization—and when they formed themselves into a confederation they only gave the central authority certain specific powers, reserving to the individual states all the other rights appertaining to sovereign powers. The dangers that have risen from this system we will avoid if we can agree upon forming a strong central government—a great central Legislature—a constitution for a Union which will have all the rights of sovereignty except those that are given to the local governments. Then we shall have taken a great step in advance of the American Republic. If we can only obtain that object—a vigorous general government—we shall not be New Brunswickers, nor Nova Scotians, nor Canadians, but British Americans, under the sway of the British Sovereign. In discussing the question of colonial union, we must consider what is desirable and practicable; we must consult local prejudices and aspirations. It is our desire to do so. I hope that we will be enabled to work out a constitution that will have a strong central Government, able to offer a powerful resistance to any foe whatever, and at the same time will preserve for each Province its own identity—and will protect every local ambition ; and if we cannot do this we shall not be able to carry out the object we have now in view. In the Conference we have had we have been united as one man—there was no difference of feeling— no sectional prejudices or selfishness exhibited by any one ; —we all approached the subject feeling its importance ; feeling that in our hands were the destinies of a nation ;

and great would be our sin and shame if any different motives had intervened to prevent us carrying out the noble object of founding a great British Monarchy, in connection with the British Empire, and under the British Queen. (Cheers.) That there are difficulties in the way would be folly for me to deny; that there are important questions to be settled before the project can be consummated is obvious; but what great subject that has ever attracted the attention of mankind has not been fraught with difficulties? We would not be worthy of the position in which we have been placed by the people if we did not meet and overcome these obstacles. I will not continue to detain you at this late period of the evening, but will merely say that we are desirous of a union with the Maritime Provinces on a fair and equitable basis: that we desire no advantage of any kind, that we believe the object in view will be as much in favor as against these Maritime Colonies. We are ready to come at once into most intimate connection with you. This cannot be fully procured, I admit, by political union simply. I don't hesitate to say that with respect to the Intercolonial Railway, it is understood by the people of Canada that it can only be built as a means of political union for the Colonies. It cannot be denied that the Railway, as a commercial enterprise, would be of comparatively little commercial advantage to the people of Canada. Whilst we have the St. Lawrence in Summer, and the American ports in time of peace, we have all that is requisite for our purposes. We recognize, however, the fact that peace may not always exist, and that we must have some other means of outlet if we do not wish to be cut off from the ocean for some months in the year. We wish to feel greater security—to know that we can have assistance readily in the hour of danger. In the case of a union, this Railway must be a national work, and Canada will cheerfully contribute to the utmost extent in order to make that important link without which no political connection can be complete. What will be the consequence to this city, prosperous as it is, from that communication? Montreal is at this moment competing with New York for the trade of the great West. Build the road and Halifax will soon become one of the great emporiums of the world. All the great resources of the

West will come over the immense railways of Canada to the bosom of your harbor. But there are even greater advantages for us all in view. We will become a great nation, and God forbid that it should be one separate from the United Kingdom of Great Britain and Ireland.— (Cheers.) There has been a feeling that because the old colonies were lost by the misrule of the British Government, every colony must be lost when it assumes the reins of self-government. I believe, however, as stated by the gallant Admiral, that England will hold her position in every colony—she will not enforce an unwilling obedience by her arms; but as long as British Americans shall retain that same allegiance which they feel now, England will spend her last shilling, and spill her best blood like wine in their defence. (Cheers.) In 1812 there was an American war because England empressed American seamen. Canadians had nothing to do with the cause of the quarrel, yet their militia came out bravely and did all they could for the cause of England. Again, we have had the Oregon question, the Trent difficulty, question after question in which the Colonies had no interest, yet we were ready to shoulder the musket and fight for the honor of the mother country. It has been said that England wishes to throw us off. There may be a few *doctrinaires* who argue for it, but it is not the feeling of the people of England. Their feeling is this—that we have not been true to ourselves, that we have not put ourselves in an attitude of defence, that we have not done in Canada as the English have done at home. It is a mistake: Canada is ready to do her part. She is organizing a militia, she is expending an enormous amount of money for the purpose of doing her best for self-protection. I am happy to know that the militia of Nova Scotia occupies a front rank; I understand by a judicious administration you have formed here a large and efficient volunteer and militia organization. We are following your example and are forming an effective body of militia, so that we shall be able to say to England, that if she should send her arms to our rescue, at a time of peril, she would be assisted by a well disciplined body of men. Everything, gentlemen, is to be gained by Union, and everything to be lost by disunion. Everybody admits that Union must take place sometime. I say now is the time.

Here we are now in a state of peace and prosperity—now we can sit down without any danger threatening us, and consider and frame a scheme advantageous to each of these colonies. If we allow so favorable an opportunity to pass, it may never come again; but I believe we have arrived at such a conclusion in our deliberations that I may state without any breach of confidence—that we all unitedly agree that such a measure is a matter of the first necessity, and that only a few (imaginary I believe) obstacles stand in the way of its consummation. I will feel that I shall not have served in public life without a reward, if before I enter into private life I am a subject of a great British American nation, under the government of Her Majesty, and in connection with the Empire of Great Britain and Ireland. (Loud cheers.)

Dr. TUPPER then gave, as the next toast, "British American Commerce," coupling with it the name of the Hon. Mr. Galt, Finance Minister of Canada.

Hon. Mr. GALT, in reply, said:—I must confess that I feel very great reluctance in rising to address you at this late hour of the evening. I feel that the remarks made by gentlemen who have preceded me have exhausted this subject. We must all of us have listened with satisfaction to the views which have fallen from previous speakers. Though it be true that England's position is due in a great measure to her adherence to constitutional usage, yet at the same time, we cannot but see that after all, the commerce, industry, and intelligence of the people are the true sources of her greatness. I feel proud to be permitted to say a few words this evening—an evening which I consider as forming an era in the history of British America. Whatever may be our views with regard to constitutional questions, there can be no doubt entertained by any of us that our interests are identical in endeavoring to increase the trade and commerce that should exist between the different families of British America. I believe the Union of these Provinces must cause a most important change in their trade. Union is free trade among ourselves. Perhaps insurmountable difficulties may prevent us carrying out any such thing whilst separated, but when united our intercourse must be as free as between Lancashire and Yorkshire. The free intercourse between the States of the American Union—free trade in the interchange of products, has had more to do with their marvellous progress than anything that was put in their constitution. Give us Union and the East shall have free trade with the West. We shall have a common interest in each other's proceedings. We shall feel that the political connection is the introduction to the commercial connection. We have had a commercial connection with the great cities of the States, but we have not had political union with them. We have not that affection for them which we have for the cities of Britain. We desire to foster this affection. But, whilst we may all be agreed that in a political and commercial sense we should be united, yet there may be grounds that forbid the banns. It may be said that the extravagance of some of the members render this union undesirable. In regard to this question I think those gentlemen who hear me will be perfectly satisfied to leave it in the hands of the men who represent the Lower Provinces in the Conference. If the union with the Canadas is to be attended with such disadvantages, we may be sure they will see it. I don't wish that this audience should go away with the idea that we Canadians, in coming down here, and bringing this subject before you, are actuated by any other object than feelings of patriotism. Therefore, I will briefly say this, that notwithstanding the differences that may exist in the tariffs and excise laws of each of the Provinces, there is practically very little difference indeed in the amount per head. New Brunswick raises probably the highest, Nova Scotia the least, and Canada occupies a central position. Looking also at the respective debts, we find that they bear the same proportion per head as in the case of the Excise and Customs. If we are united we must have an Intercolonial Railway. I am an advocate of this great work, and it becomes an absolute necessity if a union of these Provinces is to take place at all. Under the last proposition seven-twelfths was to be built by the Lower Provinces, but if the Union is agreed upon, and three millions of Canadians are to bear a share of the cost proportionate to the 600,000 in the Lower Provinces, you will get the best of the bargain. But the railway is not to be looked upon as a question of cost, but as a bond of union, that will unite us in peace and in time of need—and God forbid the latter should ever arrive. I may venture to say that there is nothing we can more lament than the deplorable war that is disturbing the neighboring States. Situated as we are, we cannot look upon the calamities that are decimating our neighbors without feeling the deepest regret. We cannot but trust that nothing may arise to break up the friendly relations that exist between us; but, at the same time, it is our duty to provide against all contingencies. If ill-feelings should arise, then the Intercolonial Railway would be of the highest importance to us. It would enable the strength of the Maritime Provinces to be available for Canada, and allow us to obtain that assistance from Great Britain which she will ever accord us when we need it. Let us trust that the difficulties which now stand in the way of the great object we have in view will be firmly taken in hand, and overcome; and that the people of these Provinces, feeling that union is strength, will do their utmost in assisting the men who are struggling to bring it about. (Cheers.)

A few other toasts, which did not bear directly on the question of Union, were then proposed and honored in the usual way. Amongst these was one in reference to Agriculture and Emigration, which called forth an eloquent speech from the Hon. T. D'Arcy McGee, Minister of Agriculture for Canada, characterised by wit and humor. The wit, though bright and genial, was evanescent, and pointed by allusion to local objects and persons. Shortly after Mr. McGee's speech, the company separated.

THE DELEGATES IN NEW BRUNSWICK.

Leaving Halifax the morning after the *Dejeuner* there, the Delegates from the Maritime Provinces, and several of the Canadian Ministers, proceeded to Fredericton, the seat of Government for the Province of New Brunswick, where they held a consultation with His Excellency Lieut.

Governor Gordon, concerning the object of their mission, and where an informal Conference, similar to that at Halifax, was also held. This Conference was of the same private and confidential character as those at the two previous places, and no public record of it has yet appeared.

PUBLIC DINNER AT ST. JOHN, N. B.

The Delegates from Nova Scotia and Prince Edward Island, together with several of the Canadian Ministers, having visited, by invitation, the Commercial Metropolis of New Brunswick, the City of Saint John—were entertained at a Public Dinner in St. Stubbs' Hotel, given by the New Brunswick Delegates, on the evening of the 14th September. The local press describes the entertainment as a very superior one, highly creditable to the hosts and to the caterer of the establishment, Mr. James McIntosh.— The Chair was occupied by the Hon. Colonel John Hamilton Gray, M.P.P., (one of the New Brunswick Delegates), and the Vice Chair was filled by the Hon. Charles Watters, M.P.P., Solicitor General of the Province.

The cloth being removed, and the usual loyal toasts given with all the honors, the Chairman proposed—

" Our Friends from Canada, Nova Scotia, and Prince Edward Island—"

In doing so, he referred, in felicitous terms, to the generous reception which had been given to himself and his brother Delegates from New Brunswick by the Governments and peoples of Nova Scotia and Prince Edward Island.

The GEORGE ETIENNE CARTIER, Attorney General of Lower Canada, was the first to address the company in response to the toast. After alluding to the visit made to the Lower Provinces by some of his friends and fellow countrymen in Canada, during the summer of 1864, and dwelling on the grateful impressions of hospitality which they carried home with them, he said—there are matters upon which men are sometimes called to express themselves which are often considered tiresome, but to give expression to the feelings of the heart was never tiresome, and this he would now take delight in doing. (The subject which most deeply engrossed his thoughts concerned the welfare and prosperity of his country, and by that word he meant the whole of British America. Prosperity such as this great country was capable of attaining to, could never be fully enjoyed until the several sectional parts of it were united under the same political and commercial systems—their respective populations brought into closer relations with each other, and all the maritime facilities alike afforded to all which Nature had so bountifully bestowed upon some of the parts. This was what Confederation proposed to accomplish. Canada has population and territory sufficient to make a great nation in course of time. But she wants what the Lower Provinces possess—an outlet to the sea. As the Lower Provinces now stand they are comparatively weak and powerless—and the wealth, labor, and industry which Canada possesses, go, in a great measure to enrich such cities as New York, Boston and Portland. This must continue to be the case until the inter-colonial railway, of which he had ever been an advocate, shall be built; and as soon as the Colonies were confederated, the construction of that work would undoubtedly commence. He said it had been urged against Confederation, that such a change in our constitution would make us republican, and gradually lead to a final separation from the mother country. But he believed it would have the contrary effect—that it would bind us more closely to that country, and probably secure to us the vice-royalty of a prince of the reigning family. With regard to the question of defence, which was inseparable from the general subject, he was confident that when England saw we were self-reliant to a great extent, and capable of organizing a large military and naval force for mutual protection, and which union would only enable us to do—she would cheerfully come to our assistance, with all her vast power, in any difficulty that might arise

Canada had been accused of insincerity in her dealings with the Maritime Provinces, and this led to the formation of a strong prejudice against accepting the proposals of his province for confederation; but he assured every one who listened to him that Canada was unjustly accused; and that her Ministers did not come there to urge them by undue means into the adoption of any scheme of union; but fairly to point out to them the enormous advantages, which, in a commercial point of view, their merchants, traders, and manufacturers would derive from having a market of four millions of people for the exchange of their several commodities, instead of being restricted to the small and scattered populations which now compose the Lower Provinces, where their industry is hampered by Custom House regulations, different in each. After a few further remarks, the honorable and learned gentleman sat down amidst loud and long continued cheers.

The Honorable GEORGE BROWN, President of the Executive Council of Canada, then rose and spoke to the following effect. He agreed with the sentiments expressed by his friend Mr. Cartier. Canada had no wish, even if she had the power—which she had not—to force these Provinces into a Union—she only desired to propose fair terms under which such a measure might be effected. It remained for these Provinces to accept or reject them. He hoped to see all the Provinces united, and they would no doubt then constitute one of the first nations in the Western Hemisphere. They had every advantage—a sea coast on the east, with great fishing, mining, and agricultural resources; and a vast territory on the west, containing countless millions of arable land. In Canada there were three millions of inhabitants — there were thirteen millions of acres of land only half cultivated, and thirty millions of acres actually in the possession of settlers, but under no cultivation, with millions upon millions of acres yet lying unreclaimed from their wilderness state, which would, at some future day, be inhabited by thrifty farmers, producing breadstuffs for the Lower Provinces, while they received the manufactures of those Provinces in return. What a happy and prosperous state of affairs would thus be presented when compared with the present isolated condition of the Provinces! New Brunswick, for instance, instead of being confined to its own small market of 250,000 consumers, would have four millions of customers. Far away on the western slopes of the Rocky Mountains were the rich gold fields of British Columbia, awaiting the enterprise and capital of our people, and in the direction of which immigration was now steadily flowing. It was not unreasonable to suppose that rich deposits would also be discovered on the eastern side of the Rocky Mountain range, which would be the means of attracting vast crowds of the surplus populations of Europe, thousands of whom would halt in their progress westward and settle upon the fertile lands of all these provinces, thus adding to the common wealth by their productive industry and enhancing the greatness of the Confederacy. He had no doubt that one of the first results of Confederation would be the construction of a railway from Halifax to the Pacific, affording an outlet to the Atlantic, through British, and not through foreign territory, for the rich products of Canada and the far west.—There was another practical view of the question, which should not be lost sight of: it was incumbent upon these provinces to make some provision for protecting themselves in times of danger. It was evident that the British Government had determined to throw them, in a great measure, upon their own resources, of which the withdrawal of the British troops from Canada was an unmistakeable sign. United, the provinces could readily organize a force of 500,000 men for field duty, besides about 70,000 marines.—The honorable gentleman then referred to the great commercial resources and the extent of shipping now possessed by the provinces in their youth, and showed how rapidly these would increase when there would be freer intercourse between them all, and a closer identity of interests.—He could not speak of what had taken place at the Convention at Charlottetown; but this he would say, that all the members of it were desirous of having a larger measure of union than the one at first proposed, if the details could be arranged in a satisfactory manner. The Canadian members of Government present at the Convention were clothed with no official authority, but a new Conference would shortly take place, in which all the details of a plan of Confederation would be examined with the greatest care, which, if it went into operation, would place us all on an equal footing as British Americans, instead of being as now, sectional provincialists with divided interests. The honorable gentleman resumed his seat amidst loud cheers.

The Honorable CHARLES TUPPER, M.P.P., Provincial Secretary of Nova Scotia, next addressed the assemblage. He had for a long time, he said, favored the project of a federation of the provinces. He referred to the circumstance of having deliverd a lecture before the Mechanics' Institute of St. John in favor of this measure. It was then stated in some of the local papers that in so acting he was not influenced by patriotic motives, but rather from a desire to obstruct the government of Nova Scotia against which he was in opposition. He re-delivered the lecture in Portland, (N. B.,) on which occasion he combatted the arguments or assertions brought against him, and clearly defined his position in reference to the question. One of his first acts, after coming into office in Nova Scotia, was to agitate for a confederation or union of some kind with the other Lower Provinces. To a union with Canada he was not at that time so favorable, because of its large debt. But he was anxious to hear the statesmen from that country give their views on the measure; and having heard them, he was free to confess that many of his apprehensions regarding a union with Canada had been removed. He believed that the Canadian Government were actuated by honest and patriotic motives in seeking a political alliance with their fellow subjects in the Lower Provinces, which would give strength to each and every portion of the Confederacy, which they could scarcely hope for in their present disunited state. They were weak and defenceless, living at the threshold, and it might be, at the mercy of a great military nation. To command the respect of such a neighbor, and the maintenance of peaceful relations, it was necessary to show that they had the power to enforce both the one and the other; and there was no surer way of accomplishing this than by a union of all the provinces. After a few further remarks the honorable gentleman resumed his seat amidst applause.

The Honorable Colonel J. H. GRAY, President of the

Executive Council of Prince Edward Island, expressed himself warmly, but briefly, in favor of Confederation. He had, before leaving England, in order to take up his residence in the land of his birth, resolved to use his influence in favor of this measure, and he hoped to see it effected at least in his lifetime, when a railway from Halifax to Vancouver's Island would bring us in speedy communication with the rich and ancient countries washed by the Pacific, bearing their treasures to us, and carrying the fruits of our industry to them.

The Honorable GEORGE COLES, M.P.P., (P. E. Island,) then followed in a short and playful speech. Canada, he said, had come down to the Maritime Provinces, and his little daughter, P. E. Island, had been wooed, but had not yet been won. The blandishments of the wooer had not altogether prevailed. Before he would consent to the wedlock, he should understand fully whether Canada, with her expansive territory and great debt, was able to maintain her in the connection as well as she was in her present condition. The prospect, however, he frankly confessed, seemed to favor a happy and prosperous Federal Union.

"The Colonial Union," having been proposed as a sentiment by the Chairman—

The Hon. A. T. GALT, Finance Minister of Canada, promptly responded to a call made upon him, and proceeded to review the financial condition of the several provinces. While Canada, he said, did not *appear* to occupy as favorable a position in a financial point of view as the Lower Provinces, each one of which had a surplus in its favor at the end of the fiscal year, yet Canada should be credited with the vast improvements which were being constantly made to develope its resources; and this year, (1864), she would have a large balance in her favor against her expenditure. Her debt might appear large, but her population was larger in proportion to her debt than that of New Brunswick, and the actual taxation on the citizens of Canada was not, all things considered, so heavy as the taxation in New Brunswick. Alluding to the efforts that had been made in Canada to improve the communication between the St. Lawrence and the ocean, and to the large expenditure of money for the construction of railways, all tending to the same result, those things, he said, were undoubtedly a heavy charge upon the public treasury of Canada, but the people were deriving vast benefits from the outlay, and its advantages would be felt more sensibly hereafter when the back country was opened up, and its immense resources to some extent developed. He was glad to find that in Nova Scotia and New Brunswick efforts were being made to open up their wilderness country. These efforts would, of course, entail new obligations, but their ability to meet them would be enchanced, as was the case in Canada. Though much had been said in reference to the debts of the respective Provinces from time to time, their position did not appear to be correctly known. Taxes imposed on the people in the provinces were derived from two sources—Customs and Excise. From these sources the debt and expenses of government are paid. In the case of Nova Scotia, if he rightly remembered, the taxes were $2.32 per head; in Canada, $2.50, and in New Brunswick, $2.56. Thus it would be seen that Canada would not be such a burthen to her sister Provinces as some persons imagined. As regards the Intercolonial Railway, it was well known that the Canadian Government had some time ago agreed to bear five-twelfths of the cost of constructing that work, and that the other seven-twelfths were to be borne by Nova Scotia and New Brunswick. Should the Union be consummated, this work must be done, and Nova Scotia and New Brunswick will only have to bear their share of the cost in proportion to their population, which will be very considerably less than the seven-twelfths. Under the old arrangement, before a Federal Union was contemplated, Canada's proportion would be very much the smallest, being but $2.50 per head, while that of New Brunswick would be $14 per head. He then referred to the commercial advantages of a union, which would confer upon the Colonies benefits similar to those which have been enjoyed by the United States in consequence of their union, their free trade and uniform tariff.—In framing the constitution for British America, the errors of the Republican Union were avoided.

The rebellion which distracted that Union was, in some measure, caused by slavery, and to a very great extent, by what was known as state rights. Of course, the question of slavery could never be an element of discord with the united provinces, and as regards "state rights," collision might be easily avoided in reference to that subject by clearly defining the powers of the central Goverment as totally distinct from the authority which should be vested in the local legislatures. [After a few further remarks, as the local report reforms us, Mr. Galt sat down, having left the most favorable impression on the minds of his hearers as to the advantages of Colonial Union.]

Speeches were made by several other gentlemen, amongst whom were, the Hon. William McDougall, Provincial Secretary of Canada; the Hon. Mr. McCully, one of the Nova Scotia Delegates; the Hon. Mr. Palmer, one of the Prince Edward Island Delegates; the Hon. Mr. McGee, Minister of Agriculture for Canada; and the Honorables Messrs. Gray and Tilley, New Brunswick Delegates,—but it appears that no report of their speeches was taken; at least, no report has been published. The St. John papers, however, state that their speeches, as well as the foregoing, were all highly in favor of a Union of the Provinces.

THE VOYAGE TO QUEBEC.

The Government of Canada having named the 10th of October as the day on which it would be desirable to commence the new Conference at Quebec, the beautiful Steamship *Victoria*, commanded by Capt. Pouliot, and owned by the Canadian Government—was despatched to the Maritime Provinces for the purpose of conveying the Delegates to the ancient capital of Canada. She arrived at Pictou, N. S., on the 5th of October, where the Nova Scotia Delegates came on board of her, together with His Excellency

Sir Richard Graves McDonnell, Lieutentant Governor of the Province, and also his amiable Lady and their servants.

Arriving at Charlottetown about noon on Thursday, 6th of October, a delay of four hours was made, which time was employed in driving around the City and suburbs, under the guidance of the Hon. Colonel Gray—also in a brief visit to His Excellency Governor Dundas, at Government House, and in partaking of a sumptuous Luncheon at Inkerman House, the residence of Col. Gray. Shortly after three o'clock the same day, the party—including the Prince Edward Island Delegates, with the exception of Mr. Secretary Pope and the Hon. Mr. Coles, who had proceeded to Quebec by way of Portland—were conveyed to the *Victoria*, anchored in the roadstead, and in a few minutes she was ploughing her way to Shediac, N. B., at which place it was arranged that she should call for the New Brunswick Delegates. Arriving off the harbor of Shediac about 10 o'clock, p. m., she anchored there until the morning, and then steamed closer in to the harbor, when, after the delay of a few hours, five of the New Brunswick Delegates came on board—two others, Messrs. Secretary Tilley and Hon. Mr. Chandler, having proceeded by the Portland route. The *Victoria* then at once proceeded on her voyage up the Gulf and River St. Lawrence

The voyage was rendered interesting by the presence of many ladies, whose number included the wife and daughter of the Provincial Secretary of Nova Scotia; the wife and daughter of the Hon. A. G. Archibald, Delegate from the same Province; the daughter of the Hon. Col. Gray, of New Brunswick; two daughters of the Hon. W. H. Steeves, and a daughter of the Hon. Charles Fisher, two Delegates from the last named Province; and the daughter of the Hon. Col. Gray, and Mrs. Alexander, sister of the Hon. Mr. Haviland, of Prince Edward Island.

The Steamer was most abundantly provided with every

comfort and luxury that could be desired, and these were dispensed with an unsparing hand by direction of the obliging Captain, in regard to whom and his staff of officers, and male and female servants, it is only just to observe that they were untiring in their exertions to contribute in every possible way to the happiness of their guests.

Notwithstanding all the discomforts of a sea voyage, when the chilling blasts and the lowering skies of autumn succeed the warm sunshine and the gentle breeze of summer—notwithstanding, too, that other discomfort attending the payment of tribute to Neptune—too rigidly exacted when the weather is least agreeable—yet the trip up the St. Lawrence had many attractions for the voyagers—the deck of the noble Steamer was seldom deserted by promenaders during daylight and long after dark—the bold scenery of the St. Lawrence, after passing the mouth of the River, being a special object of admiration. To attempt a description of the scenery of the majestic River would be out of place in a compilation of this kind, especially when glowing descriptions can be readily found in the pages of the poet and tourist.

On Saturday evening, the 8th, a violent gale and snow storm occurred, which continued during the whole night, in consequence of which the ship made little progress— the engine being stopped at frequent intervals to enable the officers to take soundings, and use every precaution that could secure the common safety. Early on Sunday the gale abated, and putting on full steam, the *Victoria* pursued her voyage in gallant style, reaching her wharf at Quebec at an early hour the same evening.

Apartments having been provided by the Government of Canada, at the St. Louis Hotel, for all the Delegates and their lady companions, they were immediately, on landing, conveyed thither, where they were most sumptuously entertained during their whole stay in Quebec, as the guests of the Canadian Government.

THE CONFERENCE AT QUEBEC.

On Monday, 10th of October, at 11 o'clock, the full Conference met in the Parliament Buildings—the whole Canadian Ministry, consisting of twelve, being present; there were five Delegates from Nova Scotia; seven from New Brunswick; two from Newfoundland; and seven from Prince Edward Island. The names of all the gentlemen who sat in Conference are as follow:—

CANADA.

Sir ETIENNE P. TACHE, Premier,
Hon. J. A. McDONALD, Attorney General, West,
Hon. G. E. CARTIER, Attorney General, East,
Hon. WM. McDOUGALL, Provincial Secretary,
Hon. GEORGE BROWN, President of Executive Council,
Hon. A. T. GALT, Financial Minister,.
Hon. A. CAMPBELL, Commissioner of Crown Lands,
Hon. OLIVER MOWATT, Postmaster General,
Hon. HECTOR LANGEVIN, Solicitor General, East,
Hon. JAMES COCKBURN, Solicitor General, West,
Hon. T. D'ARCY McGEE, Minister of Agriculture,
Hon. J. C. CHAPAIS, Commissioner of Public Works.

NOVA SCOTIA.

Hon. Dr. TUPPER, Provincial Secretary,
Hon. W. A. HENRY, Attorney General,
Hon. R. B. DICKEY,
Hon. JONATHAN McCULLY,
Hon. A. G. ARCHIBALD.

NEW BRUNSWICK.

Hon. S. L. TILLEY, Provincial Secretary,
Hon. JOHN M. JOHNSON, Attorney General.
Hon. PETER MITCHELL,
Hon. CHARLES FISHER,
Hon. EDWARD CHANDLER,
Hon. W. H. STEEVES,
Hon. JOHN H. GRAY.

NEWFOUNDLAND.

Hon. F. B. T. Carter, Speaker of the House of Assembly,
Hon. Ambrose Shea.

PRINCE EDWARD ISLAND.

Hon. Col. Gray, Premier,
Hon. Edward Palmer, Attorney General,
Hon. W. H. Pope, Provincial Secretary,
Hon. George Coles,
Hon. T. Heath Haviland,
Hon. Edward Whelan,
Hon. A. A. McDonald.

The Conference was organized by the unanimous election of Sir Etienne P. Tache, Chairman, who, on taking the Chair, commented briefly on the vast importance of the object that was to be brought under the consideration of the Convention; he said he relied on the forbearance and co-operation of the Delegates to enable him to discharge the duties of the Chair; and then, in a few eloquent sentences, he tendered to the gentlemen composing the respective Delegations from the Maritime Provinces, a cordial welcome on behalf of the Government and people of Canada. He fervently hoped that their Mission would be productive of great advantage to all the provinces, and would be agreeable to themselves.

The Provincial Secretaries of the several Provinces were then elected Honorary Secretaries to the Conference, and Major Hewitt Bernard was appointed Executive Secretary.

The first and second days of the Conference were chiefly occupied in regulating the modes of proceedure ; and as soon as these were disposed of, the Delegates addressed themselves to the general question of a Federal Union. Some admirable speeches were delivered by several of the Delegates, (which were not reported, as the Conference sat with closed doors ;) and all, without one dissenting voice, pronounced in favor of Union. The main principle having been affirmed, the Conference entered at once on the work of arranging the details of a Constitution for the proposed Federation.

"DRAWING ROOM" AND RECEPTION OF THE DELEGATES.

On the evening of the 11th October, His Excellency the Governor General held a "Drawing Room" in the Council Chamber of the Parliament Buildings, when the Delegates from the Maritime Provinces were formally presented to His Excellency before a vast and brilliant assemblage, including almost every person of note or influence in the Naval, Military, Volunteer and Civil Services of the Province, together with the leading members of the best society to be found in the social circles of Quebec and vicinity. A lengthy description of the "Drawing Room" appears in the Quebec papers of that date, but it is now unnecessary to take any further notice of it.

INVITATIONS TO FESTIVITES.—BALL IN THE PARLIAMENT BUILDINGS.

While the Conference was proceeding with its arduous and important duties, invitations were received from Cities and Corporations in both sections of the Province, to partake of their hospitalities. The Stadacona Club, (Quebec,) the Board of Trade, (Quebec,) the Cities of Montreal, Ottawa, Belleville, Kingston, Toronto, Hamilton, and other places to the remote western boundaries of the Province, forwarded invitations to the Conference Room, proffering their hospitalities. To the distant Corporations and Cities answers of acceptance were returned through the Chairman, conditional as to the time when the business of the Conference should be completed.

On the evening of the 14th a very brilliant Ball was given in the Parliament Buildings, under the auspices of the Canadian Ministry. It was attended by the same classes—the same distinguished persons and society as attended the "Drawing Room" on the 11th. His Excellency the Governor General, His Excellency the Lieut. Governor of Nova Scotia and Lady, the Members of the Canadian Government, the Delegates from the Eastern Provinces, and about 800 others, formed a large and most agreeable party, by whom the pleasures of the dance were kept up without interruption, and without an incident to mar the harmony of the occasion, until nearly 3 o'clock on the morning of the 15th.

PUBLIC DINNER UNDER THE AUSPICES OF THE QUEBEC BOARD OF TRADE.

SPEECHES OF DELEGATES.

The first and only public occasion on which the Delegates from the Lower Provinces had an opportunity of expressing their opinions on the question of Confederation, was at the Dinner given to them by the Quebec Board of Trade on the evening of the 15th of October. It took place at Russell's Hotel, in Palace Street, and was pronounced by the Quebec journals as the most successful public banquet ever witnessed in Quebec. The attendance was very numerous, including the leading members of the mercantile community, the principal officers of the Army in Garrison, the heads of the Civil Service, several members of both Houses of Parliament, and nearly all the Canadian Ministers. The Banqueting Room was superbly decorated, displaying on its walls mottoes in reference to the several Provinces. The viands were of the best description, including everything which a rich and populous city like Quebec could afford, to gratify the taste of an epicure. A. Joseph, Esq., President of the Board of Trade, occupied the Chair, and the Vice Chair was occupied by H. S. Scott, Esq. The Stewards arranged themselves at different tables, and by the most judicious and delicate management, provided for the comfort and convenience of their numerous guests.

When the cloth was removed, and the usual patriotic toasts had been duly honored, the Chairman proposed, amid loud cheers, "The Health of His Excellency the Governor General." It was drank with all the honors, the Band playing "The fine old Irish Gentleman." The next toast on the list was "Our Guests—the Delegates from the Maritime Provinces."

The CHAIRMAN, in rising to propose this toast, said that the merchants of Quebec had reason to feel a legitimate pride that they had here, as their guests, this evening, gentlemen occupying such a high position in the sister provinces, assembled in this city in order to discuss a highly important subject. (Cheers.) And while the merchants of Quebec did not think they were called upon to express an opinion on the question of confederation itself, they all heartily desired some change in our present position—they desired a thorough commercial union—they desired that the unequal and hostile tariffs of the several provinces should disappear. (Cheers.) We wanted one tariff instead of five. We wanted a commercial union, in order to bring about closer ties, and we wanted that union under one flag—the flag of old England. (Loud cheers.) We wished, too, that this union should be strengthened still further by the iron ties of the intercolonial railway. (Cheers.) It had long been the habit to call the maritime colonies by the name of the sister provinces; but notwithstanding this appellation they were strangers to us and we were strangers to them, as was shown by the diversity of the tariffs. But let us hope that a new era was about dawning upon us, now when we saw the great statesmen of the British North American Provinces assembled in this city, in this month of October, 1864—let us hope that if we did not obtain a political union, we should at least have a commercial union. (Cheers.) There was but one matter to which he would briefly allude before proposing the toast of the evening.

As they were all well aware, a vast number of our people were interested in ship-building, and he was glad to know that it was a highly important interest among the inhabitants of the Lower Provinces also. Referring to the Reciprocity Treaty, he might say that it was not framed with any particular view to the interests of the eastern section of the Provinces; but we were as willing to stand by it as others, and when the proper time came we should unite with Nova Scotia, New Brunswick, Newfoundland, and Prince Edward Island, and say that we should also have free-trade in ship-building. He would now propose the toast of the evening—"Our Guests the Delegates from the Maritime Provinces," and he spoke the wish of the merchants of Quebec, when he said he trusted the Delegates would receive this small compliment to themselves in the same open, cordial, unreserved spirit in which it had been tendered. (Loud cheers.)

The toast having been duly honored—

The Hon. Dr. TUPPER, Provincial Secretary of Nova Scotia, replied on behalf of that Province, as follows:—Mr. President and gentlemen,—I gladly avail myself of this opportunity to return thanks on behalf of myself and co-delegates from the Province of Nova Scotia, for the kind and hospitable manner in which we have been received in this country. I feel that our thanks are not only especially due to the Ministry of Canada for the very hospitable and generous manner in which we have been received, but that they are also alike due to the city of Quebec, the city of Montreal, and the city of Toronto, in fact, I may say to the people of Canada, who of one accord seem to join most heartily in rendering our visit to this great Province agreeable as well as useful. (Loud cheers.) I feel not a little embarrassed in rising to address you. The magnitude of the question which has called the delegates from the Maritime Provinces to this meeting is one which actually appals me to contemplate, when I reflect that from the time in which the immortal Wolfe decided on the plains of Abraham the destiny of British America to the present, no event has exceeded in importance or magnitude the one which is now taking place in this ancient and famous city. You will understand me when I say that

I feel embarrassed as I approach its consideration before so intelligent an audience. (Hear, hear.) But this is not the only source of embarrassment which I feel on the present occasion, because I need not tell you that, assembled as we are to discuss the great and momentous interests of British North America—assembled as we are to devise, under the authority and with the sanction of the crown of Great Britain, a better and more useful system of government for these Provinces, we are obliged to preserve to a large extent that confidence in our interchange of opinion which is essential to the discussion of so great a question. (Cheers.) I need not tell you how embarrassing it would be if the immatured opinions at which we may have individually arrived were thrown broad-cast before the people, to become matters of contention before we had, by mutual concessions and mutual compromises, arranged and matured a plan of action that we could, with confidence, submit to the intelligence of British North America. (Cheers.) But beyond this I have another source of embarrassment. I need not remind you that, from the time when we had the pleasure of receiving that large deputation of the members of the Canadian Government at Charlottetown down to the present, we have had a series of social meetings in Prince Edward Island, in Nova Scotia, and in New Brunswick, that we have several times been before the public in connection with this question; and when I tell you that the question has been already discussed by gentlemen connected with the Government of Canada—men who occupy not only the proudest position as statesmen in British North America, who have not only a British, but I may say a European reputation, you will understand how difficult it must be for me, familiarised as you must have been undoubtedly by the intelligent Press of this country, which has discussed this question and made you acquainted with the speeches of these men—you will, I say, understand the embarrassment I feel in rising here to-night to attempt to offer anything new in addition to that which has been before offered. When it is understood that the object of this meeting of delegates is to ascertain whether the time has not come when a more useful system of government can be devised for those British American Provinces, I need not say that its importance is one which it is impossible to overrate. Uninformed as the public mind in the Lower Provinces was on this question, the visit and the statements made by the gentlemen connected with the Government of Canada have aroused a large and marked degree of attention, which I believe will be fraught with the best consequences in its effects upon these Provinces, (cheers); and as these gentlemen in order to lead the public mind of the Lower Provinces to an appreciation of this question, took the opportunity to place before us statements of the vast resources of this great colony of Canada, I may, perhaps, be excused if I invite your attention to some of the facts connected with the growth and increase of the Lower Provinces. (Loud cheers.) It is true you have a magnificent country, embracing an immense territorial area; it is true you have a comparatively large population of 3,000,000; it is true you have land teeming with inexhaustible resources, on every hand; but as was observed by your able and talented minister, Mr. Cartier, great as is your country, large as is your population, inexhaustible as are your resources, the Maritime Provinces have something to you equally essential to the formation of a great nation. (Cheers.) We shall bring into the federation with Canada a territorial area of 50,000 or 60,000 square miles, and an additional population of 800,000 souls; and I need not say to the gentleman who has just sat down, and who has made such complimentary allusions to the Lower Provinces, that the prospect of the addition of a population of 800,000 souls must necessarily excite the attention of the manufacturers of Canada. (Cheers.) We should bring a revenue to the common purse of something like $3,000,000, and when I tell you that Nova Scotia has something like doubled her revenue within the last six years, you will understand that we do not require a union with Canada to draw from her resources. We should add, at the same time, to the trade of the common federation something like $35,000,000 in our exports and imports. I need not tell you how much Canada owes to the mighty St. Lawrence; but this highway, great and magnificent as it is, is but an imperfect one, inasmuch as it is closed to all commerce some five months in the year, not to speak of the humiliating position in which this great country is left, when you feel that you are dependent upon a foreign, if not a rival state, for access to the ocean, one of the essential requirements of commerce, without which no country can be permanently great. (Cheers.) You can readily understand how important it is that Canada should obtain means of access to the ocean not only for five months but for twelve months in the year—means of communication not only with the ocean but with the parent State. (Cheers.) Why is it that the Intercolonial Railway is not a fact? It is because, being divided, that which is the common interest of these Colonies has been neglected; and when it is understood that the construction of this work is going to give to Canada that which is so essential to her, its importance will be understood, not only in connection with your political greatness, but also in connection with your commercial character, as affording increased means of communication with the Lower Provinces—for the inexhaustible resources of the Great West will flow down the St. Lawrence to Quebec, and from there to the magnificent harbors of Halifax and St. John, open at all seasons of the year. I would ask you, too, to contemplate the inexhaustible wealth of the ocean which surrounds the Maritime Provinces, in the fisheries which we there have; but it is not only in that respect that the Maritime Provinces are prepared to show you that they will be able to bring something to the treasury of British North America. If you look at the Colony which I have the honor to represent you will find that its mineral resources cannot be excelled on this side of the Atlantic. You will find a vast country occupied by as valuable coal deposits as are to be found on the surface of the earth. You will find iron mines in the Province of Nova Scotia which, in quality, will successfully rival the finest Swedish iron. You will find iron and coal associated with limestone. In fact, you will find in Nova Scotia all those chief natural characteristics which have made Great Britain the chief commercial mart of the world. There are also our gold mines, not yet developed. Still they are valuable, and in illustration of their worth I may tell you that the receipts from rents and royalties have, within the last six months, enlarged to the extent of $20,000. You will thus understand that our gold mines afford a prospect of remunerative employment to the large population which will inevitably be attracted by them. (Loud cheers.) When you look at these facts, you will easily understand that the confederation which shall unite the British American Colonies, which will give a common aim, and unite by a common bond the whole people, will tend to enhance their credit—to place them upon the exchanges of the world in a far better position than we can hope for in our present divided state. I fail myself to understand how the commercial union, so ably referred to by your chairman, is ever to be realized, except in connection with a political union. The public men of British North America have not, probably, yet exhausted that subject; but they have given it their careful attention, and hitherto they have been unable to devise means whereby a commercial union could be formed separate from a political union. (Cheers.) Their tariffs would require to be adjusted to meet the necessities of each people by different legislatures, and while this is the case, while we are separate, we can never hope to have such an adjustment as to give to the people of the whole of the Provinces such a commercial union as the Quebec Board of Trade judges to be so essential to our common interest. But there are other questions in presence of which even the financial credit and commercial prosperity of these Colonies sink into comparative insignificance. I do not underrate these —I believe it should be the business of the statesmen of every free country to endeavour to increase its commercial prosperity and exalt its credit, but there is that which is dearer still, and that is freedom and safety. (Cheers.) I believe the time has come when the statesman of British North America is unworthy the position he occupies, who does not feel it his imperative duty to devote his most earnest attention to the solution of the great and important question, how the lives and property and peace of the inhabitants of British North America may not only be preserved, but guaranteed against any assault. (Cheers.) Occupying the official position I do in connection with the Government of one of the Provinces, it would be wrong for me to say a single word on this subject liable to misconception or misconstruction anywhere; yet I must say that no one who regards the changed aspect of affairs on this continent within the last few years can fail to see that unless we are to be dependent for our safety on the generous forbearance of our neighbors we must be prepared unitedly to co-operate for the common defence of our country—(cheers,) and I must say also that I do not believe the time has come when Great Britain is indifferent to our defence. I am not one of those who fancy there is any large or influential class of statesmen in Great Britain who are insensible to the great advantage and importance of preserving the British American colonies as part of the empire. It may suit the Manchester school and doctrinaires like Goldwin Smith to put forth the contrary notion, but I speak under the deepest conviction of the truth of what I say, when I assert that the statesmen who have charge of the Government of the British Empire would be thrust from place and power the very moment they should propose a policy so fatal to the greatness of the Crown and the dignity of England, as would be the casting adrift of her colonies. (Cheers.) I need not say that these Provinces have a common interest. The loss of Halifax means the loss of Nova Scotia; the loss of Nova Scotia means the loss of Prince Edward Island and New Brunswick, and the loss of these necessarily involves also the loss of Canada—for we stand or fall together. (Cheers.) And the loss of these Provinces involves also the loss of the West India Islands, and the result would be, that Great Britain would sink from the mighty position she now occupies into the comparatively insignificant position of a kingdom comprising only two small islands, (Hear, hear.) I believe the day is far distant—I believe the child is not yet born who will live to hear the proposition authoritatively propounded by any Cabinet in Great Britain of the abandonment of the British North American Colonies. (Loud cheers.) I believe that a blow struck which would assail the property or liberty of British America would bring into action all the power of the British Crown—all the force of that magnificent army and gallant navy on which we confidently rely for protection. But, at the same time, the fact that this is the temper of the British mind, the sentiment of the British Empire, instead of rendering us supine and indifferent, should nerve us with increased vigor to place ourselves in the position in which we can best co-operate with the brave army and gallant navy of Great Britain for the defence of this portion of the British Empire. (Cheers.) I have little more to say, as I do not wish to trespass on the time reserved for other gentlemen from my own and the sister Provinces who will address you. But I must say that I cannot understand the caution which your chairman, the President of the Board of Trade, felt it necessary to exercise in referring to the great question of Confederation. I feel, Sir, it was wise on your part, and on the part of the influential body. for whom you spoke, that due caution should be exhibited ; but when you were speaking of a question in presence of whose magnitude the voice of faction has been hushed—for I find around this table, combined to obtain a satisfactory solution of that question, the representatives of the two great parties who have so long been in antagonism to each other, and not particularly to the advantage of the Province of Canada—I find the representatives of these great parties, almost hereditary in their antagonism, combining in the most patriotic spirit to find a solution of the great question how the best government shall be obtained for British North America. When I look at all this, I think the circumstances would have justified the President of the Quebec Board of Trade in giving a little more encouragement to the project than he has given here to-night. (Loud cheers.) And it is not only in Canada alone that, in presence of this question, the voice of faction has been hushed. There is present at this moment in Quebec, not only the extraordinary spectacle of the different Governments of the four outlying sister Provinces being represented here on this occasion, but we find side by side with the prominent members of the various Administrations, and intimately and closely associated with them, the able and talented leaders of the Opposition in their respective Provinces. (Cheers.) Under these circumstances, when—when, as I have said, in the presence of the great question the voice of faction is hushed—why should it be necessary to exercise so much caution not to commit ourselves to the conclusion at which we may arrive ? (Cheers.) The question, at all events, is of that magnitude which requires that any hostile expression of opinion should be suppressed, and that the public should be ready to give it that calm and dispassionate consideration without which it is impossible that any number of statesmen, however able, can bring it to a satisfactory issue. Dr. Tupper having again expressed his thanks for the generous hospitality with which he and his colleagues had been received in this ancient and venerable capital, resumed his seat amidst loud and prolonged cheering.

The Hon. SAMUEL L. TILLEY, Provincial Secretary of New Brunswick, responded as follows, on behalf of his Province: He said that the manner in which the toast had been received showed how deep and earnest was the general feeling respecting the grave question on which the Intercolonial Conference was engaged. His friend, the Hon. Dr. Tupper, had said he felt embarrassed, and he, too, felt embarrassed at observing a certain table (the reporters' table), but at the same time he was reassured by the great forbearance these gentlemen had shewn on a recent occasion when several of them visited the Maritime Provinces. (Laughter and cheers.) The delegates from the Lower Provinces were not here seeking this union. They had assembled at Charlottetown a few weeks ago, in order to see whether they could not extend their own family relations, and then Canada intervened, and the consideration of the larger question was the result. He considered it right to make this remark, inasmuch as it had been asserted in certain quarters that the Maritime Provinces, weak and impoverished, were endeavoring to attach themselves to Canada, in order to reap the benefits arising from such a union. This was not the case. Look at the immense amount of shipping they owned. He was in a position to state that, for the year 1864, after paying the interest on all their debts, and after providing liberally for roads, bridges, and other public works, they would have a surplus of half a million. (Cheers.) Therefore, they were not coming in as paupers—they were coming to put something into the capital that was worth having. Next alluding to the Intercolonial Railway project, he said their feeling on this subject was this: "We won't have this union unless you give us the railway." (Cheers.) It was utterly impossible we could have either a political or commercial union without it. With regard to the latter, he might say that he had at one time believed with others that we could have a commercial without a political Union; but he now held with his hon. friend (Mr. Tupper) that it was all but impracticable, as was easily shewn by the question of tariffs, to which that hon. gentleman had referred. Without going into details, he might say that it was the opinion of the Conference that union was desirable if the details could be satisfactorily arranged. Of course, in making these arrangements we should have to have due regard to the wants, requirements and even, in some degree, to the prejudices of the people. Even in the Lower Provinces the tariffs acted adversely to each other. He asked them as commercial men was it desirable that this state of affairs should continue? (Cries of "No," "No.") He saw no other way of obviating those difficulties than by a political union. He would not now refer at any great length to the defence question, inasmuch as we had here the gallant Colonel from Prince Edward Island (Col. Gray,) who had made it his special study. He would, however, remark that the anxiety respecting the subject of defence in New Brunswick was not intense among the masses of the people. This was because the population was very small, and the people felt that their individual efforts would be useless. But throw the three hundred thousand souls of New Brunswick in with the population of Canada and the other provinces, making a total of four millions; and twice as much in the way of a defence contingent might be obtained from New Brunswick, because the people would feel that they were part of a great nation. (Cheers.) If details could be satisfactorily arranged it was advisable we should be united in one great Confederation. Look, for instance, at the example offered by Canada. Since the union of Canada its population had increased from a little over a million to two millions and a half. He (Mr. Tilley) hoped for the best; and with the intelligence of which the Conference was composed, he, trusted they would overcome all difficulties; and that they would soon meet in Quebec, Montreal, or Ottawa, to consummate the union—despite the caution of his friend the President. (Laughter and cheers.)

Hon. Mr. CARTER, (of Newfoundland), returned thanks for himself and his co-delegate. He had listened attentively to the speeches made by his hon. friends who preceded him, and believed that they had stated their cases very ably indeed. The colony to which he belonged was not represented in the Charlottetown Convention; but it had responded to the appeal to take part in that of Quebec. He might safely say, for the great majority of the people of Newfoundland, that they would feel it a great advantage to enter this proposed union, and that they would consider it a serious loss to be left out of it. Newfoundland did not occupy such a high position as Nova Scotia and New Brunswick; but she would nevertheless be no burthen to the Confederation—nay, more, he believed if the Union were consummated it would be an advantage to the city of Quebec. What was wanted was increased facilities for trade. The trade of Canada would be destroyed if Newfoundland were in the hands of a foreign power. It was only necessary to look at the map to enable one to arrive at the conclusion that the stability of the Confederation would require Newfoundland. He had occasion to visit Quebec several years ago, on matters of public business, which brought forcibly before his mind the benefits which would be derived from a union of the Provinces; he had then expressed the wish that we might one day be all united in one common country under a scion of the Royal family; and it was his belief now that the wished-for union was not far distant. (Cheers.). There were, of course, many things to be arranged; but he nevertheless hoped they would be in a position to announce a successful result to their respective constituencies.—The hon. gentleman concluded by expressing a hope that he would have an opportunity of seeing his kind hosts in Newfoundland, so that he might reciprocate their courtesies. (Cheers.)

The Honorable Colonel GRAY, President of the Executive Council of Prince Edward Island, began by expressing a regret that he was suffering from a severe cold which, he said, almost rendered his voice inaudible. His friend the Hon. Mr. Tilley had referred to him an important but rather dry point—that of defence; but he would not now express his sentiments upon it, nor would he have arisen to speak, but that it was his duty to thank them on behalf of his co-delegates and of the people of Prince Edward Island for their kind and courteous hospitality. When he saw such an amount of wealth and intelligence around this board he looked upon it as a proof that Quebec was destined to occupy the first rank, if not the first place, in a mighty nation. (Loud cheers.) It would be long, indeed, before the hospitality now extended would be effaced from their recollection.—After some laudatory reference to the articles on Mr. Howe's letter to Mr. Adderley, which appeared in a Quebec journal, the hon. gentleman went on to say that he was glad to have an opportunity of raising his voice to help in bringing about that which he believed was now about to be consummated. The dream of his youth and manhood was that he would, one day, be the citizen of a great nation, extending from the extreme west to the sea-board; and he believed that dream was about to be realized. (Cheers.) What a time was that in which we met to endeavor to accomplish this great purpose! Who could tell what would occur on this continent in the next four years? The previous speakers had alluded to our commercial interests, and on this point he (Col. Gray,) could not pretend to follow them; but he would say that the colony he represented could throw something into the common treasury. It could contribute its mite—it could be to the other Provinces what Rhode Island was to the other States of the American Union. But the delegates required from their hosts something more than this feast—they required their sympathies in another direction. It was impossible to attain the result so ardently wished for unless they gave their aid in banishing all sectional prejudices and jealousies which would interfere with the great end. He would say for himself that there was not a man among them who would not come forward to spill the last drop of his blood and spend his treasure rather than the soil of Canada should be polluted by the foot of a foe. But if the people of the Maritime Provinces united with those of Canada, as a band of brothers, they might rest assured that God would defend his own work. (Loud cheers.) In conclusion, he hoped they would accept his cordial thanks for the honor conferred on his brother-delegates and himself by drinking their health.

The CHAIRMAN said they had now to drink the health of their other guests, Her Majesty's Ministers. (Cheers.) These hon. gentlemen had undertaken a great task—a task the object of which was to put an end to those sectional differences which, for years, had existed in Canada, and to which his hon. friend Mr. Tupper had referred. We had certainly to admit that, in this Province, we had been divided in a way that was not to our advantage. It was, he repeated, an important task the Government had undertaken in trying to mature a measure which would promote the material welfare of all the British North American Provinces, and give us a strong Government. If they succeeded in their endeavors to bring about the Union to which he (the Chairman) had so cautiously referred (laughter)—if they succeeded in giving us a good Government, they would not only deserve but would receive the thanks of every true Canadian. Without further preface, he therefore begged leave to propose, "The Members of the Executive Council of Canada."

The toast was received with loud cheers—the Band playing " A la Claire Fontaine."

Hon. Sir E. P. TACHE, Receiver General and Minister of Militia of Canada, said he arose to thank them in the name of his colleagues and for himself, for the toast which had been proposed and received so cordially. Under ordinary circumstances, he (Sir E. P. Tache) would have contented himself with merely thanking them for this toast, because in mixed assemblies it was looked upon simply as a matter of respect to those who, for the time being, held the reins of Government. But there was such a close connection between the principle upon which the Government was formed and the present occasion that he might be justified in saying more. They were aware that the present Administration was formed for the very purpose of carrying out the important measure which those distinguished gentlemen from the sister provinces had met in Quebec to endeavor to bring about. He had, therefore, as it were, a right to say a few words on the subject, but the hon. gentlemen who preceded him had entered so earnestly, so fully, and so clearly into the subject, that it was almost useless for him to add more. This project of uniting the British North American Provinces was not a new scheme. It had been suggested years ago by an able statesman, Lord Durham, in his Report; and though he (Sir E. P. Taché,) might not agree with all it contained, he would say that it was undoubtedly the work of a very able statesman. One of the recommendations of Lord Durham's Report had been carried out; and whatever might have been said then, it would be admitted now that the union of Upper and Lower Canada had doubled our population and trebled our resources in twenty years. (Cheers.) Little, however, was said about the union of the provinces until 1853, when the late lamented Mr. Merritt moved for a committee on the subject. Then there was very little said or done until 1857 or 1858—he believed in the session of 1858, when his hon. friend Mr. Galt moved a series of resolutions on the subject, which were submited to Her Majesty's Government, but were not acted upon, the other Governments not having taken simultaneous action in the matter. But since the last mentioned date it had been amply discussed by articles in the public journals and by *brochures*. However, difficulties of a sectional nature grew upon us, and after the defeat of the Ministry last spring, a Government was formed on the avowed basis of a Confederation of the British North American Provinces. We had been in political difficulties, no doubt, as an hon. gentleman who preceded him had said, but these difficulties were not so great—the body politic was not so sick or incurable as to make a remedy of no avail. (Laughter.) Union would benefit us all—not merely this one or the other one, but the whole. His hearers might expect something from him as to the secrets of the Conference; but if they did they were much mistaken. (Laughter.) The members were not sworn; but they were bound in honor as gentlemen to preserve secrecy. It would be highly imprudent at this stage of the proceedings to divulge anything, for we did not know what modifications or changes might become necessary. The leaking-out of half-matured points of the arrangement would create erroneous impressions and would produce a very bad effect. He would, before sitting down, form a vow or give expression to a vow—he did not know whether the phrase was good English, but it was excellent French—that at no distant period a fraternal era might be opened unto us by which the cool-headed and persevering Englishman might be drawn closer to the warm-hearted and generous Irishman, to the keen, persevering and economical (laughter)—they should reserve their laughter as he had not finished the sentence—the persevering and economical son of Caledonia, and the gay and chivalric offspring of old Gaul—each of these contributing their quota of the good qualities they had inherited from their ancestors, blended together in one grand people—Acadian or Canadian, he did not care which, for they were both dear to his heart. (Enthusiastic cheering.)

The CHAIRMAN called upon Mr. James Bell Forsyth to propose the next toast.

Mr. FORSYTH said the toast he had the honor of proposing was "The Commercial Prosperity of British North America." But if statesmen accustomed to speak in public, on important subjects, felt their position so embarrassing as they had themselves declared, how much more embarrassing was it to him (Mr. Forsyth) unaccustomed to public speaking, yet called upon to introduce this extensive subject. The Ministry of Canada had shewn great patriotism when they cast aside the bickerings and heart-burnings of past years for the purpose of uniting us in a great nation. (Cheers.) When he (Mr. Forsyth) saw around the board those delegates from the Maritime Provinces joined with our own leading men in this great undertaking, he felt that it was a subject for congratulation; and the general feeling throughout the land, from Lake Superior to Halifax, was to wish them "God speed." He would not enter into statistics, but he did think that if nothing else arose from this meeting but the construction of the Intercolonial Railway, it would be a great result indeed. He trusted, however, that we would have not only a railroad, but a uniform tariff, and not only a uniform tariff, but such a union, whether Federal or Legislative, as would give us unity of sentiment and community of interest. (Cheers.) It was most consoling, throughout all the bearings of this great question, that there was the same good feeling as ever, to glorious old England, under whose flag we lived—that ancient flag which, for a thousand years, had braved the battle and the breeze. (Loud cheers.) Without further comment, he proposed the toast of "The Commercial Prosperity of British North America."

The toast was enthusiastically received—the Band playing the "Canadian Hymn."

Hon. Mr. GALT (Finance Minister of Canada), who was loudly called for, arose amid much cheering, and observed that though he felt it was highly flattering to be thus called upon, yet that before he ventured to address such an enlightened commercial community, it would have been only fair to allow him some time for preparation.—Alluding to the lack of information so long prevailing in Canada respecting the Maritime Provinces, he said it was to be hoped that the visit of those gentlemen in whose honor they had assembled to-night would dispel that ignorance. When we saw the ability of those gentlemen and reflected that they might be one day called to the councils of our united country, it was consoling to think that, if the Confederation of the Provinces were brought about, we might have the benefit of such talents. (Cheers.) With regard to the question of commercial prosperity arising out of this subject, he might remark that, in commerce, we should never be contented with the minor advantage if we could get the major. What depressed the commercial energies of this country? Because we had hitherto been confined to two markets—England and the United States. Now a Union with the Lower Provinces would not only give us the benefit of their local markets, but would also open up to us the benefit of their foreign trade—a trade which, in one or two instances, we had once possessed but had now lost. We had in our own Province a certain amount of the maritime element; but not so much as we should have after a Union with the Sister Provinces. In the circumstances in which we were placed, it was gratifying that those points in which we might be deficient would be amply supplied by the other Provinces. We were trying to encourage manufacturing in Canada. A supply of coal was a most important element of success in this respect; and we had before us the fact that Nova Scotia possessed that element. The great resources of the Maritime Provinces had been amply shewn by the hon. gentlemen who had already spoken, and who had abundantly proved that they came not as seeking assistance from us but in a broad and national spirit. (Cheers.) He was glad their speeches would go forth to the public, and that it would be seen that the Provinces did not come together as suppliants, but with a liberal and patriotic desire to improve our lot and to perpetuate and preserve British institutions in a truly British spirit. (Cheers.) And the enthusiasm shewn here to-night was an earnest of the manner in which the realization of the great object in view would be welcomed.

The toast of "The Press," was then given, and responded to by Mr. G. A. Sala, the Essayist, and at that time correspondent of the London *Telegraph;*—the health of the Chairman was also given and responded to; and "the Ladies" were likewise remembered as worthy of festive honors; after which the company dispersed, it being then nearly midnight.

The Conference continued to meet daily between the hours of ten and eleven o'clock, and adjourning at four o'clock, resumed their sittings at seven o'clock, which were continued until a late hour when no engagements interfered. Festivities were not wholly abandoned, but were, in a measure, checked by the declared desire of the Delegates to apply themselves assiduously to the discharge of their public duties. At an early date after their arrival in Quebec, M. and Madame Tessier, lady of the Speaker of the Legislative Council, invited the Delegates to a Ball, expressly designed in honor of them. The evening of the 19th October was set apart for this interesting event; and all the Delegates and dignitaries of the Crown in Quebec, together with some of its best Society in the private walks of life, accepted the generous invitation, and, after many pleasant hours, left the Ball Room with the impression that they had enjoyed one of the **happiest re-unions** ever experienced by them.

VISIT TO, AND ADDRESS FROM, LAVAL UNIVERSITY.

On the 20th of October, the Delegates from the Maritime Provinces were, by invitation, received at the Laval University, and honored with a grand official reception, headed by His Lordship the Bishop of Tloa, administrator of the Diocese of Quebec, His Lordship the Bishop of Hamilton, His Lordship the Bishop of Kingston. The Rector of the University, and the Deans and Professors of the several Faculties, appeared in their official robes. The attendance of the students was unusually large, and the occasion was graced by the presence of many ladies and distinguished persons in Quebec at the time. The whole party having proceeded to the great Hall, where the pupils of the Quebec Seminary, to the number of four hundred, were assembled, the Very Reverend Rector read the following Address:—

HONORABLE GENTLEMEN,—There are in the lives of nations, as in those of individuals, moments of solemn import, on which their destiny hangs.

The British Colonies of North America are now in one of those critical periods, the influence of which may even surpass our prevision.

History will hand down to posterity the names of all those to whom the confidence of their fellow-citizens has entrusted with this great mission of examining the basis of our political constitutions, and of proposing fundamental modifications.

It is not the part of a literary and scientific institution to express an opinion on the all-important questions of the day; yet it cannot remain indifferent to debates which concern our common country, understanding as it does how well worthy of the best wishes of all are the eminent personages on whose shoulders weighs so heavy a responsibility.

Moreover, the prosperity of an institution such as this is

too closely connected with the future of the country not to partake in the anxiety with which, from the sources to the mouth of the St. Lawrence, five millions of British subjects await the result of your important labors.

The students of the Quebec Seminary and those of Laval University, whom you see here united, also share in our emotion; in after years some of them may, in their turn, be called on to guide the ship of the State, and to continue the construction, the foundations of which it is your mission to lay.

Whatever may be the issue of your deliberations, permit us to assure you, honorable gentlemen, in the name of all our pupils and Alumni, that your visit will be long borne in mind by them. Nor will it be without result, for, while engaged in the task of developing their intelligence, they will be animated by the grateful remembrance of the honor conferred on their *alma mater* by the presence of the most eminent and most influential men of this immense territory.

Hon. Mr. TUPPER, on behalf of himself and his Associate Delegates, read the following Reply:

To the Very Reverend E. A. Taschereau, D.C.L., Rector of the University of Laval.

VERY REVEREND SIR,—We beg to express our grateful estimate of the very flattering terms in which we have been addressed by you, on behalf of the Faculties and Alumni of this distinguished University, and of the professors and students of the Quebec Seminary.

Engaged as we are in the important duty of endeavoring, in conjunction with the Government of Canada, so to improve the political institutions of the British American Provinces as to promote the common interests of all, we are much gratified to learn that our high mission is duly appreciated at a great seat of learning from which the public sentiment of the country must be largely influenced.

The students of the Quebec Seminary, as also the Faculties and Alumni of Laval University, may rest assured that our best efforts will be exerted to find a wise solution of the great question which has been submitted to our deliberations; but in any event we will not soon forget the distinguished mark of respect which you have been pleased to offer us on the present occasion.

(Signed,) CHARLES TUPPER, W. A. HENRY, J. McCULLY, R. B. DICKEY, A. G. ARCHIBALD, of Nova Scotia.

S. L. TILLEY, W. H. STEEVES, J. M. JOHNSON, E. B. CHANDLER, J. H. GRAY, CHARLES FISHER, of New Brunswick.

F. B. T. CARTER, J. AMBROSE SHEA, of Newfoundland.

J. H. GRAY, EDWARD PALMER, W. H. POPE, A. A. McDONALD, GEORGE COLES, T. HEATH HAVILAND, EDWARD WHELAN, of Prince Edward Island.

The Seminary band then struck up a joyous strain, and the visitors proceeded to the terrace-roof of the main building, whence a magnificent view of the city, harbor and surrounding country was obtained. The Delegates were highly delighted with the prospect, and unanimously declared it to be one of the most beautiful they had ever beheld. After having thus feasted their eyes on the beauties of nature, they proceeded—accompanied by their hosts—to visit the several departments of the University, including the library, the museum of minerology and botany, the cabinets of physics and chemistry, the schools of law and medicine, and the students' residence attached, &c. It is needless to say that they were deeply impressed with the vast extent of the University and the unrivalled educational facilities which it affords.

THE BACHELORS' BALL.

The Bachelors of Quebec entertained the Delegates at a Ball at the Parliament Buildings, on the evening of the 21st October. His Excellency the Governor General and his Ministry were present; and, indeed, all the other distinguished persons who attended the Government Ball in the same place, on the 14th, participated in the hilarity happily and most successfully inaugurated by the Bachelors. The attendance was large—the display of beauty highly attractive—the entertainment in the Supper Room of the best description; and, in short, everything combined to make the Bachelors' Ball one of the most agreeable incidents remotely connected with the Convention.

DEPARTURE FROM QUEBEC.

Nothing further of any importance remains to be noted during the time the Delegates remained in Quebec. They brought their official labors at Quebec to a close on the 27th October; and on the afternoon and evening of that day, nearly all the Delegates, their lady friends, and several members of the Canadian Ministry, proceeded to Montreal by special train, most obligingly placed at their service by C. J. BRYDGES, Esq., the popular and efficient Managing Director of the Grand Trunk Railway, to whom the Delegates are indebted for much courtesy and kindness, and which will, no doubt, be ever gratefully remembered.

ARRIVAL IN MONTREAL.

VISIT TO PUBLIC INSTITUTIONS—CONFERENCE—BALL.

The Delegates and their party arrived at Montreal early on the morning of Friday, 28th October, and proceeded to the St. Lawrence Hall, where apartments were provided for them. The weather was wet and disagreeable during the whole day, which prevented a Volunteer Review from taking place, designed as a mark of respect to the Delegates, and for which extensive preparations had been made. Visits were made, however, to several of the public institutions, during the forenoon; and the Geological Survey, under the direction of the eminent Geologist, Sir William Logan, was an especial object of attraction to the visitors. The collection of geological specimens, fossils, woods and minerals, in this institution, is said to be the largest and best in America. The Delegates were fortunate in being introduced by the Hon Mr. McGee; and the gentleman in charge of the institution most ably and cheerfully explained to his visitors every object of a curious and attractive nature which it contained.

The Delegates held a brief Conference at the St. Lawrence Hall, for the purpose of revising the Minutes of the Proceedings adopted at Quebec, and adjourned until the following day.

On the evening of Friday, a magnificent Ball was given in honor of the Delegates, at the St. Lawrence Hall, at which about 1,000 persons were present—His Excellency Sir Richard G. McDonnell, Lieut. Governor of Nova Scotia, and Lady, and Sir General Fenwick Williams, Commander of the Forces, being amongst the guests. It is needless to say that the beauty and fashion of Montreal were largely represented, and that all the magnates of the City were also present, dissporting in the mazes of the dance, or indulging in the lively interchange of thought in conversational circles. The party was, altogether, an exceedingly gay and brilliant one, and afforded unmixed satisfaction to the pleasure-seekers who filled the splendid Hall of the St. Lawrence Hotel.

PUBLIC BANQUET.
SPEECHES OF DELEGATES AND OTHERS.

On Saturday morning the Delegates again met in Conference to continue and conclude the revisal of the Minutes of Proceedings, which they accomplished a little after two o'clock. A magnificent Banquet or *Dejeuner* was prepared in honor of them, the same day, and served in the Ball Room of the previous evening. The Delegates and their entertainers met in the Drawing Room of the

Hotel about 3 o'clock, and having been severally presented to General Sir Fenwick Williams, who was a guest on this occasion likewise, were introduced to the leading merchants and professional gentlemen of Montreal, and then conducted to the Banquetting Room, which was elegantly decorated. Five tables were furnished for the company, and a cross table at the head for some of the most distinguished of the guests. Large vases, full of beautiful flowers and green-house plants in full bloom, were placed upon the board in the intervals between the highly decorated dishes and wonderful specimens of the confectioner's art. An abundance of wine, of most excellent quality, was provided, and the attandance was all that could be required. The music for the feast was supplied by the band of the Rifle Battalion then quartered in Montreal.

The Chair was taken by His Worship Mayor Beaudry, and the Vice Chairs were filled by Messrs F. Pominville, Peter Redpath, the Hon. T. Ryan, M.L.C., and A. M. Delisle, Esq. When justice was done to the substantial viands, the intellectual part of the entertainment was promptly commenced by the excellent Chairman. The healths of Her Majesty the Queen, of H. R. H. the Prince of Wales and the other members of the Royal Family, and the health of His Excellency the Governor General—were given in quick succession, and received with great bursts of applause, the Band playing an appropriate air to each.

The CHAIRMAN then proposed "The Army, Navy and Volunteers."

General Sir WILLIAM FENWICK WILLIAMS, who was received with prolonged cheering, said that in responding for the Army and Navy he would only detain them a few minutes. In the first place, he had to express his regret that the gallant Admiral, who commands the fleet on the North American station, was not here to respond for the

Navy. That gallant officer could have told them how that Navy gave protection to British commerce with distant countries, even on the distant seas of China, where Admiral Hope had so gallantly distinguished himself. (Cheers.) As regards the Army, they had seen for themselves its discipline during the last three or four years in this country, but they were aware also of the very limited numbers of that portion of the British forces which he had the honor to command; and meeting them on this occasion, and especially the Delegates from the different Provinces, if he were not certain that steps would be taken to add to that small force an efficient militia, he should take more time than he would now take to impress the necessity of this upon their minds. Another arm of the force was also included in the toast—the Volunteers—one of whose most distinguished commanders he now saw before him, his friend, Col. Dyde, who had devoted his most strenuous efforts to increasing the efficiency of that branch of the force. (Cheers.) And he must be allowed to say again that, without an efficient militia, the army in these Provinces could do nothing ; but with such a militia they could do everything. (Cheers.) He thanked them for the very kind way in which he had been received, and before sitting down he begged to wish the Delegates every success in the great undertaking in connection with which they had come here, that these countries might be formed into a great and prosperous Union, under the rule of our gracious Queen, as now, and of her descendants from generation to generation, and that the same glorious flag might continue to wave over their heads for centuries to come. (Loud cheers.)

Col. DYDE returned thanks on behalf of the Volunteers for the honor done them, in not merely drinking their health, but in connecting their names with the glorious Army and Navy. The Volunteers, he believed he might safely say, had always been ready to do their duty. The Government also had of late done its duty by them, as far as the law would allow them, but they required something more than this—they required the countenance and support of their fellow-citizens. (Cheers.) The pursuit of wealth was very commendable, but there were higher objects than that to be aimed at, and every man, particularly the influential and the wealthy, owed something to his country; and if he had not the courage and the patriotism to serve his country as a Volunteer, he ought, at least, to support the Volunteer movement by his countenance and his means. (Cheers.) He regretted to say there were some exceptions to this in this community, and that some of the most wealthy and influential in it, instead of countenancing the Volunteers, discouraged them in every possible way. These cases, however, were few, and he hoped they would be fewer still. In closing he begged to say that the force under his command were ready and willing at all times to do their duty as Volunteers or soldiers. God forbid the occasion should arise that their services should be required as soldiers; but if that occasion should arise he was satisfied they would do their duty, shoulder to shoulder, with Her Majesty's troops. (Cheers.)

The CHAIRMAN said he was sure they would drink the next toast with much pleasure. They had amongst them this afternoon a distinguished gentleman, the Lieutenant Governor of Nova Scotia. (Cheers.) He proposed the health of Sir Richard McDonnell and Lady McDonnell. (Loud cheers.)

SIR RICHARD MACDONNELL, C. B., on rising was greeted with renewed cheers. He said: Mr. Chairman and gentlemen, your reception of me has been so very kind and cordial, as almost to embarrass me, accustomed as I am to public life and to the kindness of Her Majesty's subjects exhibited in various parts of the globe towards the Queen's representatives, who always find her Her Majesty's subjects disposed to aid and co-operate with them in carrying out the objects of Colonial Government, as now administered—those objects being to increase the social welfare and material prosperity of the colonists, as the most acceptable service which the representatives of the Crown can render to their Sovereign. (Cheers.) Meeting you here, gentlemen, in this fair city, which I may truly call the natural commercial centre of a Province which has been well designated as the brightest jewel in the diadem of England, allow me to congratulate you on the progress which I see everywhere around me, since a visit I was fortunate enough to make a few years ago. Allow me also, on the part of one very dear to me, whose name has been connected with mine in the toast you have drunk, to express to you the great pleasure her Ladyship feels on making this, her first visit to your city, to find herself so surrounded by friendly and familiar faces, having had occasion recently to become acquainted at Halifax with so many Canadians that in Montreal she seems to be rather at home than in a strange place. (Cheers.) I am very glad that my visit to Montreal, although it may be considered an accidental circumstance at this time, should have enabled me, in a peculiar way, as representing that Province which is the second to Canada of those Provinces over which the British flag waves on this continent, to respond to the kind invitation to a dinner in honor of the Delegates at the Intercolonial Conference. I am sure that I only express the feeling of the community at large, when I say that whatever may be the ultimate fate of the propositions which the Delegates in due time may submit to the different governments and legislatures of these Provinces, we are all ready to concede to them the merit of having given a great deal of time, labor, and thought, so far as we can see through the mist of secrecy which has hung over their proceedings, and having brought an amount of patriotism to bear upon these questions, for which I am sure these communities will always feel grateful. I think, therefore, that the compliment which has been paid to these gentlemen is a graceful one and well merited. (Cheers.) I look, too, at the constitution of the delegation; although they do not come here with any authority from the Legislatures of these colonies or from the Imperial Government, they come as gentlemen, representing pretty accurately the state of public opinion in the different Provinces they represent; not only the feeling of the responsible governments in existence in each of those Provinces, but of that, which in a free community such as yours, is no less necessary—the feelings of Her Majesty's Opposition. Great weight, therefore, is due, and no doubt will be given, to whatever proposals these gentlemen may make. At the same time I may, without breaking through the requirements of necessary caution and reserve, say, that I do hope whatever proposals they may make will be duly weighed hereafter by the community at large, to whom they must in point of fact finally report their proceedings. (Hear.) The moment is a very critical one in the history of these Provinces, and suggestions, however patriotically made, ought not to be all at once accepted without due consideration. The whole future history, both of Canada and the Maritime Provinces, will, no doubt, be materially affected for the better or for the worse by the decision which the community at large and the different Legislatures may make on these proposals. I will only say this, proceeding merely on the semi-official announcement, and not drawing for information on any other source, that I do hope when some plan of Union comes to be decided upon, it will be a Union designed to give increased strength in matters of defence, increased economy in conducting the machinery of government, and increased convenience with regard to mercantile arrangements. I do hope that some simple, as well as effective means, will be found of carrying out these objects. I trust it will not be thought necessary to build up such a Union on a mass of guarantees and mutual suspicions. If you are to become a nation, you must lay its foundations in mutual confidence. (Cheers.) If the inhabitants of the British Provinces of America—of the " New Britain" of the West—the simplest, most loyal and fittest name for the intended Confederation—have in themselves the stuff that entitles them to become a great nation, they can only become so by being willing to make mutual sacrifices and to repose in one another mutual confidence. (Cheers.) On the other hand, if you once begin with the system of guarantees against one another, where is it to end? Are we to have guarantees to defend an English minority in a local Legislature in Lower Canada and to defend a French minority in a Parliament of the general Confederation? I do hope, and believe, there is sufficient good feeling between the inhabitants of these Provinces—having travelled over them lately and conversed with the leading men in each—to enable you to find some simple, effective mode of Union that will give you both strength and economy in conducting your government. (Cheers.) I may say that there is one portion of Her Majesty's subjects in these Provinces whom I have always been accustomed to look upon with peculiar interest, in consequence of circumstances connected with a former visit of mine to Canada. I allude to my fellow-countrymen of French descent, and I may add, that in the course of my recent trip through Canada, I never met any person who was not animated by the most friendly feelings towards that portion of Her Majesty's subjects, and I believe that none would be a more valuable acquisition to the Union. (Cheers.) It is impossible for a traveller like myself to visit this country and traverse a portion of what I may call a fragment of ancient France, without feeling deeply interested in its present welfare and its future destiny. It is true, that severed long since from its parent country, it has not had the opportunity of being immediately linked with all the glories of old France. At the same time, French Canadians cannot, and should not, forget that they have been spared much tribulation, which, under other circumstances, might have been inflicted on them by the political storms which, since their separation, have swept over the old country; and they may permit me, before I sit down, to express the great pleasure with which I see Her Majesty's French subjects here enjoying, at this moment, an amount of civil and religious liberty, and of social advantages, which is not equalled in the case of Frenchmen elsewhere, or any other people or race on the face of the earth. (Cheers.) As an old servant of Her Majesty's Government, I feel proud and happy when I see those of another race enjoying under the beneficent sway of the British Crown these great advantages. The fact that it is so, is the highest compliment that can be paid to the excellence of British institutions. (Cheers.) I therefore hope, whatever shape the present movement may take, it may result in increased happiness and prosperity to my French fellow-countrymen in this land. (Cheers.) As I have said already, I am satisfied that the end you have in view, with mutual confidence one towards another, may just as easily be attained by simple as by complicated means. It may or may not happen that the views of the Delegates will be carried out, but whether the whole of their proposals be accomplished, or only a portion of them, I may say for myself and my brother Lieutenant-Governors, that the Delegates may rely on finding every disposition on our part to co-operate and assist them in every way in our power by giving the fullest developement to whatever projects Her Majesty's Government in their wisdom may approve when submitted to them. They may rely upon us for this, as men equally interested as any others of Her Majesty's subjects in this part of the world, and perhaps more interested than any others in all measures for promoting the happiness of those over whom for the time being we have been appointed to preside. (Cheers.) I feel that I may be thought perhaps to have touched on somewhat delicate ground; at the same time I think the hour has come when public opinion should be brought to bear a little on matters in which the general public is so deeply interested. I only hope that the future of these Provinces may be worthy the materials for a glorious future which they contain, and I conclude with a very pithy sentence which I notice on this programme of toasts, and the sentiment of which I heartily adopt as my own—

> "Then let us be firm and united—
> One country, one flag for us all;
> United, our strength will be freedom—
> Divided, we each of us fall."

(Loud cheers.)

The CHAIRMAN said he now came to the toast of the evening. (Cheers.) They were all aware that a number of gentlemen from the Maritime Provinces had assembled in Quebec with the representatives of our own Province, to discuss the necessity or propriety of uniting these Provinces. These gentlemen were present, and several of them would be called on to respond to this toast. He was sure, from the feeling which had been exhibited since these gentlemen entered the Province, that the toast would be received with the greatest enthusiasm. He begged to propose—" Our distinguished guests, the Delegates from the Maritime Provinces." (Great cheering.)

The Band—" Cead mille faeltha."

The Hon. Dr. TUPPER said, deeply as he felt the kindness of the company, he had not risen to respond on behalf of the Delegates of Nova Scotia, but to state that, in forming that delegation, His Excellency the Lieutenant

Governor was enabled, through the kindness and patriotism of the Opposition, to avail himself of the services of the Leaders of the Opposition, both in the Legislative Council and in the House of Assembly. At the recent festive gathering in Quebec he (Dr. Tupper) had the privilege of responding on behalf of the Nova Scotia Delegates, and of placing before the public of Canada, through the medium of their intelligent press, his own views on the great question of the day. He now rose to ask Mr. Archibald, the talented and courteous Leader of the Nova Scotia Opposition, to respond to the toast on the present occasion, and to give us the benefit of his sentiments.

Hon. Mr. ARCHIBALD said that having been called upon by the hon. gentleman who conducted the administration of Nova Scotia to respond to the toast just given, his loyalty to the Province required him to respond. He accepted the task that was imposed on him, but he must say that his difficulty was largely increased by the observations by which he had been introduced to the meeting. These observations only showed how much more effectually and ably that gentleman could have responded than he (Mr. Archibald.) He, however, would tell the gentlemen present, on behalf of the Province he represented, that he returned his warmest thanks and the thanks of his co-delegates for the manner in which the toast had been introduced by the Mayor, and for the kindness with which it had been received. (Cheers.) And while on his feet he might be allowed to thank not only the people of Montreal, but of Canada at large, for the kindness, the untiring kindness, with which they (the Delegates) had been welcomed since they entered the Canadian borders. (Applause.) The people of the Lower Provinces had long heard that the Canadians were men of noble sentiments, generous and hospitable, but their anticipations had been far outstripped by their experience—an experience of one universal round of kindness and festivity. Whatever might be the results of the political arrangements which were in progress—whatever the effect of the negociations, one thing was certain, that the Delegates would carry away a most pleasing recollection of the hospitality of Canada, and of the kindness of the reception they had met with everywhere. He might say, if we were permitted to divulge secrets, that a very marked impression seemed to be made on some of the members of the delegation—the more susceptible of them, who were present last evening in this room, and who, from their sensibility to the attractions of the other sex appeared to be in favor, if not of Confederation, at any rate of Union. (Cheers and laughter.) From the little acquaintance he had with Canadian gentlemen, he found that there existed here a very limited idea of the Lower Provinces, of their resources, and of the character and habits of the people. He was not surprised at this. The business relations of Canada connected it with the United States, and the old world and its communications carried it beyond the Lower Provinces. The people of Canada saw nothing of the Lower Provinces, and had little knowledge of their resources or position; little knowledge, in fact, of that which the Lower Provinces desired Canada should know. The Delegates came here with a view to disseminate such information and state such facts as would shew that Nova Scotia would cheerfully assist in the construction of a nation. (Cheers.) The Lower Provinces would require to learn much of Canada, and Canada of them. The magnificence of the proportions of Canada, the grandeur of the country, the greatness of the land which its people inhabit, insured the attention of the Lower Provinces more to her than their smallness was likely to attract her to them. (Applause.) But if the Lower Provinces could not equal Canada in grandeur and magnificence, they far exceeded her in the number and variety of their resources. Many of those gentlemen who had paid the Lower Provinces a visit a short time ago at first supposed that the country produced nothing but an abundant supply of fog and fish. (A laugh.) He hoped, however, that the visitors came back to Canada convinced that these two articles of commerce did not constitute all the resources of the maritime Provinces. (Cheers and laughter.) If the Canadian visitors brought back any report of the climate he was sure it would be to the advantage of the Lower Provinces, for when they were there it seemed that nature was desirous to propitiate their good will, and gave the most lovely and cheerful weather, while, on the other hand, when the delegates came to Montreal, the climate of Canada gave them no right to suppose that Nova Scotia enjoyed a monopoly of rain and fog. (Loud laughter.) He would not assume to speak of the resources of all the Lower Provinces, but take as an instance his own little Province of Nova Scotia, which was hardly known. He would tell them an instance of this: A friend of Colonel Gray's returned to England after having been in Nova Scotia for a long time. Being congratulated on arriving at home she was reminded that among other pleasures this one was in store for her, that she was in a place where she would again hear her own language spoken. (Cheers and laughter.) The fact was that Nova Scotia was not inhabited altogether by Hurons, Iriquois and Micmacs, and he did not think that the Canadian gentlemen had any such idea. (A laugh.) He would now say a few words respecting the resources of Nova Scotia. In the first place, she had no predominant interest, although there were a great many interests there. The people of Canada imagine that they possess the finest agricultural soil on the continent, but he could take any Canadian who wished it to Nova Scotia, to some of the fertile valleys of the west, and point out land equal to the best in the western peninsula. (Hear, hear.) But though the agricultural interest in Nova Scotia was an important one, it did not predominate. A large portion of the people were engaged in the fisheries, and drew from their inexhaustible stores immense quantities of that which added to the richness and value of the country. (Applause.) And this pursuit trained up a large body of hardy men, who, if we become one nation, would be ready in the hour of danger to bear the flag of England. But the fishing and farming interests were not all; for Nova Scotia was extensively engaged in manufactures, and in the export of lumber. In that interest which was mixed up with the lumber interest, namely, shipping, he believed that, man for man, the people of Nova Scotia had a larger tonnage than any country in the world. (Cheers.) It was a fact, that for every man, woman and child in Nova Scotia there was about a ton of shipping. (Applause.) But, passing over the agricultural, the fishing and lumbering interests, he would come to a still larger and more important one, which stood out on the borders of the broad Atlantic. On the entire coast of Nova Scotia there were inexhaustible mines of that which influenced the industry of the world—coal. (Applause.) These mines were planted by the hand of nature, ready to be transported to supply the wants of the people of the Atlantic coast. No change of circumstances or political relations could ever prevent the people of Nova Scotia from having that material which all the Atlantic States of the neighboring country must have, and which they could get from no other place. (Applause.) Since 1858 when they were opened to free mining, twenty-five large coal mines had been opened, and it could be easily seen that with such resources the future of that country did not depend on the relations of any other country. As the Delegates from Canada travelled over the country what did they find? That there were in one harbor no fewer than 80 square-rigged vessels, representing a capacity of 16,000 tons, employed to convey coals to the Americans on the Atlantic border. (Cheers.) This was a scene repeated in many harbors; nevertheless, with all this supplying power, the Province was unable to supply the demand for coal. He did not speak of these things in a boasting spirit of his country—a country which he hoped would soon be the country of the people of Canada. (Loud cheers.) He only mentioned these facts to show the people of Canada that if Nova Scotia came into this Union, and if it came to ask Canada to associate with her, it was in no cringing attitude. (Cheers.) Nova Scotia came not asking Canada to accept her, or let her into the Union, but she told Canada that with the magnificent back country of the latter, and with her territory and wealth, and her desire to become a great nation, Nova Scotia had a frontier and resources of which she need not be ashamed—(applause)—but if Nova Scotia enjoyed, as she did to a large extent, all the advantages of freedom and of responsible institutions, why was she desirous to change her relations? He believed the condition of the people of the British North American Provinces was exceptional. He believed that if things could continue in the future as in the past, no class of people in the world would have a greater share of blessings than the people of these provinces. (Applause.) We had all the privileges of freemen without their burdens. (Hear, hear.) But the time had come when we could not expect this state of things to continue. The people of old England were a heavily taxed people, and they were not going to be taxed for ever to support us, while we were doing nothing. (Hear, hear.) We feel that circumstances are occurring on our border which render it necessary that we should be stirring on our own behalf, and besides all this, can we help feeling that it is humiliating to have everything done for us while we do nothing for ourselves. (Hear, hear.) The time had arrived when we were about to assume the position of a great nation, and such being the case, we should not shrink from its responsibilities. The people of the Lower Provinces entertain a magnificent idea of the grandeur which awaits us all. A united nation, we shall become a great country, and the time is not far distant when a colossal power, growing up on the continent, shall stand with one foot on the Pacific and the other on the Atlantic, and shall present to the world, even on this side of the Atlantic, the proof that monarchial institutions are not inconsistent with civil and religious liberty, and the fullest measure of material advancement. (Loud cheers.)

Lieut. Col. the Hon. JOHN HAMILTON GRAY, of New Brunswick, rose to respond on behalf of that Province—when the cheering had ceased he proceeded to say,—that being placed in the same position as his honorable friend on the right, who had just addressed them, he had, on the part of New Brunswick, to acknowledge with thanks the kind reception of the toast. And he must say that the embarrassment he would naturally feel under ordinary circumstances in addressing such an assembly faded away before the cordiality of their welcome. That reminded him, that while it was unquestionably the duty of statesmen to consider the bearing any question of importance might have upon the material interests of the people entrusted to their care, yet it was equally their duty to remember that there were times and occasions when kindred emotions and kindred sentiments rose superior to the cold calculations of interest, and pointed the way to honor and to patriotism. (Cheers.) The present was such an occasion. At no period before in the history of British North America had any question of such importance been presented to the people. It was not simply that the Delegates from the maritime provinces were here assembled to enjoy a hospitality so generous that no language could properly express their appreciation of it, but their presence—the presence of this vast assemblage—was the public recognition of the fact, that a question was now before the people of the greatest importance, momentous in its character, and pregnant with influence over the future destinies of this vast country. The public men of the maritime provinces had for years looked forward to a union with Canada. They had hoped for it—they had spoken for it—not simply a commercial connection, but a political connection—merging our interests, our character, our wealth, in one common union. He could not forget that at a time, in 1837 and 1838, when Canada was threatened with invasion from abroad—the several Legislatures of the maritime provinces had by unanimous votes, by acclamation, placed at the disposal of their Sovereign their entire revenues, property and wealth, to aid their brethren in the west. (Loud cheers.) He could not fail to recall that since that day their public men had striven for this union. Year after year they had turned their attention to the construction of the great Intercolonial Railway which would bring us closer together. Their Legislatures had passed Bills—had granted subsidies—arrangements had been made with Canada, yet year after year from causes which it would be difficult to explain, the object had eluded their grasp, and it was only when it appeared beyond attainment, when the hopes of their people, their Legislatures and their public men, were fading away, that they turned their backs on this cherished idea, and the Parliaments of the maritime provinces had directed certain of their leading men to assemble at Charlottetown in Prince Edward Island, and consider how best a union could be effected among themselves, since one with Canada seemed unattainable. When assembled for that purpose, the Ministry from Canada came down and proposed, that, instead of remaining longer divided, we should come together, and see if we could not lay the foundations of a great empire which should perpetuate on this continent the principles of British constitutional liberty. (Cheers.) He need not say that a proposition so entirely in accordance with the cherished purpose of their lives was received with unqualified satisfaction. He need not say that the statesmen of Canada, fully sustaining their character for talent, had, on that occasion, placed before the assembled Delegates of the maritime provinces such clear, simple, yet masterly arguments why the larger union should take place, that no hesitation was felt in foregoing the immediate object of their meeting, and in placing the circumstances which had arisen before their respective governments. Those governments then delegated them to meet the Canadian Ministry at Quebec. (Cheers.) It was not his duty, on the present occasion, because he thought it would more properly come from one of their own Ministry, to give the details of the conclusion at which they had arrived;—the conclusion itself was known to all. He, therefore, would make no observations on that topic, but if they would permit him, he would call their attention, for a few moments, to the resources and position of the maritime provinces. They came not seeking to enter into this Confederation as suppliants. They came not to draw upon the resources of Canada. No! Though they respected the superior position of Canada, though they admitted the rapidity of her progress in all the material elements of greatness; they yet thought they could give something which would aid her, would enable her to take a higher position amid the nations of the earth. (Cheers.) Ten years ago he had visited Montreal on a public mission of importance to his own Province, and he could only say that the rapid advance made by this City in the intervening period was sufficient to paralyze the most powerful imagination. He now saw costly structures where before there were none. He saw numerous buildings which indicated not only wealth, but refinement, rising in places which were then open fields, almost a morass, broad streets and noble edifices. It was impossible for any man not to see that this City was fast making strides which would soon place it among the first commercial cities of the continent. (Cheers.) In the vastness of the matters with which they had to deal, Canadians had paid but little attention to the maritime provinces. Probably some few who had visited them were not entirely ignorant of their advantages, but, as they did not lie immediately on the shortest at present available route to Europe, the tendency of the Canadians had been rather to look in some other direction; another day, however, would shortly come. They would be better understood and appreciated. The maritime provinces were worthy of their regard. The amount of capital, the extent of the resources they would bring into the Union, their exhaustless mines, their broad coal fields, their deep sea fisheries, their hardy and enterprising population would form no inconsiderable elements in the foundation of a great nation. The revenue of the four maritime provinces for the year 1863 by the official returns amounted to $2,340,000, but so far as had yet been ascertained for the year 1864, there had been an increase of 20 per cent, bringing the amount to nearly $3,000,000, (three millions,) an increase which, judging from the past financial history of those provinces, might fairly be counted upon as still progressive. The imports and exports of those four provinces from the same returns, for the year 1863, amounted to $44,200,000. He believed those of Canada had amounted to between $80 and $90,000,000. Thus it would be seen the trade of the maritime provinces approached to nearly the half of that of Canada. (Cheers.) The population of the maritime provinces, as shewn by the census of 1857 and 1861, (they were not taken in each of the Provinces in the same year,) was 804,000; but allowing for the natural increase since those periods, might now be safely put down at 900,000. With reference to the shipping trade of the maritime provinces, he would observe the registered tonnage by the returns of 1863 amounted to 645,530 tons, which at $40 per ton, a not unreasonable valuation, represented an available transferable property of $27,821,200—in one article alone—and he would observe as an evidence of the soundness of the financial position of those four Provinces, that during the present year, 1864, after paying all debts and liabilities, they would have a clear surplus of between $450,000 and $500,000, to be applied to the future exigencies of the several Provinces as the respective Legislatures might determine, each disposing, of course, of its own surplus. These figures appeared large, but they indicated plainly that in the contemplated arrangement, the maritime provinces could take an honorable position. While, however, the revenue and position of Canada could not but be appreciated, he must make one observation: great as was their trade, powerful as were their commercial connections, and extensive as was their domain, they stood for six months in the year without the power of access to one mile of sea coast, or one wave of salt water, accept through the territory of their neighbors. When, during those six months, Englishmen or Canadians desire to send the proceeds of their industry from Europe to Canada, or from Canada to Europe, they must pass, he would not say through a hostile territory, for he hoped it was a friendly one—(applause)—but, at any rate, a passage had to be asked through territory not their own, through lands not under British control. They held their trade at the beck and bidding of a nation that might be their foe—a position inconsistent, apart from all other considerations, with the dignity of any country which desired to take a proper position in the world. (Cheers.) The maritime provinces proposed to add their marine to that of Canada. This done, and British North America would become the fourth Maritime Power in the world—England, France, and the United States would, alone have a marine superior to ours. Canada, standing alone, cannot claim that position, nor can the maritime provinces. Isolated, our position is sinignificant — but unite us, and there was no country, save England, from whom we claim our birth—save the United States whose power was derived from the same parent source—save France, from whom many of those here present had sprung, could take rank before us. (Loud cheers.) He could not but call attention to the fact, that in Canada were combined the talents and characteristics of the most industrious and energetic, as well as of the most cultivated and *spirituel* races in the world. (Cheers.) If we turned back a few years we found, written on the pages of the history of this country, records of heroic deeds. From the plains of Abraham the ascending spirits of Montcalm and Wolfe—united in their death—left us the heritage of a common country and a glorious name. (Cheers.) Many men have believed that a mere commercial union, a Zolverein, might accomplish the object now sought to be obtained; but in the opinion of practical men, men of sense, integrity and experience, this could not be done.

UNION OF THE BRITISH PROVINCES.

For the last 10 or 15 years the Provinces had been separately carrying on great public works, for which the public credit had been pledged, and it must be apparent to all that it was the duty of each Province, as it was indeed a point of honor, to maintain its credit intact. While this was the case, it might become the interest of one Province, nay a necessity, to impose duties on articles that might be inconsistent with the interests and position of the other Provinces. Trade would be governed by no great or permanent principles. The tariff would fluctuate with local expediency, and be varying and uncertain. Therefore, in the absence of any general arrangement, by which the individual liability of each province could be removed and the general credit afterwards effectually maintained, it was apparent that a mere commercial union, of the kind referred to, was impossible. It would fade away before the neccessities of the occasion. But apart from this question of a commercial union, would they permit him to express the opinion that they wanted something more—they wanted a National Union, one that would enable them to take an honorable place among the nations of the earth. (Cheers.) Turning to the subject of National Union, the honorable and gallant Colonel said he would not appeal to the company simply as men, having a proper pride in their country and in themselves, but he would speak to them from a material point of view. He would ask them to bear in mind how little each man contributed towards the defence of his country. He asked them to turn their eyes to Europe, to Russia, to France, to England, to the United States, and tell him upon what spot they could place a finger where the people contributed so little towards the defence of their hearths and their homes as did we in British North America. (Cheers.) If, in England, would they not have to contribute largely of their incomes towards the support of the Army and Navy? No doubt it was a glorious thing to be able to boast of the triumphs of the British arms, to claim a share in the achievements of her warriors, to speak of their victories as ours; but we had not contributed much from our treasury to the support of the one or the attainment of the other; we had sent our sons and our brothers to take their places in the field, and thank God, in the hour of difficulty and trial, they had shed lustre on the country of their birth. They had shared in the rewards and honors which a generous country could bestow; but what had we contributed to the support of the Army and Navy? Not one farthing. England drew from the industry of her own Isles alone the means of their maintenance. We would be unworthy of our heritage and race if we did not take cognizance of the fact, and when the mother country pointed out to us, that in her opinion the time had come for us to do something for ourselves, we did not show that we were prepared to do so. (Cheers.) Without violating any rule of secrecy, he might state that the maritime provinces had gone hand in hand with the representatives of Canada, and were prepared to place all their resources, all their wealth, all their power in one general fund for the maintenance of the liberty and honor of all. (Prolonged cheers.) He had had the opportunity that morning, and a source of great gratification it was to him, to visit the Volunteer Armories in this City. He was much pleased to see the nucleus of an organization thus established around which the country could rally in time of difficulty or danger. (Cheers.) He had already trespassed on their time, (no, no, go on,) but he had only a few words more to say. He had to ask them all sincerely, that if they approved of this great scheme, this union of their common interests, that their first step would be to sanction by the expression of their strong and earnest opinion the construction of that work which was alone required to bring us together, which would give them, even in the depth of their long winters, free access to the sea, which would make the people of the maritime provinces and of Canada no longer strangers to each other, but brothers in identity of interests as well as of race. This question of the Union of the Provinces was one of deep importance. And, (continued the honorable gentleman), I now call upon you, Canadians, by your own name, here in the presence of your own hills, which rose to their majestic height ere yet your race began,—here in the presence of your own St. Lawrence, hallowed by the memory of Cartier, and spanned by the stupendous work which shews that in the onward march of progress and improvement, you are not behind—by the memory of the past, by the spirit of the present, by the hopes of the future,—I call upon you to rally round a proposition which will tend to perpetuate the glory of your name, and promote the prosperity and happiness of your people. (Great cheering, during which the speaker resumed his seat.)

The Hon. JOHN AMBROSE SHEA, of Newfoundland, on rising to return thanks on behalf of the Colony which he represented, was greeted with hearty cheers. He said—since the arrival of the delegates in this country they had been the recipients of the most princely hospitality, and such was truly the character of that which they were now permitted to enjoy. Though remembrance of such scenes as the present would not soon be effaced from their memories, these demonstrations had a much higher significance than mere good fellowship; they demonstrated how much general interest was taken in the question of Confederation. Canada had many great advantages that he was perfectly willing to admit, but it would be his duty to mention a few facts which would shew that it would be no disadvantage for her to unite with Newfoundland. (Hear, hear.) In considering an union of the Provinces, it became necessary to take into account the position of the proposed Confederation with regard to safety and defence. (Hear, hear.) In this view, the position of the Island of Newfoundland became one of marked significance. Look at it stretched right across the Gulf of St. Lawrence, commanding both passages by which the vast trade of the Gulf region and of the St. Lawrence river finds its way to the ocean. Were this Colony in the hands of a hostile power in war time, the trade of Canada would be hermetically sealed, as if perpetual winter prevailed here. (Hear.) Considering this, the statesmen lately assembled at Quebec at once considered that the Confederation would be insecure unless Newfoundland were made a portion of it. (Applause.) Nor was it a colony the least entitled to consideration on account of its commercial and financial standing, and the benefits thence to be derived. And, perhaps, he would be pardoned going into somewhat minute details—more, indeed, than many of his hearers might desire. Well, then, Newfoundland had a coast of twelve hundred miles, with some of the finest harbors in the world, in which ships of the Navy might repose in security. (Hear.) The agricultural capabilities of Newfoundland were not, he admitted, of the highest order; its soil and climate were not well calculated for the highest conditions of agriculture, but still it derived considerable advantage from them. Some agricultural operations had been conducted with marked success. It possessed large tracts of country highly valuable for grazing purposes, and but for the presence of a race of dogs, for which its people exhibited marked partiality, farming would be very profitable to those engaged in it. (Laughter.) The main stay of Newfoundland, the main element of its wealth was, however, its fisheries; in which was employed 30,000 men, able, hardy, industrious, fit sailors for anything in which daring and energy were required. In the article of fish it had commercial relations with almost every maritime nation in Europe, with Brazil and the United States. With the Colonies of British North America, however, its relations were very limited. The imports of Newfoundland were from five to six million dollars annually; the exports were six or seven millions *per annum*. The exports almost invariably exceeded the imports. Three hundred and fifty vessels were employed in seal fishing, manned by about fourteen thousand men, the very best and most active portion of the community. The Revenue of Newfoundland was higher than that of any of the British North American Provinces, man for man of the population, because it imported almost everything it required. With a population of 130,000 it had a revenue of $500,000 to $550,000. The debt, he was happy to say, was not very large compared with the other colonies, being about $900,000. Represented by public buildings of various descriptions, the province had ample tangible value for all the money it had expended, while such was the credit in which its securities were held, that the government had no difficulty, even at the present moment, when the rate of interest in England was unusually high, in raising money at $4\frac{1}{2}$ *per cent*. (Loud applause). They had a Savings Bank in St. John's, guaranteed by the government, in which were deposited the earnings of its industriours people to the extent of nearly $900,000. (Hear.) The country had not been sufficiently explored to enable him to say a great deal as to the mineral deposits which lay within its bosom, but it was known that there were some very important lead mines; copper mines, too, had been found in various localities, and it was believed that a very valuable gold mine would be found on the gulf where investigations were now being made under the direction of Sir W. Logan, to whom he took the opportunity of returning thanks for the great assistance he had afforded the people of the Island. (Hear.) There were about 1,200 vessels entering and clearing annually, going to all countries. With regard to the financial position of the Island, he might say that, perhaps, it was sounder than that of any of the colonies or States of America, in spite of the unusual vicissitudes of trade. In proof of this he would observe that in 1846 a serious calamity befel the town of St. John's; it was visited by a serious conflagration, which swept the whole business part of the place, leaving no store nor wharf, so that some thought the city never could recover from its effects. The amount of loss was between five and six millions, not one fourth of which was covered by insurance. The city did, however, recover, and no man failed to meet his business engagements in consequence of the calamity. (Cheers.) The Bank of British North America was then the only Bank doing business in the community, and at the time of the fire the amount of paper it held was larger than it had been for several years; yet he could assert that not a single man failed to discharge his obligations to the Bank; nay more, when the Bank which had been doing business twenty years at last wound up its affairs, the whole of the paper held was handed over to another Bank and taken at its face value, without any reduction. (Hear.) These statements might appear extravagant, but he made them in presence of gentlemen acquainted with the facts, and his position relieved him from suspicion of indulging in misstatements. (Applause.) Under these circumstances Newfoundland might claim to come into the Confederation on honorable and independent grounds. It would contribute its share to the general stock of advantages to be enjoyed. (Hear.) He had said that the imports amounted to between five and six millions. Now, of this they received from one million five hundred thousand to one million seven hundred and fifty thousand in value from the United States, chiefly in flour, butter, and other articles of that description. A very small proportion of imports came from Canada. Why? Was it because the United States offered superior commercial advantages? This was not the case; they could generally purchase on better terms in Canada than in the United States. (Hear.) It would, no doubt, be said that political arrangements could have no effect, could exercise no control, over matters of this kind. That doctrine, however, had its limits, which were in some cases very remarkable; but let them look at the inter-colonial railroad as an illustration. That road would be productive of the most important commercial advantages to the people of these Provinces, and yet every one knew that might have remained for years without any progress towards completion had it not now become a political necessity. How did Newfoundland stand towards Canada at the present moment? Its people had to go to the United States to do business, for they had to pass by way of Halifax and Boston to reach Montreal. It took nearly a month to carry letters between Canada and Newfoundland and back, and the rate of postage was double what it was between the Colonies and Great Britain. If arrangements had been made designed for the purpose of preventing commercial intercourse they could not have been made more effective than these. (Hear, hear.) A commercial union would do away with such anomalous and almost barbarous features, which all the colonies evidently felt it necessary to uphold in the present position of affairs, notwithstanding the fact that they were regarded in England as remarkable illustrations of strange political heresies. These must be got rid of. They must establish steam communication between Newfoundland and Canada. That Island had what Canada required, and wanted what Canada furnished. Newfoundland was obliged to pay a million dollars hard money for what it obtained from the United States, without having any reciprocal advantages to obtain from them; it was owing to fiscal impediments between the colonies that its trade went thither. With free trade it would be a purchaser in Canada for her woollens, her leather goods, her cutlery and products of these manufactures which were every day growing up within her borders, and must, no doubt, considerably increase. Give Newfoundland the means of entering into trade relations, and trade would soon spring up. (Applause.) Under the proposed Confederation the town of St. John's would become the most easternmost part of the great Union, and by making it a point of call for the magnificent steamers of which Canada was so justly proud, it would be placed within six days of the mother country. A close connection with that country was what he believed all the colonies desired, and speaking for his own Province of Newfoundland, he would say he hoped the day was far distant when she would have forced upon her any other allegiance than that she now rejoiced to acknowledge, however remote the contingency of change in this respect might be. (Cheers.) When such issues were involved it would be unwise and short sighted, if due weight were not given to it by the men charged with the grave task of laying the foundation of a new empire. (Applause.) He would say but one word more, for he felt he had already trespassed too long upon his hearers' patience. (No, no.) It was that the question of Confederation had never been, in the colony he represented, much discussed in its press; he he and his fellow laborer were here simply as expressing their own opinions on the subject; but he did not hesitate to say that he would think it a grave error if the people failed to enter into what had been the unanimous feeling of the Conference, and hesitated to become members of the Confederation, charged with so high a mission of grandeur, whose future it was impossible for the wildest imagination to over-estimate. (Cheers.)

The Honorable Colonel GRAY, Premier of the Prince Edward Island Government, then rose and said:—We had heard from our friends from the other three Provinces a great deal of the commercial, political and military element. Now, as his friends had rather transgressed upon the usual time that had been devoted heretofore to these subjects, he proposed to have something said of the social, and asked permission for his friend and co-delegate, (Hon. Mr. Whelan,) to respond, on behalf of Prince Edward Island, as there were none better able or more worthy, as a son of Erin, to give effect to their feelings, in answer to the cordial and appropriate motto with which they had been welcomed: "*Caed mille faeltha.*" (Cheers.)

The Honorable EDWARD WHELAN, M. P. P., then rose amid loud and protracted cheers, and spoke as follows: He was grateful to the gallant Colonel for the call with which he had been honored, and also for the handsome but wholly undeserved terms in which his name had been announced. While any man, no matter how great his ability, might be justly proud of the position in which he was placed, he could not subdue a feeling of embarrassment at the consciousness that he stood in the presence of some of the first men of British America, and before others who had renderered eminent service to the crown in the four quarters of the globe. He felt assured, however, that his embarrassment would receive the generous consideration of the many kind friends around him, who would readily forget and forgive in a stranger the errors he might commit, whether, like angels' visits, they should be "few and far between," or "thick as leaves in Vallambrosa." He would, however, bear in mind that the best quality of an after-dinner speech was brevity. Speeches, on such an occasion as the present, should be, if possible, like the champagne before them, bright and sparkling, and as soon disposed of. (Cheers.) Now, his first duty was to thank that distinguished audience, in the name of the people of Prince Edward Island, for the honor conferred upon their representatives in connection with the other delegates, not only for the splendid entertainment before them, but for the cordial and overpowering welcome they had received on their visit to this fair city, the great commercial emporium of Canada, the grandeur of whose busy marts and palatial residences bear testimony to the enterprise, public spirit and refined tastes of her sons. (Applause.) He was well aware that the compliment was not so much to the gentlemen composing the delegation as to the colony which they had the honor to represent. He accepted it in that spirit, and thanked their generous entertainers for it. Politicians are generally cunning fellows, and those in the several Maritime Governments showed this quality to great advantage when they appointed members of the Opposition, to which, in Prince Edward Island, he had the honor to belong, but from the cares of which he hoped to be soon relieved—(laughter)—to aid them in perfecting the great scheme of Confederation, because if the people of the several Provinces should be so unwise as to complain that their liberties and cherished institutions have been taken from them, the Opposition would have to bear the censure as well as those in the Administration. Members of the Government might say, in reply to any complaint, that the gentlemen opposite have been quite as bad as themselves. The sequel, he hoped, however, would prove that Confederation would be the means of enlarging our liberties instead of restricting them, and that our noble institutions would be strengthened and consolidated, instead of imperilled, by the proposed alliance. The present was his first visit to Canada. He was so deeply impressed with the greatness of the country in every respect, which so far exceeded his expectations, that he ardently hoped it would not be his last. It was great, he said, in its industrial, commercial and natural resources, in the countless treasures of its vast forests, its inexhaustible mines, its gigantic public works, whose value is estimated by many millions of dollars; in the vast lakes which were small inland seas, and the mighty river which flows past us, being the natural highway to and from the Lower Provinces, inviting an interchange of our commercial relations, and an expansion of the resources of them all. It was great, too, for the history it has bequeathed to all time, and which may now be referred to without disturbing the sensitiveness of the gallant people, who, only a little more than one hundred years ago, acknowledged the sovereignty of Great Britain. He had read that history, and while in Quebec he did not fail to visit some of the places which were made famous by the marvellous enterprise and heroism of Wolfe. Montmorenci, at which the first dash was made for the conquest of Quebec, was a place of stirring interest which no visitor could pass by. The Falls were not, perhaps, very wonderful in themselves, (in being directed to the upper portion of which he was indebted to a most agreeable and intelligent French Canadian girl,) but the historic associations which they recall give them an enduring claim to attention. He visited the Cove and walked up the narrow pass which led Wolf and a few followers to the Plains of Abraham, where a soldier's death closed his conquest of Canada. He was delighted to visit in the Governor's Garden the monument to the memory of Wolfe and Montcalm.

It was a generous and noble impulse in the Earl of Dalhousie thus to commemorate the names of both heroes, both foemen worthy of the great struggle in which they were engaged, both illustrious in their lives, and honored and lamented in their death; one the idol of the English nation, the other the embodiment of all that is virtuous and chivalrous in the French character. (Cheers.) The names of the two great Generals, thus united and thus commemorated, beautifully symbolized the close union now subsisting between the French and British races in Canada. (Cheers.) But of all the attributes of the greatness of Canada, there was one other which he could not overlook. It was to be seen in the personal character of the people of Canada, in the large and generous heart which seemed to throb alike from one end of the Province to the other. Unaffected by distinctions of race, nationality or creed, it appeared to feel, and give visible manifestations of the feeling, that it was capacious enough to enfold within its tendrils every section of British America. The only fear was that the caressing, as in the case of the Delegates, might be too warmly given, and that they might suffer a most agreeable death from the operation. This was not intended to apply to the fair ladies of Canada, (laughter,) for the Delegates being all married men, were, of course, like Cæsar's wife, above suspicion as regards a breach of the marital engagement, for if not so circumstanced they would be as dead as Julius Cæsar long ago. (Laughter.) He would now, with the permission of the chair, offer one or two observations touching the important business which had brought the several Delegates to Canada, and in doing so he would so express himself as not to violate the confidence which the Convention seemed to consider so essential to the success of their deliberations. Politicians sometimes take extraordinary liberties with the patience of the public, and perhaps they did this when they resolved upon holding a secret Conference; but it may be, that they had so many dark sins to confess to each other that they imagined it would not be safe to let the public listen to the confession. He would, however, bear testimony to the fact that the confession was a most satisfactory one. Each felt that he was entitled to political absolution for many sins done by his province, and now behold (said he, touching the champagne glass,) how earnestly we are all doing penance. (Laughter.) The Confederation of the Provinces may not follow immediately in the steps of the Conference, but that it will come, or that our condition will become very much worse than it is at present, seems morally certain. Nothing can be worse than to become the prey of a military despotism, not far distant, wherein every vestige of liberty is daily offered as a sacrifice to the Moloch of Ambition, and wherein the ties that were supposed to bind two people of common origin and common language, are now brittle as glass, and an opportunity is desired to cry "havoc and let slip the dogs of war" upon unoffending colonists. If we want to avoid such a misfortune the people of British America must become more united than they are at present. The Convention, whose labors have just closed, took the first step in that direction. In the Colonies we have been strangers to each other too long, as much so as if we lived under separate sovereignties. We have been jealous and apprehensive of each other; mutually restricting our trade and placing obstacles in the way of our prosperity—not knowing and not respecting each other as we should. In our separate and disjointed condition, we have not been and never can be, treated with due respect by our powerful foreign neighbors. Even England is concerned for our feeble and defenceless state, and gently chides us for our apparent supineness and indifference. The Confederation, if perfected, will remove that stain, and give all the colonies a national and indivisible character. It will be seen that we are willing to struggle and make sacrifices for our own protection; and then should an evil day and evil counsels bring a conflict upon us, we may rest assured that the red right arm of Britain will be bared to aid us in repelling aggression. (Loud cheers.) He had only seen, a day or two ago, an able article in the London *Telegraph*—a paper of great influence and ability—in which this view was clearly set forth—that England would be always willing to help us if we first helped ourselves. Alluding to the proposed Confederation, the writer said:—" Firmly believing that the project will be immensely beneficial to the Colonies, we are convinced that it will be equally acceptable to the Home Government. As the matter already stands, England is committed to the protection of every acre of her soil, be it on the Indus, the Murray, the St. Lawrence, or the Thames. Doubtless the responsibility is great, doubtless the work is arduous; but the duty exists. The best way, indeed, to lighten it, is to call upon our colonies themselves to take measures for their own defence, assuring them that whenever the odds are too heavily against them, whenever the danger becomes serious, we pledge the British Empire to their aid." (Loud cheers.) Mr. Whelan continued—Commercial and pecuniary motives, if no other of a sterner nature prevailed, should certainly teach us to unite. There should be no hostile or restrictive tariffs between the several Provinces—no dissimilar postal regulations—no dissimilarity in our currency and exchange. Our commerce, which now flows into other channels, where we get little thanks for it, would diffuse its enriching streams amongst ourselves, and nothing could possibly prevent us from becoming a great and powerful Confederacy. The union proposed by the Conference, in which there were mutual concessions of small sectional claims, and a unanimous desire for conciliation, will not, when its deliberations are more fully known, alarm any man. Large sectional rights and interests are proposed to be preserved. The connexion with the British Crown will not only be not impaired, but will be strengthened; and for the preservation of those free institutions which we all value so much, and which we hope to transmit to future generations, he thought there was but one remedy, and that remedy was union. (Cheers.) But let no man imagine that this much desired object can be effected at Quebec or Montreal. The great work is but commenced. The halls of the several local Legislatures, the constituencies of each Province in public meetings assembled, and at the hustings, are the places in which the great question must be settled. It will be the duty of the public men in each and every Province whose representatives are now in Canada to educate the public mind up to the adoption of their views. The task may be a tedious, difficult and protracted one; but no great measure was ever yet accomplished, or worth much, unless surrounded with difficulties. Defering reverently to the public opinion of his own Province, he would cheerfully go amongst his people, and explaining it as well as he could, he would ask them to support a measure which he believed will enhance their prosperity. Few and comparatively poor as the population of the Island of Prince Edward may be now, its fertile fields and valleys are capable of supporting a population at least three times greater than it is at present. It was once designated the garden of the St. Lawrence, and it was a valuable fishing station for Canada during the occupation of the French under Montcalm. It still possesses all the qualities of a garden, and its rivers and bays still abound with fish. He desired that those great resources should become as well known now and in the future as they were in by-gone days; and regarding the advantages which modern improvements and institutions afforded as auxiliaries to the natural resources of his Colony, he was satisfied that she could not fail to become very prosperous and happy under the proposed Confederation. (Loud cheers.)

The CHAIRMAN then proposed "Our Sister Colonies," which, having been duly honored, the Band laid aside their instruments, and sung a thrilling melody, each verse of which ended with the chorus:

"Then let us be firm and united—
One country, one flag for us all;
United, our strength will be freedom—
Divided, we each of us fall."

The song having been encored, was sung again, and cheered rapturously—

The Hon. T. HEATH HAVILAND, M. P. P., of Prince Edward Island, volunteered a response to the toast as follows: As a member of the smallest province of the whole, he would not detain the audience long. At the same time he desired to draw attention to some peculiar facts connected with the present movement. They might recollect that this was not the first time that states had met together to organize a constitution, for in times gone by the states of Holland had met to resist the tyranny of the Spanish Government; and the old Thirteen States of America had also assembled under the cannon's mouth and the roar of artillery; but the peculiarity of this meeting was that it was held in a time of peace, with the approbation, and he believed, with the sanction of Her Majesty, that the colonies might throw aside their swaddling clothes, to put on themselves the garb of manhood, and hand down to posterity the glorious privileges for which their ancestors contended from age to age in the old country, and which had been brought into these new countries under the protecting shadow of the flag that had braved a thousand years the battle and the breeze. (Hear.) Although Prince Edward Island had only 80,000 inhabitants, principally engaged in agriculture, yet small as it was it did not come as a beggar to the Conference doors. Its revenue was certainly not very great, but there was yet a surplus of about £4,000 sterling to the credit of the Province over and above the £36,000 it had spent for the Government last year. Thus, it did not come as a pauper, but was honestly prepared to do something—all in its power—to organize here in America a constitutional monarchy which should be able to spread those institutions in which there was the soul of liberty. (Hear, hear.) The despotism now prevailing over our border was greater than even that of Russia. The liberty of the press was gone. Liberty in the States was altogether a delusion, a mockery and a snare. No man there could express an opinion unless it agreed with the opinion of the majority for the time being; as for the rights of the minority, they were not recognized; they did not exist, and the majority rode rough-shod over all. (Hear, hear.) Well, Prince Edward Island, though it was small, was prepared to take a burthen upon it, and share with the other maritime Provinces in contributing towards military defence. (Hear, hear.) He believed the day would come when the battle of civil and religious liberty would have to be fought in America, and he felt that it would be fought between Canada and the United States. When that time came Prince Edward Island would be prepared to contribute its quota of men and money in order to aid Canada in defending those free institutions which are so dear to us as British Americans. (Hear, hear.) There was a point of importance connected with this subject. There was an iron band wanted to unite the Colonies—the band of the Intercolonial railroad—and that completed, the interior connected with the seaboard, the colonies would be able to go on hand in hand together in commercial and military undertakings. (Hear, hear.) Some years ago he had the honor of being in Montreal during the visit of His Royal Highness the Prince of Wales, who would, some day— might that day be distant—rule over this country. Then he was here a stranger, and the maritime provinces were hardly known. It was with the utmost difficulty he could find so much as a newspaper from the Lower Provinces in the reading rooms. Now, however, he felt like belonging to a nation, for he thought ere long we should be a nation with interests no longer distinct, but one people under the same old time-honored flag which now floated over us. (Applause.)

The CHAIRMAN gave, as the next toast—" Her Majesty's Canadian Ministers," which was received with great enthusiasm, the Band playing *"A la Claire Fontaine."*

The Hon. GEORGE E. CARTIER, M.P.P., Attorney General East, having been called upon, rose amidst great cheering. Being asked to speak in French, he said, in that language: I hope my French Canadian fellow citizens will remember that at this moment we are honoring the visit of the Delegates from the Lower Provinces, by all of whom the French language may not be understood. He then proceeded in English, and, after some complimentary allusions to the sumptuous banquet before them, he apologised for the absence of his chief and colleague, Sir E. P. Taché, and also for the absence of his other colleague, the Hon. John A. McDonald, Attorney General West, who were unable to be present. He then addressed himself to the subject of Confederation as follows:—Mr. Mayor, the question which, we may say, brings us together this evening is of great moment. Every one knows that throughout the British North American Provinces at this time people are discussing the question whether it is possible for the British American Provinces to form a strong government under a system of administration, which will allow all the general interests of the Provinces concerned to be dealt with by a general government, and will leave all purely local matters to a local government. This is the question which is agitating all public men, and every one taking any interest in the politics and the welfare of British North America. I cannot lose sight of the fact that not quite ninety years ago there was a great Confederation doing all in its power, on the other side of the line, to carry out democratic institutions, and that General Washington, supported by a French General, was trying to induce the people of Lower Canada, (which was then the most populous of the Provinces on this side of the line,) to join the American Union in 1784 and 1785. What was the answer of the Canadians? Our ancestors understood what democratic institutions were. (Cheers.) They did not respond to the address of General Washington, though at that time the rights to which they were entitled had not been granted to them. Yes, they preferred to stick to the monarchial form of government. (Cheers.) At this time we are trying to help the monarchial elements to take deeper root in these British North American Provinces. I know, Mr. Mayor, that it may be expected from me, perhaps on account of what has fallen from some of the speakers, to disclose the proposals of the Conference at this entertainment; but, Mr. Mayor, that cannot be the case. The proceedings of those who have taken part in these deliberations are confidential; they must first be made known to our Governments, and they have to be made known to the Imperial Government. Every one must understand the delicacy of the trust reposed in us. But though I may be prevented by the confidence with which these grave matters are to be discussed among the gentlemen who are deputed by their respective Governments to deliberate on them, from stating the results arrived at, at all events I don't think I am committing any indiscretion if I proceed to submit them in a sort of hypothetical way. (Cheers, and laughter.) You have already heard several eloquent speeches on the subject. As for myself, I have no pretensions to eloquence; I am a mere dry politician. I go to work when there is anything to be done, and I say very plainly to my friends what I think, perhaps sometimes too plainly, but at all events I am sincere. (Cheers.) I do not say this to draw your attention to me, for you may perhaps be disappointed; but if you do give me your attention, I may have something to tell you. (Cheers.) Now, without revealing anything, you all know that at this moment I happen to be in the Government of Canada allied to a gentleman who for fifteen years has been my great opponent in Upper Canada—I refer to the Hon. George Brown. (Cheers.) Now, when a great matter of public policy came before us, though that gentleman and myself had been pitted against each other, he for Upper Canada and I for Lower Canada, yet we resolved to try whether we could not concur in a great scheme of Confederation, either of the Canadas, or of all the Provinces. I must say this, gentlemen, that in none of my most important political decisions did I ever take the advice of any one. (Cheers.) As a politician under the British system, I know that we are carried on to power in order to give advice to the Governor of the day; but when a gentleman takes office, he ought to understand that a man should not be merely the reflex of public opinion, but should try to lead public opinion. (Cheers.) I don't mean to say that the public voice should not be listened to. But at the same time there are prejudices in the minds of the public, which, however, like unfavorable winds, may be turned to good account. A good pilot will use the wind to make the ship go in the direction he wishes, and in the end every one is satisfied, both the pilot and the crew and the passengers. Well, with regard to this question of Confederation, and with regard to my political alliance with Mr. Brown, I must say that he has kept faithfully to his work. I don't know what you have to say of me, but for my part I have such an amount of self-esteem that it matters not what amount of good or of bad you say. (Laughter.) Then, Mr. Mayor, it is obvious that there are general questions which might be subjects to be taken up by the General Government of the British North American Provinces. As to Lower Canada, I am not one of those who will not recognize that the union of Upper and Lower Canada has not done a great deal of good. I am confident, and I have stated it on many occasions, that the union of Upper and Lower Canada has achieved wonders for the two Provinces. The prosperity to which we have risen under the union of the Provinces, encourages a still larger union. (Cheers.) I am not one of those who would like to see Upper and

Lower Canada separated, and become two distinct Provinces, and warring against each other. What would be the consequence of this state of things? Montreal would soon be a city in a corner, for I confess that the prosperity of Lower Canada is due, to a great extent, to the trade of Upper Canada. (Cheers.) It is well that the cause should be stated. As I am one of the representatives of Montreal, I tell you that I would never consent to any system of government under which Upper and Lower Canada would have a different system with respect to the tariff and trade of the country. (Cheers.) In fact we see to-day that a great part of those who were formerly opposed to the union of the two Canadas are now in favor of it. Why? Because the Union has bestowed on the Province a great part of its advantages. I must repeat to you what I stated while in the Lower Provinces, that while we possessed the personal and the territorial elements which go to constitute a nation, we were wanting in the maritime element. (Cheers.) During six months of the year we had to knock at the door of our neighbor in order to carry on our trade. This cannot be tolerated. This Confederation must be carried out. I know that every citizen of Montreal will understand that at this critical time we should look to Nova Scotia, to New Brunswick and Prince Edward Island for the elements wanting in Canada to make a great nation. I don't mean a nation distinct from the mother country. (Cheers.) I wish that all the power granted by the mother country to the Colonies should be combined in order to make, as far as we can, one great nation. If we can do this, I think we shall have done a good deal. With regard to the General Government, I suppose that some gentlemen would like to know my hypothesis. Is it right that there should be a Custom House erected against the trade of each Colony? No. Is it right that there should be a difference of currency? Is it right that there should be a difference between the system of weights and measures? Between the mode of becoming a British subject? That there should be a difference in the postal service? Is it right that there should be a difference in regard to the question of the defence of the country? (No, and cheers.) Can, for instance, the Island of Prince Edward, or Nova Scotia, or

New Brunswick, successfully devise separate systems of Militia, so as to secure themselves against invasion? No, they cannot. Then suppose portions of Nova Scotia, or New Brunswick, or Prince Edward Island, were invaded by an American army, the question would present itself, shall the forces of England be transported to the invaded Province for its defence? Well, we know that there is a school in England which disregards the claims of colonists on imperial protection. I speak of the school of Mr. Bright and Mr. Cobden. Canada possesses better means of defence in men. Would this be sufficient to defend her against invasion? I believe it would not. But if we should be united under one Government, the battle would have to be fought somewhere, and the forces of British North America would have to be brought together somewhere to meet the foe. In this case there could be no doubt that England would see that we were really in earnest, and strengthen our hands to the extent of her ability. I see that there is a great objection on the part of some to this system of general Government, because we had not at once a Legislative Union. But we had to take into consideration all the objections of the different Colonies. And if we succeed in presenting a scheme which will form the foundation of a general Government, to take charge of such general subjects as interest every one, shall we not have done a great deal? (Cheers.) Now, I am told that in Lower Canada there is a great objection to the scheme, because it is asserted that the British inhabitants of Lower Canada will be at the mercy of the French majority. Certain prejudices are being impressed upon the minds of the British people of Lower Canada against the Confederation, because it embraced a general Government and also local Governments. I think the British inhabitants of Lower Canada should not be frightened by this argument. (Hear, hear.) The British inhabitants of Lower Canada ought to bear this in mind, that in Upper Canada the French Canadians will always be in a small minority. In that section the French Canadians will have to trust to the good judgment of the British majority, and is it too much to ask the British minority in the Lower Provinces to trust to the good judgment and to the justice of the French Canadians in the local Governments? If, then, I have no objection to the local arrangement as regards Upper Canada, why should the British population of Lower Canada object to the local arrangement because they happen to be represented according to their numbers? I say this to my friends of both races, I will never consent that any injustice should be done either constitutionally or otherwise to my fellow-citizens of any religion, language or race. (Cheers.) In treating of the question of race with regard to this great Confederation, looking to England, you will find three distinct nationalities. Each of these has contributed to the glory of England. Who would like to take from England the glory conferred on her by any one of the three nationalities? By the son of Erin or the Scot? (Cheers.) I think the glory of England might not have been equal to what it is, if the three nationalities had not been united. Was it surprising that some should try to find difficulties in the way of the formation of a Union because there happened to be different races and religions? I have already spoken about the elements which are necessary to constitute a nation. Every one knows that England is great; she has achieved a great deal more than any nation whose history we know. The Romans could not keep their colonies, because they were wanting in one of the elements which England possesses— the commercial element. Without detracting from the power of England, I think, when we come to analyse it we will find that it will not be so great, without taking into account her commercial power. As soon as a colony is conquered by the bravery of her soldiers and seamen, the work is taken up by her merchants, who cause the colony to prosper to such an extent that it is the interest of England to bring her army and fleet to protect it. The prosperity of the two sections of Canada illustrates this fact. With our prosperity we are enriching the American States, whereas we ought to be enriching our own States. We ought to be enriching such harbors as St. John and Halifax. And then, with regard to Newfoundland, as had been stated by the Hon. Mr. Shea, Newfoundland stands at the bottom of the St. Lawrence, and is the key to foreign trade. When we are politically connected with Newfoundland, this will afford an opening that we cannot yet appreciate. It may be said that by a sort of Zolverein we might achieve the same result as we hope to do by political union. That cannot be the case. If we succeed there will be a local Government to take cognizance of such matters as the civil law, regulating property, &c., which are local, and naturally fall within the province of local government. But I know that in this city and elsewhere it is sought to turn public opinion against us by saying that if you have a local government you must resort to direct taxation for the support of the government. This would never be the case, for a subsidy was to be paid by the general Government to each of the Local Governments to cover their expenses, and there would be some small items of local revenue which would be sufficient. There will be, therefore, no direct taxation if the Government be wise and prudent. As I stated at the outset, I am impressed with the conviction that this Confederation should not be carried out if it deprives us of our connection with England. But I am of opinion that the scheme, if successful, will increase the *prestige* of the monarchial form of government. (Cheers.)

The Hon. Dr. TUPPER then rose and proposed, in a brief but eloquent speech—"The Mayor of Montreal and Montreal City," which was suitably responded to by His Worship, and on his resuming his seat, there were loud calls for the Hon. T. D'Arcy McGee, one of the Members for Montreal City:

Mr. McGEE rose amidst prolonged cheering. He said he had no intention at that late hour and after the long sitting, to try anything in the shape of a speech. When we, he said, were down on a visit to the Lower Provinces, our hospitable entertainers were always pleased to hear us speak, and I feel that I shall best discharge my duty in showing myself a good host by being a good listener. (Cheers.) However, as one of the leading politicians and member of the Government had been prevented from attending, and as the other member for the City of Montreal—Hon. Mr. Rose—had, he perceived, withdrawn, he could not allow the meeting to separate without saying a word of welcome. They were welcome to us as fellow subjects long estranged, now about to be united. They were welcome as accomplished gentlemen, of whose powers his hearers had had specimens that evening. They were welcome as the kind hosts and entertainers in the Lower Provinces of many of those whom he saw around him. They were welcome for the work in which they had been engaged. (Cheers.) If you asked, wherefore this Conference with closed doors at Quebec, why all this mystery, why this assembling together of their Excellencies' advisers at Quebec, leaving Governors and Lieutenant Governors in the meantime deprived of their counsels,—if he were asked the reason of all this, he would give the answer in one word, *circumspice*. Look around you and you will see the reasons for the gathering. Look around you to the valley of Virginia, look around you to the mountains of Georgia, and you will find reasons as thick as blackberries. Were they to believe that things would go on in the future as they had gone in the past? It was necessary that those engaged in the work should have with them, and he trusted they would have with them, the public opinion and the countenance of the people of Montreal, and of the people of Canada. If they had assumed, thirity-three of them, to go into a chamber and sketch an outline which was to be submitted to Her Majesty, to the Imperial Parliment, and to our Parliaments, they found their justification in the circumstances of British North America, and of Republican North America, and in the intimation conveyed to us from the most undoubted sources from the seat of the Imperial Government. They had not acted in an empirical spirit. They had gone there to build, if they had to build, in a reverent spirit, upon the old foundation— (Cheers)—not a showy edifice for themselves, with a stucco front, and a lath and plaster continuation—(laughter)—but a solid foundation that would bear the tempest and the waves, that would stand for ages, and afford an exemplification of the solidity of our institutions. (Cheers.) He trusted that they would emulate the races from whom they sprung, the Norman, the Celtic, and all that went to make the concrete of the British Empire, the land of stable government, the land of old renown, where freedom in the broadest sense was enjoyed by all. One of the New York journals, friendly to us, the New York *Albion*, warned us last week not to make premature rejoicings over our success, reminding us of the premature rejoicings over the laying of the Atlantic Telegraph a few years ago. He would take the liberty to inform that journal that we had not been experimenting and sounding out of our depth. We did not proceed so far without having a very safe intimation of what England's sentiments are. If we want explanation from England we have only to put our hand upon the book which contains the law of England, and as long as we had that explanation in our libraries we could always learn what they would think in England of what we had been doing. (Cheers.) Before he sat down he must express his great regret that the Delegates were obliged to leave us at an early hour on Monday morning. The next day being Sunday, would be no day for sight-seeing, and the preceding day was a regular damper. (Laughter.) The speaker proceeded to touch upon what the Delegates might tell their constituents upon their return home. They might say that we desired the Confederation for the sake of self-defence, common advancement, coming into Union well dowered. They might say that Canada desired this Union, though at present the public mind was not fully alive to the advantages to be derived from it; that if she goes into it, she goes into it for no small or selfish purposes; that the people of Canada are year by year becoming more liberal and enlightened in their views; that we did not speak of cutting each other's throats for the love of God; they could say that in Canada religious bigotry was at a discount. He could point them to the place where that bigot withered upon his stock, that where he was held in honor no man is now so mean as to do him reverence. That we have not amongst us bigotry of classes or bigotry of race; or the belief that no good could come out of Nazareth, or any religion but their own. That the day of these small things had passed away in Canada; that we respected one another's opinions, and had shown ourselves fit to be freemen by allowing every class, every sect and every creed, to manage their own affairs—(cheers)—so long as they did not trouble the peace and happiness of the community. He thought they might say all this in regard to Canada. Their limited stay would not permit them to see for themselves the progress that we had made in freedom, which gave every man the fullest scope for the exercise of his own rights, but he was sure they could say to their constituents that Canada would come into the Union with the view of securing the common prosperity and welfare. (Cheers.)

Hon. Mr. GALT, being loudly called upon to speak, rose and observed that he was sure he would fail in doing justice to the kindness with which they called upon him, were he to make a speech after what they had heard that evening. He hoped that the discussion of this public question would induce gentlemen to look at it in all its bearings, and that they would find that what was good for Canada would be good for the Lower Provinces, and for all sections of the British dominions. He was sure they would look at this question not in a selfish point of view, but in one which has regard to the benefit of all, and which would raise this country to a position in which it would be honored. In this question of Confederation it was perfectly true we had put our confidence in those who were associated with us, and who have lived with us. It is necessary that the French Canadians of Upper Canada should have confidence in those with whom they have lived, and that we in Lower Canada should have confidence in the fair dealing of the French Canadian people. (Cheers.) If our institutions have borne any fruit at all, they have borne the fruit of harmony. He believed we were united in one common movement for the benefit of both Upper and Lower Canada. He believed the Union would be productive of good to both Canada and the Maritime Provinces. If we want an open port, we could find it in St. John or Halifax. He was not disclosing any secret when he said this, that so far as the protection of the interests of the people of Upper and Lower Canada was concerned, there was no secret to be kept—the arrangements were made in a way to do honor to his friend Mr. Cartier. (Cheers.) It was not a light thing for people to trust their prosperity and happiness in the future to others. But he was sure that a very prudent effort had been made to try and bring about a state of things that would rescue us from the troubles that threatened us. (Cheers.)

It was now 8 p. m., the speeches having commenced about four o'clock, the Chairman left the Chair, and the meeting broke up.

DEPARTURE FOR, AND ARRIVAL AT, OTTAWA.

The Maritime Province Delegates, accompanied by their lady friends, together with several of the Canadian Ministers, and many acquaintances from Quebec and Montreal—left the latter city on Monday morning, 31st October, by special train *en route* for Ottawa. Having travelled a short distance by railway, they embarked on board of a beautiful steamer at the first convenient landing place on the river Ottawa, and proceeded without delay along the course of that renowned and picturesque stream. Its charming scenery, diversified by innumerable islets resting gently on its tranquil bosom, were objects of great attraction to the many persons on board the steamer who had seen them for the first time only. The frequent recurrence of the small islands, as the vessel wound her devious way through the narrow channel, was a source of inexpressible delight to the voyagers. Although the garish beams of day had given place to that beautiful compromise between daylight and darkness which is known by the name of twilight, yet the soft rich landscape could be easily seen, and was, perhaps, more impressive at that hour and at that season, when the emerald glories of summer seem to be struggling for ascendancy over the varying tints of early autumn. Moore's Canadian Boat Song—inspired on this river more than half a century ago—recurred to many minds at the time described, and sweet voices were not wanting to blend with the gentle airs of heaven the melody whose burthen is—

"Blow, breezes, blow, the stream runs fast,
The Rapids are near, and the daylight's past."

Having arrived at one of the usual stopping places, named Carillon, where freight and passengers are received and landed, His Worship the Mayor of Ottawa, M. K. Dickinson, Esqr., and several members of the Ottawa Reception Committee, came on board, to whom the Hon. Mr. Galt severally introduced the Delegates from the Maritime Provinces. About two hours more brought the whole party to Ottawa. It was then quite dark, but from the water the scene presented in the heart of the city was highly interesting. It seemed to be one mass of moving light, which was soon found to be an immense torch light procession, composed of the Fire Brigade in uniform, together with a large body of other citizens.

There were numerous carriages in waiting at the landing place, which conveyed the Steamer's party to Russell's Hotel, escorted by the torch light procession. It was impossible to estimate the number of the dense crowd which filled the street, but it seemed as if the whole population of Ottawa had turned out on the occasion, sending forth rapturous cheers after cheers as welcome notes to their guests.

Before the crowd separated, the Hon. JOHN A. MCDONALD was called for, and appeared at one of the windows of the Hotel, from whence he briefly addressed the assembled multitude, thanking them on behalf of the Government of Canada, and also on behalf of his friends from the Lower Provinces, for the very warm-hearted welcome they had just received. He expressed his gratification at the prospect of Ottawa soon becoming the Capital of Confederated British America, and briefly referred to his own exertions, in the Legislature and Government to procure for the young and rising city so great a distinction. Immense cheering followed for some moments, in the midst of which Mr. McDonald retired, when—.

The Hon. Dr. TUPPER appeared in one of the carriages

in the crowd below, and addressed the assemblage for about fifteen minutes, referring, in the course of his eloquent remarks, to the stupendous importance of the work in which the Delegates had been engaged. He stated that it was their constant aim to preserve sectional and local interests as far as it was in their power to do so. The result of their labors would, he had no doubt, meet with much hostile criticism, but he hoped the intelligent people and their energetic and enterprising press would not prejudge the scheme until all its details could be placed before them, in order to do which some unavoidable official forms were necessary. He then thanked the people for their cordial reception, and retired amidst enthusiastic cheers.

On the morning of the first of November, about 10 o'clock, His Worship the Mayor, the Hon. Mr. Skead, M.L.C., Mr. Scott, Mr. McGilvray, Mr. McKinnon, Mr. S. Keefer, and other members of the Reception Committee, had carriages in waiting at the several Hotels where the visitors were located, to drive them round the City of Ottawa. After a short time most agreeably spent in driving through the several streets, which presented in every direction marks of great enterprise and wealth, the party embarked on board of one of Mr. Dickinson's steamers, and took a trip of two or three miles on the river below the Rideau Falls. The sun shone out in all its effulgence, and although the wind was keen and cold, still it was exhilarating, and the objects worthy of note on both sides of the river challenged earnest admiration. The buildings to be dedicated to the use of the Parliament and the Government Offices, now nearly completed and ready for use, could be seen to much greater advantage on the river than in the city. The boat having been turned, she steamed to the foot of the Chaudiere Falls, penetrating the boiling cauldron further than ever any vessel had done before.

The visitors having been afforded ample opportunity to admire this marvellous work of nature, the boat again turned, and crossed the river to the Lower Canada side, where carriages were in waiting. After a short drive through the bush, the party arrived at the Suspension Bridge over the Chaudiere Falls, and thence returned to their several Hotels.

At half past twelve o'clock the visitors proceeded to the Parliament Buildings, through the various apartments of which they were conducted by the Contractors and their friends. The Delegates warmly expressed their admiration at the exterior design and construction of the edifices, and what then promised to be the splendour of the interior arrangements. An hour having been spent in examining and passing through the several parts of the main building, it was announced that

THE DEJEUNER,

for which the most extensive preparations had been made by the Contractors, was served in the room to be used as the future Picture Gallery of the Parliament Houses. This part of the building appeared to be nearly finished, and was most handsomely decorated for the occasion. The walls were hung with diamond shaped frames of flowers, in the centres of which were inserted brief inscriptions expressive of welcome; and the time-honored flag of England spread its ample folds wherever a place could be found for it on the walls. The decorations about the tables were of the most elegant description, and the viands included every luxury and delicacy that could be desired. About 160 persons sat down to the several tables, and this number included the ladies of the Delegation Party, and the ladies of many of the citizens of Ottawa and vicinity, whose presence largely contributed to the pleasure of the entertainment.

There was no particular Chairman appointed for the occasion. The Contractors being the Hosts, divided amongst themselves the duties which usually fall to the lot of a Chairman. There were four tables arranged in the form of a paralellogram. At the centre of one table sat Mr. McGreevy, with the Hon. Mr. Tilley, of New Brunswick, on his right, and Hon. John A. Macdonald, on his left. At the centre of the opposite table sat Mr. Ralph Jones, with Hon. Col. Gray, of Prince Edward Island, on his right, and Mr. Rose on his left. At the third table sat Mr. Haycock, with Col. Gray, of New Brunswick, on his right, and Mr. Cauchon on his left. At the fourth table sat Mr. T. C. Clarke, with Dr. Tupper, of Nova Scotia, on his right, and Mr. Johnson, of New Brunswick, on his left.

Mr. McGreevy gave the first toast—"The Queen"—which was received and honored with great enthusiasm, the Ottawa Band playing the national anthem.

Mr. Jones next proposed, "The Governor General," which was received with unbounded applause.

After a short pause, Mr. Haycock, one of the other Chairmen, proposed, "The Canadian Administration," coupling the toast with the remark, that they were much better able to speak for themselves than he for them.

The Hon. John A. Macdonald briefly returned thanks. [The honorable gentleman intended to have spoken at some length on the question of Confederation, but illness induced by fatigue from assiduous devotion to public affairs, compelled him to curtail his observations, which the whole company deeply regretted, as no public man in Canada was considered so well qualified by talent, experience and statesmanship to speak on the question of Confederation as the Honorable Attorney General for Canada West. His illness excited deep sympathy, and when he resumed his seat after the brief expression of his thanks, he was applauded as if he had made the most brilliant oration ever delivered—thus manifesting the profound respect entertained for him at Ottawa.]

The Hon. Mr. GALT having expressed regret for Mr. Macdonald's illness, and having pronounced a high eulogium on the great and universally acknowledged ability of the Attorney General West—

Mr. T. C. CLARKE, one of the Chairmen, rose to propose the next toast. He said the pleasant duty devolved on him of proposing, "The Delegates from our sister Provinces and their fair wives and daughters." On behalf of the people of Ottawa and of the Contractors, their hosts on this occasion, he tendered them a cordial and sincere welcome. (Cheers.) Their only regret was that their guests would be with them for so short a time. He might mention one circumstance in respect of which this entertainment differed from the magnificent Dejeuner at Montreal. There the ladies were permitted to look down on the gentlemen from the gallery; here they sat down with the gentlemen, participating in the welcome given to the Delegates. (Cheers.)

The Honorable WILLIAM A. HENRY, Attorney General of Nova Scotia, replied on behalf of that Province, and said; "Our hosts, ladies and gentlemen—By an arrangement among the Delegates, the pleasing duty devolves upon me of responding on behalf of Nova Scotia in this city, to the toast which has been so handsomely proposed and enthusiastically received. From the time of our first landing at Quebec we have been the recipients of universal kindness and social hospitality. We have, heretofore, had the pleasure of making the personal acquaintance of many of your public men on several previous occasions, when they have visited England and the Lower Provinces on occasions of general importance; and we have recently had the pleasure of seeing many of your citizens during the excursion they made to the Maritime Colonies last summer. We, therefore, felt that we were not coming here amongst strangers, or to a *terra incognita*, but were coming among brothers, equally with us the descendants of Englishmen,

Frenchmen, Scotchmen, and Irishmen. If any thing were wanting to convince us of the hospitable intentions of you all, it would be afforded by the magnificent reception we last night received at your hands. (Cheers.) We were, indeed received like conquerors, like warriors returning from a great victory, and indeed a great victory has been achieved at the Conference, whose labors have just terminated. We have triumphed over personal jealousies and local and party considerations, having sacrificed all these to the great object we had in view. (Hear.) The reception you have given us is all the more pleasing, as it has taken place in Ottawa, a city selected by Her Majesty the Queen to be the seat of government for Canada, and in a building the corner-stone of which was laid by His Royal Highness the Prince of Wales. I feel the extreme difficulty of speaking upon a subject about which a dozen speeches have been already made, and borne, by the enterprising press which has reported them, to every hamlet in this Province—a difficulty arising from the fear of following in the same paths already so well trodden by others. I have, however, great pleasure in communicating for myself and my colleagues our warmest thanks to the Contractors engaged in the construction of these magnificent buildings, for the very pleasing banquet they have so liberally provided. It is matter for additional congratulation to see present so many of the leading citizens of Ottawa, for it is an earnest of their hearty sympathy with us in our labors, and of the deep interest they take in the success of the great work in which they are engaged. (Cheers.) The splendour of the entertainments we have received since we left our homes has abundantly convinced us of the hospitality of the people of Canada, and I can assure you that whenever a Canadian lands upon our shores he will at all times find the inhabitants of our Provinces ready to reciprocate these numerous acts of kindness. Were no political consequences immediately to flow from our present efforts, the intercommunication we have had with you will not be barren of results, for we shall have learned to know each other better, and have discovered the necessity and benefit of more frequent intercourse. The people of Nova Scotia entertain no mean or selfish views when they propose to enter into a Confederation with the other colonies. They know that their position commands many advantages not equally enjoyed by the rest. They feel that their principal port, Halifax, is one of commanding importance. Situated as it is upon the most easterly peninsula of British North America, and of paramount importance to be retained by England while any portion of the West Indies remains connected with the British empire, it will be the last spot of territory on this continent to be yielded up by the Parent State, and will always receive even more than the other colonies the protection of the home government. The time, however, may come, and may not be far distant, when, with great political changes from which we cannot expect to be always exempt, the protection of the Parent State may be withdrawn, and if we wait till that unfortunate event arrives, it may be too late to form associations for our local defence. We feel that we may be likened to one of a number of rough, unhewn stones, which some political architect may hereafter appropriate, and if no measures are taken to secure to us a proper position, to secure that important place in a grand structure which we conceive to be our right, we may by accident, or the force of events, either occupy an elevated station or form part of a mere pavement, to be walked over and trampled on. (Applause.) We know that these colonies are made of the right material; and that descendants of the countrymen of a Wellington and a Napoleon, of a Marlborough and a Clyde, possess when united elements of immense and almost invulnerable strength for their defence, and will not be found unworthy of their common ancestry. It is not improper for me in this connection, speaking on behalf of Nova Scotia, leaving the interests of the other colonies in this respect to other gentlemen, to refer to the the heroes of Kars and of Lucknow, both natives of our Province. Having entertained for some time these general sentiments, the Legislature of Nova Scotia, by resolutions adopted last session, took measures for effecting a Legislative union of the Provinces of Nova Scotia, New Brunswick and Prince Edward Island. Similar resolutions having been adopted by the Legislatures of the two other Colonies, a meeting of Delegates appointed by each, took place at Charlottetown in September last. We would have gladly included your Province in our invitation to join our Union, but were somewhat afraid of approaching and attacking the giant Canada. (Laughter.) We were induced to limit our plans for a Union among the Lower Colonies. But it having been communicated to the Canadian Government that we were about to meet for the purpose mentioned, your Government sought and obtained admission to our preliminary Conference. Without interfering with the more local object we had in view, the members of the Canadian Government who attended, presented for our consideration more extended views of Union, when the consideration of the smaller scheme was postponed, and for the time thrown aside, with a view of considering a larger measure. We were subsequently favored by an invitation from the Canadian Government to meet in Conference at Quebec, to consider how far a general Confederation was practicable. The invitation was accepted by all the Colonies, and the Delegates were chosen, not exclusively from the several governments, but were selected from the ranks of parties representing all classes and interests in the several communities, in order that all party prejudices and sectional feelings might be laid aside in the contemplation of an object of such vast importance. (Applause.) The importance of the matter was, indeed, so vast that it was not surprising my friend the Hon. John A. Macdonald, weakened as he was by indisposition, had faltered in the task, and quailed before the responsibility of addressing the public upon it. (Applause.) Public men, in addressing an audience at the present time, labored under unusual difficulties, and felt in a manner tongue-tied, as a certain reticence had to be observed, even although the desire to obtain detailed information as to the new constitution was so intense. Difficulties of a grave character had to be surmounted. Look at the sacrifices of opinion we had to make at the Conference. First, each individual forming part of the Delegation entertained his own views upon every one of the infinite number of important questions to be solved, and drawn as they were from different classes of opposing politicians in the several provinces, with the influence of party relations upon them, and the interest of each province clashing to a certain extent with those of the others, while the Delegates who represent them feel a natural obligation to conserve their interests, it required the greatest exercise of moderation and frequent modification of personal, party and local views and interests to arrive at anything like a successful issue. (Hear, hear.) None but those who have taken part in the Conference, or have deeply weighed the importance of the considerations involved, can have any idea of the difficult task of reconciling antagonistic views and interests, and nothing but the absorbing feeling of the importance of their mission and its results could have produced anything like a satisfactory conclusion. I have, however, the gratification of being able to announce that although on minor points differences arose and were decided, each individual member of the Conference is fully satisfied with its general results, and willingly pledged to bring to a favorable termination the result of our deliberations. I have said we were received like conquerors from a great battle; when such heroes are honored by the complimentary ovations of the friends and countrymen to whom they have returned, the pleasure they enjoy is invariably alloyed by sad reminiscences of the sacrifices made by the fate of the brave comrades who have gallantly fallen beside them. The pleasure of the distinguished reception you have given us is unalloyed by any such melancholy reminiscence. None of our comrades have been left behind us on the field. Our victory has been a bloodless one, and although all are not now present, I can assure you they are all alive and in good fighting order, fully willing and prepared at any moment when necessary to buckle on their armour, and encounter any opposition that may arise to the ultimate success of the all-important object upon which we have so harmoniously deliberated and agreed. (Applause.) I will not trespass upon your time by referring to the items upon which the Conference deliberated, but there is one subject which I feel it is impossible for me to pass over. The time has now arrived when we ought to have direct communication between Halifax and Quebec by railway, on a line not subject to foreign control, so that the inhabitants of our country may be able to visit the inhabitants of yours, without the necessity of going off British territory on their way. I have, therefore, the pleasure to announce, as one of the results of the Conference, the determination to take immediate measures for the completion of the Intercolonial

Railway. It is agreed to be one of the first objects of attention in the United Parliament. (Hear, hear.) It is impossible to over-estimate the commercial and social advantages of that great intercolonial highway. Offering facilities on the one hand for the interchange of the natural productions of each province, and highly calculated to break down the barriers which perpetuate political and social distinctions, it will be a means to the great end we all have in view. It will be a glorious day when we can get into a railway car at Halifax, and in three days be at the capital in Ottawa. (Cheers.) When the means of communication are provided, our people will avail themselves of them, and I shall glory in the day when the inhabitants of my country can put their foot on Canadian soil and say, "this is my heritage," while the Canadians too can visit the Maritime Provinces and feel an interest in every inch of their soil. (Loud cheers.) In all unions there must be a compromise of feelings to a certain extent; and as in the delicate union between the sexes there must always be a yielding of individual opinion to insure happiness, so it is in all unions, and the wider the circle and the greater the object, so in proportion must concessions of opinion be made. In contemplation of this great object the people of every section must be prepared to yield a portion of their feelings and interests to the common stock, and in the contemplation as well as in the working out of the Union this sentiment must not be forgotten. Having fulfilled our mission, our work may be but half done. We must return to our constituents, and impress them as far as we are able with our own views and sentiments. They have not seen as we have done; they have not learned, reflected and deliberated as we have, and we have still before us the important duty to instruct them in our views. We all feel proudly the position we occupy in the performance of that duty, and would be glad to use our best endeavours to procure the acceptance of the measure. We hope and trust that the people to be affected by it may in their deliberations forget all old party interests, private prejudices and local affections, and that the opposite of these feelings, reacting in, and reflected by their several legislatures, a favorable issue to the appeal to be made to them will abundantly result. We hope to be able with the materials at hand to raise a structure, which, bound together with the cement of patriotism, will be a monument of the wisdom of the present generation, and a tower of strength capable of resisting as well the minor effects of domestic broils as the attacks of the stoutest of foes from without. We will then feel we have a government as free as the world can exhibit, resting as it must for its support upon the continued love, confidence and affections of a free and enlightened people, and under the fostering care of a gracious Queen, whose name is held dear in every quarter of the globe, and upon whose kingdom the sun never sets. (Loud applause.)

The Hon. JOHN M. JOHNSON, Attorney General of New Brunswick, also responded to the toast. After thanking the company for the manner in which the toast had been received, he referred to the late meeting of the Conference, and said the public men who composed it had been forced to take such action from influences both within and without. The politicians of the Lower Provinces had been led to meet together to bring about a legislative union of those Provinces, when statesmen from Canada appeared and invited the consideration of the subject of a union of all the Provinces. Accordingly, the Conference was held, when all agreed to set aside their own peculiar opinions for the common good, and that the advantages of union were so great that all minor differences on political matters should be sunk and forgotten. This was the way he hoped the people would meet the question—either declare against it like men, if they believed the union to be without advantage, or if they believed it would prove beneficial, to lay aside all questions of mere party, in order to secure it. He then proceeded to shew what benefits the union would confer upon Canada, and alluded especially to the resources and wealth of New Brunswick, which would be enjoyed by Canada in case a union of the Provinces was effected. He desired to see it accomplished only under the British flag, and that no matter in what part of the British North American Confederation one might be, there would only be heard as a national anthem the strains of "God save the Queen." (Cheers.) He returned thanks also on behalf of the ladies whom they had so kindly toasted. The ladies of the lower Provinces had come here in love with union, and those not in it were prepared to enter into it. (Cheers and laughter.)

The Honorable GEORGE COLES responded for Prince Edward Island. He said the reception given to the Delegates in this city, last night and to-day, went beyond his expectations. He had thought the same at Quebec, but on coming to Montreal and Ottawa his admiration of the good-feeling and hospitality of the people of Canada had been still further increased. (Cheers.) He stood here in a different position from the gentlemen from the other provinces, who had just addressed them, both of whom were members of their respective Governments, while he (Mr. Coles) happened to be one of the Opposition. They were aware that the Oppositions of all the Provinces had entered into the Delegation to assist in carrying out the views of their respective Governments. Generally, when an Opposition joined in carrying out the views of Government, they were looked upon with suspicion by their constituents. But the present case was one which stood entirely by itself, and he claimed that in going for Federation the Government of Prince Edward Island were carrying out his views—views which he had entertained for many years. (Cheers.) In former times he had found many opposed to his sentiments on this question. It was the same as in the case of a proposed matrimonial union, when the friends of the family are very apt to raise objections on the grounds of disparity in wealth, standing, &c., but in spite of these objections they had gone to work, and for the last two months—first at Charlottetown, and then at Quebec—they had been trying to draw up the marriage settlement—(cheers)—and he had to announce to them that they had succeeded in framing a marriage settlement, which, though in some respects not what some of them might have wished, he hoped would, taken as a whole, give satisfaction to the entire family. (Cheers.) The marriage ceremony had yet to be performed. When that took place he hoped the families thereby allied would not be such strangers to each other as they had been in the past, and that the people of Canada would more frequently visit the people of the Lower Provinces, who would be happy to return the Compliment. (Cheers.) Mr. Coles went on to speak of the advantages of Prince Edward Island as a delightful summer residence, and of its various resources—particularly the inexhaustible treasury it had in the fisheries of its waters. At present hundreds of thousands of pounds worth of fish were taken from their waters by the American fishermen. He trusted that soon Canada would take that fish for the consumption of her inhabitants, and send her fishermen to catch them. (Cheers.) He thought they had reason to congratulate themselves on the result of the labors of the Conference. That thirty-three men, representing the various political opinions of six different Provinces, could have assembled and so amalgamated their opinions as to agree upon a constitution suited for that great Confederation, was something, he believed, such as the world had never seen before, and shewed that the Delegates were worthy of the position they held. (Cheers.) He said this although there was no man more disappointed than himself with respect to some parts of that constitution, but by mutual concession they had arrived at a result which they could all agree in supporting and submitting to the people, for he held that it must be submitted to the people. They could not force it on the people; they must endeavour to shew them that it was for their benefit, and thus induce them to accept it. (Cheers.)

Mayor DICKINSON then proposed, "The prosperity of British North America," and remarked that prosperity depended upon Union. (Cheers.)

The Hon. A. T. GALT, Finance Minister of Canada, then rose and replied to the toast as follows:—Mr. McGreevy, ladies and gentlemen—Before attempting to respond to this toast, I must express the pain I feel that Mr. Macdonald is unable from indisposition to make the remarks he intended. I know the loss you have sustained in not hearing from our friend the exposition he had proposed to give in reference to the inter-colonial union. I feel it a public loss, and hope his illness will be temporary, and that on an early occasion in Toronto he may be able to offer the explanations he is unable to give to-day. (Hear.) It falls to my duty to respond to both toasts at once. I desire to thank you most cordially for the way in which you responded to the toast of the Canadian Administration. We receive it, not as representing any political party in this Province, but as representing the Government, whoever they may be, who administer affairs. But on an occasion like this, when events of the greatest importance to Canada are transpiring, it is perhaps the more important to us to know that we have, at least for the moment, the cordial support of the people of the country, as we have a very difficult task to perform and desire to feel sure that there is confidence in our desire, if not in our ability, to do our duty to our common country. We have heard from the lips of eloquent gentlemen something about the Confederation of the Provinces—about the object here had in view—which is to give to the general Government of the British North American Provinces that amount of strength necessary to attend to common interests and to reserve to the local Legislatures the power to attend to sectional matters. All know that in proposing Confederation we have not to deal with a homogeneous people, but we have within our borders two different races—races equally distinguished in war and civil attainments—and we are bound to attend to the interests of those of French as well as of English origin—both being alike to be considered and respected. I trust that in the question soon to be submitted to the people of this country, it will be found that while on the one hand all necessary powers have been given to the general Government, there has been reserved, at the same time, to the local Governments such control over their own affairs as will preclude internal agitation. (Hear.) I should have been glad to have entered into the details of Confederation, but time will not permit, even were I competent. I will, therefore, rather follow the lead of those friends who have preceded me and say a few words respecting the general benefits we hope to receive. Whatever our views about monarchial and democratic governments, all are agreed upon this—that the material prosperity of the country should be promoted. All government is designed to effect this end. It is the only means whereby intellectual and material prosperity and development may be brought about. I believe we are making a move in the right direction in Confederation, and if we give more strength to the monarchial element on this continent it is because we think that through this form of government we can more effectually add to the peace and happiness of our people. In regard to the various interests of all the Provinces, we cannot but feel that the different circumstances in which we are all situated, the different systems of taxation, the different tariffs, must be detrimental to all. We can all appreciate the advantages that arose when the union in Canada took place. Those who can recall twenty years can remember the position in which Lower Canada then stood. They can recall the advantages which arose from the union of these provinces. It can be seen that in that short period—twenty years—this country has grown to a position in importance such as never could have been hoped for as long as she remained in a disunited state. We can feel that although there have been difficulties connected with the union of the two provinces, still the advantages that have flowed from that union have far outstripped all difficulties that have arisen from it. And in removing the difficulties of Canada, and considering the greater question of Confederation, we feel that in doing so we are not taking a step in a retrograde direction, but are taking it with a desire to an extension of the union. It is because we feel that disunited Canada was weak, united she became stronger; and now we ask the other Provinces to join us in the race of improvement and progress, and in extending through the whole of the British dominions in North America the advantages we now derive from union, which give us that essential power which is capable of controlling the various matters and maintaining our strength. At the same time we desire in this Confederation to give the internal management to the people themselves, the control of the local affairs which they are best able to manage. I feel I am trespassing on you in speaking at this late hour of the day. (Go on.) I certainly did not expect to be called upon on this occasion; at the same time, I am glad to be allowed to say a few words on this subject, because there is none who have felt more strongly than I have done the disadvantages of Englishmen in Lower Canada being in a minority. It is a source of much happiness to me to be present on an occasion when we are celebrating the advent, with the Delegates from all the lower Provinces, of that which is to unite us in one common country. Since the union of the Canadas we have been in harmony one with another—mutual confidence has existed; and when, on an occasion like this, I see here the representatives from all the Provinces coming forward to join us, I feel that it is removing farther and farther away from us any danger that might arise; and by increasing the area in which our politics range we shall have less danger; and whilst we shall be able to go forward in the race of improvement and free government, we shall be able to go forward hand in hand with less risk of difficulty occurring among ourselves. (Cheers.) With regard to the question of the commercial prosperity of these colonies, I have already said that there can be no doubt whatever that the union of these Provinces will tend to promote our prosperity. We have seen the effects of union in regard to matters of free trade in the United States. I know perfectly well that if one thing more than another has tended to promote the prosperity of that great country, it has been the free trade that has existed between its various parts. Now we desire to bring about that same free trade in our own colonies. It is almost a disgrace to us, if I may use the term, that under the British flag, in the dominions of our Sovereign in British North America, there should be no less than five or six tariffs and systems of taxation; and we cannot have trade between one Province and another without being subjected to all the inconveniences which occur in a foreign country. Surely it is our business to remove these difficulties, and we ought as subjects of the Crown, whose interests are identical, to be united. I am confident this great Union will tend to the promotion of all our interests; but whilst we own that the commerce of our respective countries will be benefited by it, we must remember that the vitality and life of the matter is confidence. It is confidence that is the life of our commerce. If we remain as we are now we are certainly comparatively weak. Let us combine our strength, and bring together all the elements of colonial power which we possess, and for national defence as well as as for national improvement, let us be a united people. (Cheers). I had intended, ladies and gentlemen, to have said a few words more with reference to matters connected with the proposed Confederation, but perhaps I had better not do so; but at the same time there is a subject on which I feel that I may be excused if I say a few words, and that is the arrangements proposed with regard to the government of the country. (Hear.) The newspapers, which are very generally correctly informed on all these points, have given the public to understand, in general terms, what the Conference or Delegates, to a certain extent, may be said to have decided to recommend to their respective legislatures. It is, therefore, quite well known to all that the form of government is one which is intended to be of a Federal character. A Legislative Union, it is perfectly true, would in many respects, perhaps, have been that which we in Canada, having been accustomed to it in the past, would have desired ourselves. But at the same time, considering that we had not merely to consult the interests, but even the feelings of the people of the several Provinces, it becomes very evident that it is not practicable to carry out a Legislative Union, and therefore it is proposed that the Union of the Provinces should partake of the federal rather than the legislative character. In that view a question has suggested itself to the minds of the people of Ottawa, that in reference to the buildings in which we are now so pleasantly occupied, there might perhaps be some change of policy. (Hear.) I think I may be forgiven if I say a word on that subject. I think that you and those who with us have to-day been permitted an opportunity of seeing the magnificent buildings erected in Ottawa must be gratified to know that in the decision the Conference has come to, that Ottawa is to be the Seat of Government, we are only doing that which every preparation was made for. (Cheers.) Ottawa, it is well known, has been selected by Her Majesty the Queen as the seat of Government for Canada, and one that can readily understand that when the other Provinces join with Canada, if it is our good fortune to have the measure carried, the question would arise as to where the future seat of Government would be; and in regard to that matter, I have the satisfaction of repeating this afternoon the statement which my friend Attorney General Macdonald made last night, and referred to also by my friend Dr. Tupper, that Ottawa has been selected by the Conference as the seat of Government for the Confederation. (Loud cheers.) That selection has not been made without some reference to the future. It is true that Confederation has at this moment in view the annexation, if I may use such a term, of the Maritime Provinces, but we cannot fail to see that in the great West there is a vast territory which must, at some time hereafter, be united to these Provinces; and in view of this extension to the West, we cannot fail to perceive that Ottawa, while it possesses all the elements for the seat of Government that made it to be chosen by our Sovereign the capital of Canada, possesses also that security and accommodation necessary to make it the capital of British North America. (Loud cheers.) Therefore, while our friends in Ottawa are most anxious to have us here, I am quite certain our reception this afternoon by our respected hosts must increase our anxiety to come up. (Cheers.) Still, I can only say this —that it depends entirely upon yourselves when we shall get here. You have here in Mr. McGreevy and his co-contractors the gentlemen who are in the way. If you can only get them to finish the buildings we will come here to-morrow. (Cheers.) I know there is reason for delay in this respect, and one can see for himself there are a great many difficulties. There are heating apparatus, ventilating apparatus, roofing, and things of that kind yet to be done, but I think that within a very short period my friend Mr. McGreevy ought to be ready to allow us to come here. We would be only too glad to come; and I am quite sure from the hospitality we have received we need not have the least hesitation in placing ourselves in the hands of the people of Ottawa. (Cheers.) With your permission, Sir, I would like to propose a toast. When we cease to enjoy the hospitality we are now receiving, I believe we are going to receive that of the city of Ottawa. I therefore hope you will allow me to propose the health of the Mayor and Corporation of Ottawa.

The toast was drunk with great enthusiasm.

Mayor DICKINSON responded. He begged on behalf of the citizens of Ottawa to return his most sincere thanks for the manner in which the toast had been proposed by the Finance Minister, and responded to by the company present. The occasion which had brought them together was one of no little importance, not merely to those within the sound of his voice, but to their children's children, whose interests were deeply involved in the result of the deliberations of the delegates who were now with them. In his official position it was, perhaps, out of his province to enter into political matters, but he might say, in his individual capacity, and he believed he might also say on behalf of his constituents in the city of Ottawa, that should the final result of the proposed amalgamation of these Provinces be as pleasurable to all concerned as this first opportunity of social association with their brothers and fair sisters of the other Provinces had been to the citizens of Ottawa, it would, indeed, be most satisfactory in its character. (Cheers.)

Colonel GRAY, of Prince Edward Island, asked the company to fill their glasses. It was not his intention to detain them with a speech, as he saw that their fair companions were already looking forward with agreeable anticipation to a more congenial task—one better suited to their capacities, although he would not say to their understandings. (Cheers.) The delegates had come to this city as strangers, and it was now his duty, as Chairman of the Convention of the Maritime Provinces, to ask them to join in drinking a bumper to the health of their hospitable entertainers. (Cheers.) They had been much delighted to-day with what they had seen. Nature and art had combined to render this fair city peculiarly attractive, and as regarded this superb structure in which they were now assembled, and which not only rivalled the Tuileries of Paris, but in his opinion, even the Houses of Parliament on the Thames—(cheers)—they all agreed that it was but a fit and proper building for the purpose to which it was to be devoted—one in which should sit the representatives of a free people, who soon would have their territory washed by the Atlantic at Halifax and by the Pacific at Vancouver Island. (Cheers.) It needed no prophet to foretell that the day was coming when they would take their places among the first nations of the world. (Cheers.) He asked them to join in drinking the health of their worthy hosts the Contractors for these public buildings. (Cheers.)

Mr. CLARKE briefly responded.

The party then separated, it being about half-past five o'clock, to prepare for the festivities of the evening.

BALL AT OTTAWA.

On the evening of the same day a Ball was given to the Delegates, under the auspices of the City Authorities, at the British Hotel. The assemblage was not so large as were the like *reunions* in Quebec and Montreal; but all the appointments were of the most elegant description, evincing unbounded liberality on the part of the promoters of the entertainment; while the decorations of the Ball Room surpassed those witnessed at the other places. Mr. Dickinson, the worthy and popular Mayor of the City, together with the whole Committee of Management, were most assiduous in their attentions to their guests, and succeeded in making the entertainment one that that will be long remembered with feelings of the liveliest gratitude and pleasure.

DEPARTURE FOR TORONTO.

RECEPTION AT KINGSTON, BELLEVILLE AND COBURG.

The Delegation party having engaged to be in Toronto on the evening of the 2d November, left Ottawa on that morning at nine o'clock, by a special train of the Ottawa and Prescott Railway. A rapid and agreeable drive of two hours brought the party to Prescott, where they were transferred to a special train of the Grand Trunk Railway, then in readiness for them. After a warm hearted farewell to some of their friends from Quebec, Montreal and Ottawa, who had accompanied them thus far, the special train hurried the delegation party on their way to Kingston, without waiting to stop at most of the intermediate stations.

The train arrived at the Kingston station at two o'clock. There an excellent dinner was prepared for the party by direction of Mr. Brydges, the Managing Director of the Grand Trunk Railway. The party were precluded by their engagements from spending much time over the sumptuous festivity; but the Delegates from the Maritime Provinces felt that they were deeply indebted to Mr. Brydges, not only for his hospitable entertainment then, but for the many other manifestations of his generous spirit while travelling with him on the Grand Trunk Railway, and the Hon Dr. Tupper, of Nova Scotia, became the exponent of the feelings of his co-delegates, by proposing Mr. Brydges' health at the Kingston dinner. He said:

Since we left the shores of the Atlantic Provinces we have had the pleasure of drinking many toasts, but I am sure that on no occasion of the kind has any toast been offered which could be drunk with greater pleasure or enthusiasm than that which I am now about to propose for your acceptance. I give you "The health of Mr. Brydges." (Cheers.) No one in Canada has had an opportunity of contributing more to our enjoyment. Madame de Stael used to class travelling among the evils of life, but I am sure that if she had the opportunity of travelling with our friend she would have classed it among the pleasures. (Cheers.) I see I have but to mention the name of Mr. Brydges to secure a cordial response. The great company of which he is the representative in this country, has accomplished to a great extent that which it has been the object of the Maritime Provinces to bring about—that is, union, and I trust the iron band which connects Upper and Lower Canada, and contributes so much to the prosperity of both, will be extended at an early day to Halifax, on the Atlantic coast, so that with the same speed and comfort with which we have travelled to-day, we may travel all the way from the Atlantic Provinces to the great lakes. (Cheers.) I can only hope that the gentleman to whom, at no distant day, will be entrusted the Government of all British America, will exhibit the same administrative ability that Mr. Brydges displays in his management of the Grand Trunk Railway, for he would then raise the condition of the whole country to that which it must be our, and our sons', ambition to see it occupy. I propose the health of Mr. Brydges, who has so handsomely contributed to our enjoyment. (Cheers.)

Mr. BRYDGES, on rising to respond, was received with renewed cheers. He said—I assure you, I have been taken entirely by surprise, but I beg sincerely to thank Dr. Tupper for the very handsome manner in which he has been pleased to propose my health, and you, ladies and gentlemen, for the kindness with which you have received the toast. In anything I have been able to do to promote the comfort and convenience of the ladies and gentlemen who have visited Canada from the Lower Provinces, I have simply discharged a duty, and I assure you it has been an exceedingly pleasant one. There is no question which has more engaged my attention, connected as I am with one of the leading institutions of the country, or elicited a more zealous disposition to promote it, than to see these great Provinces united into one consolidated whole, and a means of closer intercommunication established between them, so that in future days there may be many and various opportunities of meeting each other afforded the inhabitants of the different Provinces. (Cheers.) I am sure you will not expect me to make a speech to-day, especially as the time has nearly arrived when we must depart. But I assure you I shall ever appreciate, to the highest possible extent, the warmth with which you have been pleased to acknowledge any little kindness I have been able to shew you. I can only regret that it has not been in my power to make you more comfortable. I would only further say that I trust the day is not far distant when I shall be able to realize the hope which I formed when first connected with the Grand Trunk Railway, and that is, that I may start some morning from Sarnia on the western confines of our Province, and find my way without change of cars to the shores of the Atlantic at Halifax. (Cheers.)

The party then returned to the cars and were soon again in motion westward.

The train arrived at Belleville at a quarter to five o'clock. The Delegates had been apprised by telegraph that an address would be presented to them by the Mayor of the town, Dr. Holden, on behalf of his constituents; and they therefore expected that there would be a gathering at the station. They did not, however, anticipate such a hearty reception as they received. A large number of the inhabitants, ladies and gentlemen, were assembled upon the platform to greet the Delegates, and the 15th battalion Hastings Militia and Belleville Rifle Company, No. 1, were present as a guard of honor to receive them. As the train approached, it was hailed with loud cheers and waving of handkerchiefs by the fair ones of Belleville. The Delegates were then conducted to a dias that had been erected for the occasion, where the Mayor welcomed them in the name of the people of the town. As the Delegates walked from the dias, the Volunteers and Militia, neatly uniformed in green and red respectively, "presented arms," and the Band of the Battalion struck up a welcome strain. The Battalion was under the command of Col. Campbell, and the Rifles under command of Ensign Bowles. Upon the dias, introductions being over, the Mayor read the following address to Col. Gray of Prince Edward Island, as representing the Delegates:

To Col. the Hon. J. H. Gray, Chairman, and the Convention of Delegates from the Maritime Provinces:

Honorable Gentlemen—

On behalf of the inhabitants of the town, and in common, we believe, with the whole of the inhabitants of the Province, the Mayor and Corporation of Belleville desire most heartily and cordially to welcome you on the occasion of your tour through Canada, after, we trust, the successful completion of the labors of the Conference at Quebec.

We shall hail with pride and satisfaction a union of the most intimate kind with our fellow colonists of the noble Provinces of New Brunswick, Nova Scotia, Newfoundland and Prince Edward Island, and we feel convinced that the commercial effects of such a union will contribute much to our prosperity, as it will, we trust, contribute much to the prosperity of the Lower Provinces, and at the same time afford a large field for emigration from the mother country. It is most gratifying to us to learn that the wise and patriotic counsels of the eminent statesmen of the Convention, as well as our own eminent and political leaders, assembled together at the Conference, have smoothed the difficulties that might naturally have been expected to arise in settling the preliminaries of the union.

In strengthening the relations which bind us as fellow-colonists, we are convinced that our inalienable rights as British subjects will suffer no diminution, that our fealty to our sovereign will remain without change, and that we shall ever remain an integral portion of the great British Empire, vieing only with the other parts thereof in loyalty and devotion to our common Sovereign.

We regret very much that the time at your disposal prevents us from having the pleasure of receiving you in a manner more befitting the high positions you hold in your several Provinces, and more worthy of the greatness of the occasion upon which you assembled to deliberate.

We trust that the remainder of your tour may afford you much pleasure and gratification.

On behalf of the Corporation of the town of Belleville,

R. HOLDEN.

Col. GRAY replied as follows:—

MR. MAYOR,—On behalf of the Delegates from the Maritime Provinces, I have to express to you our extreme gratification and our most hearty thanks for your handsome reception of us.

Ever since our first entry on the confines of Canada, we have been the recipients of so much that is kind that we have become habituated to the returning of thanks. I need not assure you that we firmly believe the object of our mission will tend to unite us in bonds of brotherhood which shall never be severed; and I would say, woe be to him who shall ever attempt to rend these bonds asunder. (Cheers.) When I look around, Mr. Mayor, and see the stalwart forms of the noble looking men who stand now before us, I see the nucleus of a force which, should the hour of need arise—though I trust that hour may be far distant—will not have to look long for the strong right arms of their brethren in the Maritime Provinces to hasten to their aid, to assist in repelling any assault that may be made by any foe upon your rights and liberties. (Cheers.) Necessity impels us to travel onwards. Otherwise we should have been glad to have given, if but an hour, to walk round to see your fair town and this portion of your fine country, which is now doubly interesting to us, and will ever have our deepest sympathy and interest, particularly on account of your proximity to the great Republic on your borders. (Cheers.)

The Delegates having been invited to partake of a glass of champagne—

Col. GRAY proposed a bumper to "the Mayor and Corporation of Belleville."

The toast was drunk with all the honors.

Cheers were proposed and most heartily given for the " The Delegates," and for " the Canadian Administration,' and the Delegates having again got on board, a parting salute was fired, and the train moved off amidst the cheers of the assemblage.

At the Colborne station, a number of persons were assembled, who warmly cheered the Delegates as the train slowly passed the station.

At Coburg, which was reached at half-past six o'clock, His Worship Mayor Daintry and the Town Council were present to receive the visitors. Among other gentlemen present were the Hon. A. Burnham, Hon. G. S. Boulton, Dr. Beatty, Professor Kingston, Judge Boswell, Hon. James Cockburn, Mr. Barrow, Head Master Grammar School, and the Very Rev. Archdeacon Bethune.

Mayor Daintry read the following address:—

To the Honorable the Delegates from the Maritime Provinces of British North America.

We, the Mayor and Town Councillors of the Town of Coburg, respectfully beg leave to avail ourselves of this opportunity of giving you a hearty welcome, and we regret that the demands on your valuable time will not admit of your passing a longer period amongst us.

We recur with pleasure to the recollection of the unbounded hospitalities extended to the Canadian visitors to the Maritime Provinces in August last, and had an opportunity been afforded us of reciprocating them in a more suitable manner, we should gladly have embraced it. The mission on which you are engaged has our cordial concurrence, and we trust that nothing may transpire to prevent our becoming intimately connected with you both commercially and politically. We look forward with great satisfaction to the time when a band of iron, as well as the ties of brotherhood, shall unite us in one common country, and we feel sure that should our vast territories be at any time invaded, you will stand shoulder to shoulder with us in defence of the empire of British America.

Wishing you a prosperous journey and a safe return to the bosoms of your families, and hoping that when we next meet it will be as the happy inhabitants of a united country, we beg respectfully to bid you farewell.

G. S. DAINTRY.

Col. GRAY, of Prince Edward Island, addressing the Mayor and Corporation, said—As Chairman of the Convention of Maritime Delegates, I have to return you our sincere, united and cordial thanks for this very handsome testimonial of your approbation of our work. I have to repeat to you what I said a little while ago to the Mayor and Corporation of Belleville, that, since we first entered upon the soil of Canada, the reception we have met with has been such as cannot fail to have the effect of uniting us still more closely in the ties of brotherhood. As regards our proceedings in Conference, although to a certain extent confidential, enough has been made known through the press to satisfy you that the enterprise in which we have been engaged has for its object to unite us indissolubly as a band of brothers. (Cheers.) And I need not say to you, on behalf of the Maritime Provinces, that, should the hour of danger ever come—though we trust that it is far distant —you will find us ready to stand shoulder to shoulder with you to repel any aggressor. (Cheers.) When the Confederation is carried out, we will have a territory extending across the continent from the Atlantic to the Pacific, and I doubt not will be able to maintain ourselves as a nation among the proudest on the face of the earth. (Cheers.) I think we must all admit that the hand of a far greater power than that of ourselves has been directing our labors. He who controls all events, I have no doubt, controlled those apparently fortuitous circumstances out of which sprung the holding of this Convention. (Hear, hear.) Who would have ventured to fortell, a twelve-month ago, that so soon thirty-three representatives of the different Provinces, then separated by so many local prejudices and interests, should have met together, and agreed with such singular unanimity on a plan of uniting these Provinces? (Cheers.) We are proud of having been received as we have been in this Province, and shall carry home to our respective peoples most grateful recollections of the kindness with which we have been treated by our Canadian brethren. (Cheers.)

The Delegates having spent an hour most agreeably under the hospitable roof of the Hon. Mr. Cockburn, the Solicitor General of Canada West, where an excellent supper was prepared for them, they returned to the train, a torchlight procession of the Coburg Firemen and a band of Music accompanying them. At the Coburg Station, the Mayor of Toronto, and several of the other civic dignitaries of that place, were in waiting to receive and welcome the Delegates on their way to Toronto.

The party arrived at the Toronto Station about half-past ten o'clock, where an immense concourse of people were assembled, including all the members of the Corporation of the City of Toronto, the Yorkville Corporation, the Corporation of the United Counties of York and Peel, and all the members of both branches of the Legislature residing in Toronto. The Volunteers and the Fire Brigade of the City had turned out in full force, the latter body bearing torchlights, and presenting a most imposing appearance in the midst of the immense crowd by whom they were encircled.

Before leaving the Railway Station, the Mayor of the City, surrounded by his brother officers of the Corporation, came before the Delegates and read the following address :—

To the Delegates from the Provinces of New Brunswick, Nova Scotia, Prince Edward Island and Newfoundland:

GENTLEMEN,—We, the Mayor, Aldermen and Common Councilmen of the City of Toronto, most cordially bid you welcome to the metropolis of Upper Canada, and beg to express our warmest sympathy with the patriotic object which brings you hither. We doubt not that the contemplated Federation of the Provinces will tend to promote their prosperity, happiness and security, and that thereby they will become a great British American brotherhood, united by the ties of nationality, mutual safety, and cordial good will.

Whilst regretting exceedingly that circumstances render your sojourn in Toronto so brief, we trust your visit may prove a pleasant one to you and to the ladies who accompany you and honor us with their presence on this occasion ; that it shall be the means of fostering a more intimate acquaintance, and securing closer intercourse between Canada and the Eastern Provinces, and that all parties shall be thereby better prepared for a more permanent Union—a Union from which we anticipate a long and prosperous career under the protecting ægis of the British Crown

F. H. MEDCALF, Mayor.

November 2, 1864.

Colonel GRAY, of Prince Edward Island, then replied as follows :—

To His Worship the Mayor, Aldermen and Commonality of the City of Toronto.

GENTLEMEN,—We, the Delegates from the Eastern Provinces, with much gratification accept the cordial welcome you have tendered us, and thank you sincerely for the deep interest expressed in the object of our mission.

We agree with you that the Federation of British America will largely promote the happiness and prosperity of this portion of the empire, and unite us in indissoluble ties of common brotherhood.

We regret that our visit to your city must necessarily be brief, but the acquaintances we hope to form will, we trust, tend to prepare us for that permanent union and prosperity which can but be secured by the guardianship and protection of the British Crown.

During the reading of the reply the assemblage cheered approvingly.

The Delegates were then conducted to the carriages which had been provided for them, and a move was made for the Queen's Hotel, amid a blaze of torchlight, firing of rockets and strains of music, three or four Brass Bands being in attendance.

Soon after entering the Hotel, some of the Delegates made their appearance on the balcony of the west wing accompanied by the Hon. George Brown. The large crowd beneath were then addressed by Dr. Tupper, Mr. Tilley, Mr. Whelan and Mr. Brown. Dr. Tupper spoke at some length, dwelling upon what the Conference at Quebec had done, in a general way, and pointing out the advantages of Union, commercially and financially. Mr. Tilley spoke briefly, stating what the Maritime Provinces would bring to the Confederation; and Mr. Whelan referred to the proposed Union from a national stand point, alluding to its probable beneficial influence in moulding the character and destinies of the several communities to be embraced by it, while they enjoyed the alliance and protection of Great Britain.

The crowd shortly after dispersed in excellent order, cheering right heartily in token of welcome to their visitors

On the morning of the third November, the Delegates were invited by the Reception Committee at Toronto to visit some of the great public institutions of that city, and shortly after ten o'clock they left the Queen's Hotel for that purpose. Their first visit was to the College of Upper Canada. As they drove up the carriage way leading to this institution, the College students were ranged on each side, all having Enfield rifles, which they carried at the "present." There were not less than two hundred students thus in attendance; they were all dressed with remarkable neatness and uniformity, and had a fine healthy appearance. The Delegates were received at the entrance of the College by the Principal and Professors of the institution, and they proceeded at once to the public hall, where there was a large assemblage of the principal inhabitants of Toronto, including many of its fair daughters. The students occupied the galleries, and received the Delegates with the most enthusiastic cheering as they entered the hall. When this enthusiasm subsided, Mr. Principal Cockburn read the following address:

To the Hon. Gentlemen and Gentlemen, Delegates from the Maritime Provinces:

We, the Principal and Masters of Upper Canada College, beg to hail your visit to this part of Her Majesty's dominions as an event of high importance to the empire of which we form a part, and as likely to influence the history of the world. As a College we take no direct part in politics, but we cannot deny ourselves the pleasure of congratulating you on the prospect of reuniting the scattered bands of Englishmen who have settled in the different parts of British America, and who have hitherto been, to some extent, socially severed, though occupying regions not far apart. It has been our pleasing duty and pride, as a corporation, to educate upwards of 3,000 youth, coming from the Red River and Newfoundland on the one hand, and from the far North to the West Indies on the other. Anything, therefore, that tends to unite these Provinces—and your visit cannot fail to have this effect—must at the same time extend the fame and influence of this " Ancient Seat of Learning."

On these walls are recorded the names of those who, having won academic laurels, have gone forth to the battle of life strong in loyalty and attachment to the institutions of our father-land Our *alumni* are wont to be found in the various fields of usefulness, in the Legislature of this country, as well as in the learned professions, and in the army and navy of the British Empire.

Gathered together from the various provinces in the proposed federation, our students cannot fail to acquire a better knowledge of each other, and thus aid in drawing closer the social tie which will render this young and prospering Empire an harmonious whole—a child not unworthy of its mighty parent.

We again give you a hearty welcome, and wish you all success and prosperity in your noble mission.

We are,
Hon. gentlemen,
G. R. R. COCKBURN, M.A., Principal.
WILLIAM WEBB, M.A.
J. BROWN, M.A.
J. CONNON, LL.D.
M. BARRETT, M.A., M.D.
J. MAITLAND, B.A.
C. J. THOMPSON.
E. SCHLUTER.

Col. GRAY, of Prince Edward Island, received the address on behalf of the Delegates, and in doing so said a few words in reply. He said it gave the Delegates great pleasure, indeed, to receive such an address from an educational institution of such long and honorable standing as the Upper Canada College. He trusted that when the proposed band of brotherhood was completed and all their Colonies were united in one, the educational institutions of the country would receive that share of prosperity which he sincerely hoped all branches of internal progress and improvement would receive. As soon as the great scheme was carried out and fulfilled, they would see a change in the affairs of British North America which it was almost impossible at present to conceive. A tide of emigration would flow in upon us, our vast tracts of wild lands would be opened up, and the free sons of free Britain would here make homes for themselves amongst a people of whom they know so little. In looking upon the boys assembled before him, he could not help thinking that amongst them there were some who, at a future day, would be the statesmen of the great country that is now being formed, and who would have the pleasure of reaping the great benefits of Federation long after the originators of the scheme had passed away. He would long remember this day with pleasure, and concluded by hoping that the institution would continue to meet with that prosperity which has so long marked it.

Three cheers were then given for the Queen, and three for the Delegates, after which the party returned to the carriages. On going away they again passed through the lines of the College boys, who gave them a parting cheer as they passed through the gate.

The Delegation party next visited Osgoode Hall—a very splendid edifice, not surpassed by any other in the Colonies erected for similar purposes—being chiefly occupied by the Law Courts and the various chambers connected with them. The party was received at the entrance of the building by the President and members of the Law Society, who cordially welcomed them and showed them through the numerous and splendid apartments.

The next place visited was the University, which was justly regarded as one of the most interesting institutions in Toronto. The Delegation party were here again cordially received and welcomed by the officers of the institution in their official robes, at the entrance to the main hall; and the whole party at once proceeded to the Convocation Hall, where a large concourse of the citizens of

Toronto were assembled. The students, ranged on both sides of the Hall, and dressed in their College robes, received the visitors with the most enthusiastic cheering. The Delegates having been conducted to a platform at the head of the Hall, were introduced to the several Professors, on whose behalf, and on behalf of the institution, the Reverend Dr. McCaul, the very distinguished President of the University, delivered an oral address, with a tone and dignity that added very much interest to the chaste and beautiful language which composed the address. The Toronto papers furnished a report of the speeches delivered on the occasion of the reception of the Delegates in that City, but it is to be regretted that justice was not done to the brilliant utterances of Dr. McCaul, or to the sensible and well-timed response of the Hon. Dr. Tupper, who, on this occasion, represented the Maritime Delegates. The following is, however, the only report of the addresses which we have been able to obtain :—

The Rev. Dr. McCaul said—On behalf of the professors and others connected with the University, he received and welcomed the Delegates from the Maritime Provinces and the ladies accompanying them. Under any circumstances, he said, he would be happy to receive so many talented and distinguished gentlemen, representing the several provinces to the east of Canada, but on the present occasion it was with more than ordinary pleasure that he greeted them, as in their presence there he recognised a realization of the great principle of the federation of the British North American colonies, by which those children of one great parent would be bound together for mutual advancement, prosperity, and strength. These colonies had justly been called the brightest gems in the British Crown, and in carrying out the principle of federation it was not proposed to remove those gems, but to re-set them in one brilliant cluster, which would shine with increased lustre, and add new beauties and splendour to the glorious diadem of the British Isles. (Loud cheers.)

The Hon. Dr TUPPER then stepped forward, and on behalf of the Delegates thanked the professors and students of the College for their hearty welcome. He said the President had rightly interpreted the intentions of the Delegates in saying it was not their purpose to sever these Colonies from the British Empire in joining them into one country; but that, as by that scheme they hoped to benefit this country, they also hoped to add new strength, and power, and glory to the old parent who had reared them. It was to encourage emigration, to give prosperity and importance to themselves, that they joined each other, and also to encourage and establish such institutions as the one they were then in, in which the youth of Canada have the great and inestimable privilege of receiving an education which will prepare them, not only for a professional or commerial life, but also enable them to take an active part in the political affairs of their country. He hoped that the institution would continue to prosper, and that when the federation scheme was carried out, they would have the pleasure of ranking the University of Toronto amongst the leading institutions of the united country. After again thanking them he retired amidst loud applause.

The Delegates were then conducted from the Convocation Hall, and were shown through the principal apartments of the establishment, including the extensive Library, the very splendid Museum and the Observatory, in all of which their admiration was constantly awakened by the innumerable evidences of taste, intellect and wealth.

The Normal School next claimed attention, and although the Delegation party found the buildings which are used for the Normal School not so attractive in architectural construction as the University, the interior arrangements and objects of interest were of a more diversified character, and attracted much longer observation. Dr. Ryerson, the Chief Superintendent of Education, so long and favorably known throughout America for his zeal and efficiency in discharging the noble duties of his office, was assiduous in his efforts to shew every attention to his visitors; and in this respect he was most ably assisted by his distinguished coadjutors in the institution. No part of the great establishment was left unexamined,—the rooms used for the scientific apparatus, (which is of the most extensive and costly description, and all the fruits of Canadian skill and science)—the Museum—the Rooms dedicated to Painting and Statuary—were all noticed with admiration and delight; and the more ardent admirers of the Fine Arts were evidently reluctant to hasten their departure from the apartments dedicated to the service of those arts.

THE BANQUET AT TORONTO.

The Delegates having returned to the Queen's Hotel, prepared at once for the Banquet or *Dejeuner* which was designed in honor of them at the Music Hall. Two o'clock was the hour appointed, and punctually at that hour the party began to assemble. The Hall was splendidly decorated. Amongst the decorations was a fine portrait of the Queen—besides two or three luminous gas stars; and mottoes representing the several Provinces. The company was very large, occupying, and, indeed, crowding in some places, seven long tables. The viands and all the other accompaniments of a sumptuous repast were of the choicest kind, and formed, at the time, the subject of many compliments to the Committee of Management. His Worship the Mayor, F. H. Medcalf, Esq., presided, and discharged the duties of his important trust with little garrulousness and excellent taste.

Having given the usual loyal toasts in reference to the Royal Family and the Governor General, the Chairman proposed the "Army, Navy and Volunteers." In doing so, he said:—

If there were not a number of eloquent gentlemen to follow me, I certainly would be tempted to make a speech on the subject. It is a toast we always hear drank on social occasions. Visions of true greatness rise before me as I stand in your presence, thinking of scenes from Cressy to Waterloo — from Blenheim to Balaklava. (Cheers.) And not only are great names associated with the military—names equally great are connected with the navy. I call to mind those of Howe, Jervis and Nelson. There is still another branch of the united service—the Volunteers of Canada, form a part of the toast. (Loud applause.) They are mentioned last, but I know they are not least; for if the occasion required it, I am sure they would be found in the foremost ranks to oppose the common foe, and prove that they are worthy sons of noble sires. Without further trenching on the time of the distinguished gentlemen who are to follow, I now give you "The Army, Navy and Volunteers." (Cheers.)

Band—" Rule Britannia."

General NAPIER rose to respond, and was received with much cheering. Having thanked the company for the compliment to the Army, he said:—Being myself a military man, you cannot expect me to resound the praises of the branch of the service to which I have the honor to belong. But I may say this on the authority of His Royal Highness the Duke of Cambridge, the Commander-in-Chief—and I can conscientiously say it—that the British army at the present moment is in a state of the greatest efficiency, and ready to do its duty whenever called upon to do so. On an occasion such as this I can only venture to address you for a brief space to make a few remarks on the Volunteers and Militia of Canada. You all know my opinions on the subject of the Volunteers. I believe them to be in deed and in truth the right arm of Canada, and should war arise—which I sincerely hope may not be the case—but should war arise, owing to the number of miles we have to defend, it would be impossible for the regular troops for a moment to make a successful resistance against a large force unless we were supported, and well supported, by an organized and effective militia. Gentlemen, I know with you, that to have an efficient militia force you must pay for it; and it is in that point of view that I hope my hon. friend on my right (Mr Galt) will put his hand deeply into your pockets, and bring out sufficient money to keep up a good militia service. (Cheers and laughter.) Let him do that, and there will be no question about your having an efficient militia. I am not going to detain you long; but before I sit down I wish to make a few remarks on another branch of this subject. I consider that a great and most important step has been taken in the organization of the militia of this country by the establishment of military schools in Upper and Lower Canada. I think it is one of the most important measures which Lord Monck and his advisers could have brought forward, because you know as well as I do that forty or fifty thousand men could not be rendered efficient unless they had officers who were well drilled themselves and who knew how to drill others; and unless they were well drilled before hand, it would be impossible, within five or six months at all events, to get men to take the field, and in the interval we would be, I will not say what. (Hear and laughter.) There have passed these schools not less than 250 gentlemen holding first-class certificates, and some 206 or 208 holding second-class certificates. I am well aware that any gentleman who may have passed these schools and taken a first or second-class certificate, is fit to take command as an officer of a company of soldiers. But besides these there were more than a hundred who attended the schools, and who, although they took no certificates, had enough of drill to make them exceedingly good subalterns, if not good non-commissioned officers. You will thus agree with me that the establishment of those schools is a most important step towards the organization of an efficient militia.

Colonel DENISON returned thanks on behalf of the Volunteer Force. He said:—It is always a matter of the greatest satisfaction to the volunteer militia generally to be coupled in any way with Her Majesty's forces. (Hear, hear.) I hope the great measure which our guests have lately been engaged in will have the desired effect, and that we will all soon be united as one grand system; and I am sure the country will be well defended by the volunteer force, aided by the regular troops, against any foe which might have the temerity to present himself. (Cheers.)

The Hon. Mr. ALLAN, M.L.C., who officiated as Vice Chairman, then rose to propose the health of the Maritime Delegates. He said :— We have here, Sir, gentlemen from all the Provinces in that part of North America calling itself British, and which acknowledges the sway of that gracious Lady, whose portrait behind the chair looks down approvingly on her loyal subjects now assembled. (Applause.) On all occasions we Canadians— and I think I may especially say so of my fellow-citizens of Toronto—are prepared to extend a hearty and cordial welcome to our fellow-subjects of the Maritime Provinces. And more especially is that the case when, as on this occasion, there are present those who are distinguished as public men and as statesmen. But, Mr. Mayor, the present visit of these gentlemen to Canada is invested with peculiar interest and significance to all of us. They have come here to-day as it were to hold out to us the right hand of brotherhood, and to invite us to draw closer those political ties of a common allegiance, of similiar political institutions, and of a community of interests It is in many respects desirable that our connexion should be of a more intimate character than has hitherto existed between us. I shall not presume to trespass upon the time of this assembly with any lengthened remarks on the great subject of Confederation, inasmuch as we are called to meet those to-day who are prepared to give those explanations in reference to this important scheme, without which it would be impossible for us to form a correct judgment. And while I would preserve a becoming reticence on the details on this occasion, feeling that, with others, I shall probably have an opportunity of discussing these details elsewhere, I may at any rate go so far as to say that I heartily believe that a close, cordial and intimate union of all the Provinces of British North America is one of the most important and most desirable objects which any body of British American statesmen could set themselves to promote. (Loud and enthusiastic cheers.) Such of us as have watched with any interest the opinions put forth from day to day by persons of all political parties in Great Britain, in regard to the colonies, must feel there is a growing feeling in England that the time has come when this country should assume a larger share in the responsibilities which are looked for on the part of all colonies aspiring to a great political status and a national existence I heartily concur with those of our fellow British subjects who think we ought so to apply ourselves as to secure a firm stand on this continent as a British nationality; and if any would doubt that the time has come when we should set ourselves to the task of using our best exertions to place these Provinces in a different position to that they already occupy, they have only to look across our borders to the great Republic, and reflect upon the changes wrought there by a military autocracy. (Hear, hear.) If, then, we would draw closer together those social and political bonds which unite us to our fellow-subjects in the Maritime Provinces, in order to increase our strength and material prosperity, we are bound to extend a hearty welcome to those gentlemen who are come here as delegates of the respective Provinces to aid in maturing a plan for that great Confederation which has been so lately brought before us. (Applause.) All honor to those statesmen of the Maritime Provinces, and all honor to those statesmen of Canada who have originated this scheme, and who have applied themselves for many weeks past to mature it, so that it might commend itself to the hearty approval, not only of Canadians, but of the inhabitants of British North America generally. (Cheers.) Sir, I feel confident that we may look forward to a long future of happiness and prosperity, not alone to Canada, but to British America as a whole, from the visit of these gentlemen on this important occasion, and therefore I am sure that you will heartily join with me in according to them a right cordial welcome. (Cheers.) Gentlemen, I ask you to join in drinking, with all the honors, not only the healths of the delegates of the Lower Provinces, but if I may be permitted to say so, (turning to the ladies' gallery,) that of the fair representatives of those Provinces also.

The toast was drank with three times three cheers.

Band—" Auld lang syne."

Hon. Mr. McCully, of Nova Scotia, responded. He said, Mr. Mayor and Gentlemen—The reception that has been given to the Delegates from the Lower Provinces, and the enthusiastic manner in which you have responded to the toast which has just been given, quite overwhelm me. I was prepared to some extent for meeting a cordial reception in this part of Canada, and I must say that since we first set our feet upon the shores of this noble Province we have been received with one continued ovation; it has been one carnival, from the beginning until now. Indeed, language fails me to express the emotions which at this moment inspire my bosom, and you will forgive me, therefore, if I should pass by various subjects which I might speak upon, in order to address myself briefly and more immediately to the important matter which has called us together, in this the future capital of Upper Canada. (Cheers.) Gentlemen, we of the Maritime Provinces were engaged a short time ago endeavouring to make such arrangements as would enlarge the sphere of our commercial operations, accomplish a legislative union, and secure future prosperity. We had learned that while commerce knew no bounds, and our sails whiten the shores of every sea, our merchants, entering into large commercial enterprises, were cramped in their energies, and our trade encumbered with hostile tariffs. While we were so engaged there tapped at our door one fine morning a delegation from Canada,—seven of your most intelligent, active, and enterprising statesmen, whom we invited to seats in our councils. They gave us to understand that they had a more excellent way. We sat down listening to them day after day. First we had our friend from Lower Canada, Mr. Cartier—(cheers)—who in a graphic manner gave us to understand that what was required to make a great nation was the maritime element. Canada, he said, possesses the territorial and the popular element, but it requires the maritime element. (Cheers.) He invited us gentlemen of the Lower Provinces to assist him and those who were with him in preparing a larger scheme than that in which we were engaged.—Next followed your Attorney General West, Mr. Macdonald. (Loud cheers.) In that pleasing, chaste, and classic style for which he is distinguished, he spoke to us half a day on the subject of governments and governmental institutions. He enlarged upon the failure of the institutions which had been adopted in the neighbouring republic, and advocated a system which he contended would build up a great empire of these Provinces. Close upon him came Mr. Galt, mighty in finance, great in statistics, and wonderful in political skill —(cheers)—he charmed us for another half day. Following close upon him came Mr. McGee—(cheers) with his agricultural statistics—(laughter)—charming us yet again. Last but not least, followed my honorable friend from Upper Canada, Mr. Brown—(cheers)—enlightening us, and producing sensations so overwhelming that we almost forgot where we were. (Great cheering and laughter.) I suppose you will hardly believe me when I tell you that the representatives of the Maritime Provinces, who had been convened for the purpose of securing a particular constitution for themselves, having heard your Delegates, adjourned with their work unfinished, if I may perhaps coin a word, unbegun. (Cheers.) We adjourned to Nova Scotia, and asked the gentlemen from Canada to come see our Province. They had seen the fair little Island of Prince Edward; we asked them to come and see the mines and minerals, the forests and fisheries of Nova Scotia. We first took them to Pictou, a great storehouse of the world's motive power, and we asked them to take a trip down one of the shafts with us, but we found them gentlemen of opposite proclivities, aspiring upwards, and not one of them could be induced to descend to look at our coal. We next took them to Halifax, and, while on the way, stopped the cars for half an hour to shew them our gold mines. You would have been pleased to have seen how the eyes of Mr. Galt glistened as he gazed upon the precious metal. (Great laughter.) Why, he said, there was a specific for all the commercial and financial crises that ever could befall the Confederation. (Laughter.) They were satisfied that Nova Scotia was a land that, after all, had some attractions about it. (Cheers.) Before we parted from our guests, we received an invitation to Canada, and to Canada we came. They took us to Quebec, where they kept us for sixteen mortal days. Though they treated us well, they, however, worked us well too. (Cheers and laughter.) We sat down to frame a constitution for this great confederation. (Cheers.) There we dug deep, and laid strong and broad the foundations, as we hope, of an Empire, and it will be for you hereafter, when the proper time comes, to pass a fitting verdict upon our labors. Though circumstances render it impossible for me to give you more than you have seen already with regard to the nature of that constitution which we have been framing, I do trust in all hopefulness that it will meet your approbation. Deal kindly by it. It has been the work of men of some experience, and I am free to say it has been to a great extent with us a labor of love. Our discussions have been characterized by the most friendly intercourse. We have expended our best energies upon the scheme which we have wrought out, and when it comes to be unfolded to you, men of Canada, men of Toronto, I trust you will deal fairly with it. Let no savage, hostile criticism attack it, till it has been read, weighed and duly considered. (Cheers.) And if, after so weighing and considering it, you have anything to say against it, let it be in a spirit of moderation. (Cheers.) I ask it with the more confidence, because I, a member of the opposition of Nova Scotia, invited to take my share in this task, have been content that party feeling and party action should, for the moment, be hushed and stilled in prescence of so great a question. (Cheers.) And I ask it, too, of the members of the Governments of all the Provinces, if they desire that this enterprise should be successful, that there be no attempt to make out of it any local political capital. (Hear, hear, and cheers—loud and long.) Nothing in in my opinion could be more fatal to the measure. Therefore, as we of the Oppposition have laid aside our feelings and prejudices to work out this scheme, then I say in all confidence, we have a right to expect of the Governments of these Provinces that they will co-operate with us, and so attempt to combine the sympathies of all the people of the Provinces in such a way as to secure from them for the measure that consideration from their hands which it merits. I suppose many of you are anxious to know all the particulars of the scheme. But it is not in my power to deal with it in other than general terms. I may say, however, that if the measure under consideration goes into operation, in the first place each of these Provinces—

Canada being divided into two—may manage its own local affairs as it likes, but that larger subjects—commerce, the post office, banks, telegraphs, ocean navigation and the great Intercolonial Railway, which has been so much talked of, currency, coins, interest, public works and kindred subjects, that these shall be fit subjects for the Federal Government and Legislature to deal with. We trust that, when the whole matter has been fairly placed before you, it will meet your approbation. Although there may be some points that may be assailable, and although we cannot expect that our scheme should come perfect from the hands of the designers, yet I humbly trust that when it is unfolded, and that when the men of Canada and Nova Scotia and New Brunswick, of Prince Edward Island and Newfoundland, shall properly understand it, it will command their cordial assent. (Cheers.) But let me say that if there is one thing connected with this grand scheme of Confederation which ought more than another to be kept in the minds of the public men of all these Provinces, it is this—that it shall not financially weigh too heavily on the people. (Hear, hear.) In Nova Scotia, from whence I come, we have an *ad valorem* tariff of ten per cent., and one of the greatest difficulties we shall have to contend with in that Province in inducing our people to come in to the Confederation, will be to reconcile them to the raising of that tariff to any very large extent, unless it be for the public defence of the country, or some great public improvement, advantage, or necessity. The hon. gentleman proceeded to say that he did not himself believe, as an individual member of the Delegation, that it would conduce to the happiness of this country if we were to get a great Confederation, and the result were to be a great addition to the public debt, unless that addition were contracted for public works, or in providing the means of public defence. Therefore, he did hope that the public men who might have the arrangement of these affairs will so manage them that our tariff should not bear heavily upon the people, because he was satisfied that the Confederation scheme would not be looked upon with approval abroad, much less at home, if the result were to be that the Provinces were to be confederated for objects purely selfish, and no provision secured for our common defence. (Cheers.) It became us all to endeavour to arrange at the outset as far as possible to economise the finances of this great Confederation, and therefore he asked that the public mind should be pointed in that direction, for he believed it lay at the basis of the success of the whole scheme. (Cheers.) He (Mr. McCully) and his coadjutors had looked with pleasure and pride upon the mighty city of Montreal as it expanded year by year, its great heart pulsating with extending trade ; they had passed thence to Ottawa, designed as the future capital of the empire, where art and nature seemed active in rivalry and enterprise, and all along they had met with the utmost kindness and hospitality ; but when they arrived at Toronto last evening the reception they there met with, he thought, must be summed up in the single word—" Excelsior." To-day they had been carried to see the public educational institutions of this city. He regarded the youth of these institutions with deep interest. He trusted at some period not far distant, that from those halls the future rulers of British America would emerge. Some perhaps were there to-day. When he got back to his own land he should not fail to endeavor to convey to his own people some faint reflex of what he had seen in Toronto. Nova Scotians were not in all respects situated as Canadians are. Very many of them derived their living from the fisheries and by navigation. They were much upon the ocean—

> "Their march is on the mountain wave,
> Their home is on the deep."

Therefore it was that some portion of the population had not, perhaps, advanced in education equally with the population of Upper Canada. But they were brave seamen, and no people could be great without the sea ; and Nova Scotia would offer her seamen for common defence. The last man he (Mr. McCully) saw in Nova Scotia said to him :—" Don't be afraid to cast in our lot with Canada. (Cheers.) Give us a fair deal, and I have no fears. I want to see Confederation (if there is to be any) in my own day and I am quite prepared to take my chance with the men of my profession—the mercantile profession—the wide world over." So he (Mr. McCully) said, whatever came of it, he desired to see Confederation, if any, in his day. (Cheers.) Canada for Canadians, if you will, but British America for us all; and all combined for mutual protection. The country that was not worth defending was not worth living in. Let all our energies be combined, not only to make it a home to be loved, but a home to be respected, and one in which we should all be safe. (Cheers.) And should the foot of the ruthless invader ever threaten Canada, he hoped he knew the people of Nova Scotia well enough to assure Canadians that they would feel as though their own Province were invaded. (Cheers.) They would be prepared to contribute their quota for purposes of common defence. No man could look upon the contest progressing in the United States without feelings of deep regret. That nation, great in prosperity, would be great even in its ruins. It was now bleeding at every pore. He (Mr. McCully) was neither for the North nor for the South. He deprecated the extreme partisanship manifested by some persons in these Provinces; he did not think it right. But he thought it our duty to prepare ourselves against any danger which might be forthcoming, and he hoped the men of Western Canada, of all Canada, and of the Maritime Provinces, would now combine their energies for the purpose of building up an American empire which should withstand all the winds and storms of the future. (Cheers.) We had already a nucleus of something like 4,000,000 of people to begin with, and if we worked together harmoniously, energetically, and heartily, we should be able to accomplish all we desired. (Cheers.) The hon. gentleman concluded by cautioning the Governments of the Provinces against attempting to make party capital of the present movement; and asked the company to accept his thanks, and the thanks of the Nova Scotia delegates, who had on the present occasion deputed him to speak for them, for the great kindness shown; and when a federation of the Provinces was an accomplished fact, he, for one, should never envy the feelings of him who could not heartily and proudly exclaim—

"This is my own, my native land."

The hon. gentleman resumed his seat amid loud cheers.

The Honorable CHARLES FISHER, one of the New Brunswick Delegates, rose to respond on behalf of that Province. He said:—If his friend who had just sat down felt embarrassed, how must he (Mr. Fisher) feel who had to follow an orator like him. When Dr. Tupper addressed the audience in Quebec he stated somewhat of the embarrassment he felt on that occasion. How much more must his (Mr. Fisher's) be now, being called to speak upon a subject which, having been discussed meeting after meeting, was to a great extent exhausted. Desirous as he was, as an *alumnus* of an institution kindred to that whose President to-day delivered to them such weighty words within the walls of University College, that his every expression should be well guarded, he felt some embarrassment in rising to address an audience hundreds of miles away from his home; but he felt also that there were there kindred sympathies—not simply those arising from a common origin, but from other causes, whereby he, a New Brunswicker, was assured of welcome and consideration in this the Queen City of the West. He referred to the welcome given those men who early settled this portion of Canada, who alike settled that portion of New Brunswick in which he was living—those men who, in a time of trouble and revolt, strong in British feeling, left their homes, and, desirous of perpetuating British institutions in this wilderness of the West, settled various portions of this territory. Thus he could claim a common ancestry, which he felt certain, though a stranger, would assure to him a patient hearing in an assemblage like this. Himself and friends had been overwhelmed with the reception they had received. From the first hour they had set their feet in Canada, up to this moment, they had had one continued ovation. He saw fully that the public mind of Canada was stirred to its inmost depths by the great question with which they had to deal. Perhaps no event equal in importance to this country since the battle on the plains of Abraham—certainly no event in more modern times, stood forward so prominently as this; and the future historian would refer back to it as full of great results. In 1785 the Congress of the United States first met for the purpose of making arrangements to sever the colonies from the mother country. How different out position. We assembled under the ægis of the protecting power of Great Britain, determined to provide means whereby our connection with the mother country should endure. Whatever other differences of opinion there might be, whatever were our local peculiarities, that was a foregone conclusion; that was a point about which there could be no discussion; all have agreed that the course we might adopt for the improvement of our condition should be taken under the protecting care, and as part and parcel of the greatest empire the world ever saw. * * * Men of every party, of every denomination—men from every section of the country, cognizant of their different ideas in politics and theology, met together resolved to lay their differences as an offering upon the altar of their common country. (Cheers.) No event had occurred in modern times equal to this. We had seen the kings and potentates of Europe meet together, but for what purpose? To divide nationalities, to destroy the liberties of peoples, according to their own will and for their own selfish purposes. But we had only one common desire, to build up one great country, with one free government, whose pervading element should be monarchial, combined with sufficient of the democratic element, that we might provide for all time a government adequate to the wants and interests of the whole people. (Cheers.) The Maritime Provinces would bring into this Confederation something near a million—800,000 people, and a territory of fifty or sixty thousand square miles. They offered a maritime element; they offered a large sea coast, ports open at all seasons of the year; they offered access to the ocean; they offered to come in with Canada on terms of equality. When this Confederation became a fact, if they examined the statistics published from time to time, they would find that in point of maritime influence and importance it would be the fourth power in the world. (Cheers.) In these respects England, France, and the United States would alone be superior to it. The Lower Provinces had many things which would be beneficial to Canada. They had important fisheries, native iron, coal, copper and lead; all of which would count in the future interchange of commodities between the different Provinces. They had in New Brunswick ten million acres of land still ungranted, eight of which were fit for settlement. Let it not then be supposed that they came in as almoners, as supplicants; they came like free Englishmen to ask a place in the Confederation. (Cheers.) Great as Canadians—as manufacturers and as merchants—might be, great as was their population, great as was their resources, he would tell the audience that their equals were to be found in the Lower Provinces. (Cheers.) New Brunswick expended annually £30,000 a year for schools, £35,000 a year for roads, and small as their Province was, they had at this moment 1,500,000 miles of roads, 7,500 of which might be traversed in a carriage and four. They had besides 200 miles of railway, equal to anything of the kind on this continent. (Cheers.) Did they know why the inter-communication between these Provinces had hitherto been so limited? It did not arise from poverty of soil, or from local and political causes. Until 1845 the country between New Brunswick and Canada was locked up. And then what was done? Why, a large tract of land was taken away from little New Brunswick and Canada, and handed over to the United States. Did they think, if this Confederation had then been formed, that the interests of New Brunswick would have been sacrificed to the cotton-spinners and the tobacco dealers? The result of the differences which took place was that this part of the country long remained a wilderness, and a large portion of it, equal to the State of New Hampshire, with a large settlement of French Canadians, was handed over to the Union. They had built roads through New Brunswick, but if they were to have complete intercommunication the Intercolonial Railway must be built, and he hoped its necessity was recognized as fully in Western Canada as it was in New Brunswick. He had almost hoped against hope for its construction, but he had ever felt that what was an advantage to New Brunswick must be supplied. When built the district between the two Provinces, now almost uninhabited, would speedily be filled up, and the two countries connected. Their trade was rapidly extending in that part of the Province. So long as five years ago their lumbermen had cut lumber within hearing of the gun fired regularly at Cape Diamond. They imported annually 250,000 or 300,000 barrels of flour into the

Province. Hundreds and thousands of barrels were yearly carried up the river St. John, to within 40 or 50 miles of the banks of the St. Lawrence. They were not entirely selfish in this matter. He had been an advocate of the railway ever since it was proposed. He had always argued for it as a link in the great chain of railways which would yet connect Halifax with Vancouver Island. He had read with great interest the descriptions of that country—especially those given by the scientific men sent out by Canada to explore it, and he had always argued that communication with that country was a commercial necessity to the West. It was a peculiarity of the British territory lying on this side of the Rocky Mountains that its very formation made it the best route to the Pacific, by which a railway could be constructed on much better terms than in the United States. We possessed the best pass by which to cross the Mountains. Another singularity was that in the approach to those mountains in the United States territory, there was a large area of desert incapable of cultivation and unfit for settlement. But explorers told us that both sides of the mountains, in British territory, were fit for settlement. They enquired would such a road pay? Had the Grand Trunk Railway paid? Ask the rapid improvement of Canada if it had not paid? Ask the hundred thousand people of Montreal the result of that great instrument of progress. Ask the increase given to the value of land and to the products of the West; ask all these, and let their testimony to the great benefit derived be the reply. When the resources of the interior were brought into action, what would be required to carry these products to the ocean? Would not a railway be needed? (Cheers.) Then, was there no pride involved in the construction of an Intercolonial Railway? Were we not liable to have our means of communication stopped by the Americans any time they chose to do so? Was it not a humiliation to them, the delegates from the Lower Provinces, to have to open their trunks for examination by an American customs officer, before they could pass from one portion of British territory to another. If a railway were constructed this would not have to be undergone. (Cheers.) But, after all, possessing as they did such complete elements for the formation of a great nation, what would they be without a free government? What would have been the trade of England, the centre of civilization and of Christianity, without her free government? The members of the Convention had met together for the purpose of framing a government adapted to these colonies, and they had endeavored to do it upon the principles of the British monarchy. (Cheers.) They had kept in view the great original of the parent state, but they had so constructed the constitution as to preserve intact the rights of each separate Province. They had felt that the social condition of the Provinces was such that there might be great difficulty in carrying out the British constitution in all its details, still its great principles they had kept and applied. They had endeavored to preserve the three leading elements which should give elasticity and power and animation to the whole. They had endeavored to preserve the monarchical, the aristocratic and democratic principles, the three elements of virtue, honor, and power, and he believed that whatever difficulties might be found in working out the details, the constitution as a whole would be found to possess the vital principles necessary to vitality and permanence. They had left to the local bodies of the Confederation local matters, and when they had found any condition of things which it was necessary to preserve, they had provided that these should be untouched forever. They had endeavored to build up a strong central power, which should have control of matters of common interest, and surely the defence of the country might be counted among them. (Cheers.) He was not one of those who had any fear, whatever might be the result of the contest in the United States, that Great Britain would throw us off; but he believed that it was a part of our duty as good subjects, who valued our privileges, to make provision for our defence to the extent of our ability. He believed further, that in Great Britain, observing this to be our determination, the whole power of the empire, should occasion require, would be put forward to defend her colonies. He was not one of those who mistrusted the people of this Province. Let the men of Canada not forget that when the alarm of war broke out in 1812, when this Province was threatened with invasion, the people of New Brunswick raised a regiment which, amid suffering and privation, passed through the Northern snow, and fought and fell heroes by the side of the militia of Canada. Surely if any one doubted we might appeal to the memory of the immortal Brock to show that we were willing and able to defend ourselves. Separated, widely separated as we were, we might be easily destroyed; but united, we should present a formidable front. We had territory enough. The first House of Commons that was elected for these united provinces would represent 4,000,000 of people, a population equal to that of many of the states of Europe. It had been well said that if some of those states which enjoyed an independent existence were thrown into one of the Canadian lakes, they would not make a ripple on the shore. (Laughter.) As in our Confederation local questions would be left to the local legislatures, he had high hopes that in the general legislature the smaller politics would be forgotten, and that a desire for national honor would arise, without which national greatness could never be attained. Then we were to have intercolonial free trade. If the Lower Provinces could do Canada no other good in going into a Confederation with her, they could give her manufacturers a million new customers, while they themselves would open up a market with 4,000,000 of people rapidly increasing in number. He did not feel disposed to detain the audience much longer, but he could not close without a few remarks on the future that lay before this country. Just imagine, when the whole territory had become populated, when into this Confederation were thrown the colonies beyond the Rocky Mountains, that we should have one continuous flow of British blood and British feeling from ocean to ocean. Then we might anticipate that the whole trade of the world would pass through our territory to India and China and far off Japan. (Cheers.) In endeavoring to form this Confederation, in endeavoring to unite this country together, in endeavoring to promote the mutual good-will of these peoples, it appeared to him we were only carrying out the original designs of the settlers of this country. They desired to extend British freedom, British power, British institutions here, and we were now going to effect this great object, that object for which our fathers bled and died. (Cheers.)

Hon. Mr. CARTER, of Newfoundland, was then called upon, and said—Mr. Mayor and Gentlemen, I am highly pleased that my hon. friends from the other Provinces have given me a little breathing time. I intend now, with your permission, to offer a few observations for myself and co-delegate of the colony of Newfoundland. Some of you may know something of that colony, but by the majority I fear that little information is possessed as to its capabilities. We have been placed, as it were, at the fag-end of this Confederation; but in another sense our geographical position places us at the very commencement of it. We are, in truth, at the gate of entrance to the St. Lawrence, which leads on to your mighty inland waters. And without us, it is not too much to say that there would be no stability to this proposed Confederation. I have no doubt myself that when the celebrated navigator, Jacques Cartier, first touched at Newfoundland, when proceeding to the discovery of Canada, he formed an opinion that these sections of country must one day become united; and in that point of view it is a pleasing thing to know that one of his collateral descendants, the Attorney General for Lower Canada, should take such a deep interest in the matter, with his friends in the Administration, as to endeavor to carry out this union, which by many of us has been long sought for. (Cheers.) For myself, I would say, that I am not altogether unacquainted with Canada, having already paid some three or four visits to this Province, and most of our people know a little about it. There has been within the last four years a growing desire that we should have more intimate intercourse one with another—that we should, in fact, form part of a great whole. In the Conference held at Charlottetown we took no part; we were not invited; and the first invitation we had came from Canada, but a short time before our visit here. To show that we have long been alive to the advantages of union, I may mention that in 1858, when a despatch was received from the Government of Canada, requesting the Lower Provinces to co-operate in bringing about a union, Newfoundland was the only colony which responded. (Cheers.) From that time up to the present we heard nothing further on the subject, but I think that when you shall have heard from me that scarcely a day elapsed from the time the telegram was received in our colony until we were appointed to come to Quebec and started on our journey, you will admit that it is a proof of the deep interest our people have continued to take in this matter. (Cheers.) Newfoundland, as you are aware, is a commercial place, and is not very celebrated for its agricultural capabilities. The reason of this is, that the attention of our people has been chiefly taken up by the prosecution of the fisheries, which have been most valuable to the people along the coast, furnishing inexhaustible mines of wealth, from which, from time to time, immensely large fortunes have been drawn. But unfortunately those who have amassed those fortunes have retired to spend them, not in the country, but in their mansions on the Clyde and the Thames; and we hope that when this Confederation shall have been accomplished we shall not find our men of wealth deserting us and spending their money in the old country but remaining with us, finding there homes as congenial to their wishes as the mansions of Great Britain. On the subject of our territorial area, it will not be unimportant that I should say a few words, though I do not intend to go into elaborate statistics, as these were very well gone into by my hon. friend, Mr. Shea, in Montreal. He there stated that we were ready to receive from Canada to the extent of some five or six millions a year if we had increased facilities, and particularly increased shipping. He also shewed that our public debt is only £200,000—that our exports always exceed our imports—that we are able to raise within the colony every penny which is required for public purposes, and that our five per cent. debentures are worth a premium of five per cent. (Hear, hear.) This is a good proof of the state of trade in this colony, and shews that we can come to join with you in the character, at any rate, of independence. We have mutual wants, and may be of great benefit the one to the other. You want the maritime element, and we are able to give it to you. You may by and by require seamen to man your navy, and where will you be able to get them more readily than in Newfoundland? A more hardy and enterprising people than that colony contains are not to be found. From their earliest days they have been "rocked in the cradle of the deep." (Applause.) Great Britain has given large bounties to create a nursery for her navy; and there is no class of her subjects who stand more ready with willing hands and stout arms to come to her defence when necessary than the people of Newfoundland. (Cheers.) Sir, the area of this country, so little known in Canada, is over 40,000 square miles, and that is no little to add, if anything were wanting to be added, to your present territory. It is larger a great deal than New Brunswick; it is larger than Nova Scotia; it is larger than either of the countries taken separately, of England, Scotland, and Ireland. And its resources, when developed, cannot fail to be of the greatest value. We have valuable mines of gold—I believe silver mines will be discovered, to be worked to advantage—and we have rich mines also of lead and copper. Will not all this, I may ask, be something to bring into the proposed Confederation as the free-will offering of Newfoundland? (Cheers.) Then, too, as I said before, we have our fisheries. We are supposed, however, to be almost altogether buried in fog, and when I meet with gentlemen abroad, the first thing they say, on hearing I come from Newfoundland, is, "I believe you are notorious for fogs, and highly celebrated for fish and dogs." (Laughter.) I desire as far as possible to dispel so erroneous an idea. These fogs do not, in truth, prevail more with us than in Nova Scotia and New Brunswick, and I can assure you that in Newfoundland you will find as cloudless and as bright a sky, and that you can breathe there as free and dry an atmosphere, as in any part of the known world. (Cheers.) Many of you may think that this subject is becoming thread-bare from being so frequently spoken about; but my excuse for mentioning it again is that the magnitude of the question is such that it cannot be too frequently referred to, provided one does not trespass on the time of others. Now the reception—the enthusiastic reception—of last night, and magnificent entertainment to-day, are strong proofs of the deep interest taken in this question in Canada. We do not come here as distinguished men—we do not come with titles or honors—we do not come ennobled; but we come as brother colonists on our peaceful mission, proclaiming the desire of our people to unite their destinies with yours. (Cheers.) We knew that you would receive us for the cause, and no stronger proof could be given us of the deep-rooted feeling which prevails in this Province, in favor of union, than is afforded by these receptions. We come here representing all shades of politics—my co-delegate from the Opposition and myself from the Government. We break all distinctions of party down for this occasion, and I hope for ever. (Cheers.) If you were to ask me by what differences we are kept asunder in Newfoundland, I confess I should have great difficulty in telling you; and were the same question to be put to my other friends from the other Maritime Provinces, I fancy the response would be the same. I hope sincerely if this Confederation is formed, that it will tend to do away with this petty party spirit and those prejudices, and that acerbity of feeling which at one time was characteristic of us; for we generally find that the intensity of the acerbity is proportionate to the narrowness of our limits. (Applause.) And what do we find here? Do we not find here, as everywhere else, a combination of men who, like ourselves, are of different shades of politics, but who have united together to promote the same reform? Have you not the ablest men from both sides of the House represented in the Administration, combining together to carry out this noble object? They are no longer fighting as the "ins" and the "outs," but striving to promote the good of the country. In such an arrangement as is here proposed, we must necessarily lose some of our individualism; but if we do we look forward to larger and brighter and greater prospects—we look to your glory and to our own. We know that as you advance we must advance, and that if you fall we are in danger of falling too. When we blend all our interests together, and become as one, we know that whatever honor and glory you may obtain will be reflected on us as well; and for these results, I care not for giving up what is called part of our individualism. [After thanking the Company for the toast, and making some pleasant allusions, in reference to the ladies, the honorable gentleman resumed his seat amidst great cheering.]

The Hon. EDWARD PALMER, Attorney General of Prince Edward Island, rose on behalf of that Colony to reply to the toast. He was well received on rising. He begged the company, on behalf of himself and his colleagues who there represented it, to accept his acknowledgements for the very flattering manner in which the health of the delegated gentlemen had been proposed and received by the Assembly; and proceeded to say:—The Island from which I came is but a small country, and it requires perhaps little to be said in its behalf; and it is fortunate it is so, as the task has fallen upon one so incapable of doing it. But notwithstanding I shall say a few words, and in speaking of the Island, I am at first reminded of a very facetious remark of a gentleman whom I trust you all know—and that is no other than Mr. D'Arcy McGee—when speaking of Prince Edward Island. "Now," this witty gentleman said, "don't you be too boastful about your little island; don't let us hear so much about it, or we will send down a little tug boat and draw you up into one of our lakes, where we will leave you to take care of yourselves." (Laughter.) Perhaps if this did happen—if you did bring our little island here, we would not have much reason in many respects to regret the exchange. (Hear, hear.) We are an agricultural community, as you are all aware; and although not a very great one, yet we can send away a million and a half bushels of oats in one year, still leaving enough for our own use. Now, as to the proposed union. Your friends came down, and we listened to them, and we resolved since then that there should be an Union. (Applause.) In the first place, we resolved that the Union should be, as far as the circumstances of the country would permit, in accordance with the British Constitution. (Cheers.) The Provinces were unanimous in this. We then resolved that each of the Colonies should preserve its peculiar privileges and institutions, and that there should be no higher power to interfere with them. (Applause.) We next agreed that as far as possible the debts of the colonies should be dealt with fairly and equally, and that the tariffs should be equal throughout. We next agreed that as regarded the outside world we should, between and amongst ourselves, enjoy free trade. (Applause.) I confess that in my Province there was at first no little anxiety with regard to this proposition, because we stand at present as happy and contented a people as any of the British Provinces. Yet I hesitate not to say that from all that has been witnessed by the Delegates representing that Island, they will not hesitate to recommend to their people the great Union which I hope soon to see accomplished. (Cheers.) We have come here and been delighted with the enterprise of your people. We have become acquainted with your vast resources—the great perfection of your machinery—the great progress of arts and manufactures among you. (Applause.) Even to-day we were surprised to witness the admirable institutions of learning which you have among you, and had great pleasure in inspecting the *minutiæ* of the operations. We saw your wealthy merchants, your happy enterprising men making their fortunes—all convincing us that this country is one with which we need not be afraid to throw in our lot. (Cheers.) It is not the great hospitality alone that we have met with since we entered within your borders—it is not the kindness which we have received individually or collectively from the people of this Province—that causes us to desire to come into this union; your excellent institutions of all kinds, and your progress in everything that goes to make up a great country, impel us to such a desirable consummation—to form part of the great empire or colony, or whatever you choose to call it, which is to be constructed out of these provinces of British America, sharing the glories of the mother country, which we all desire to see perpetuated and increased. (Cheers.)

The CHAIRMAN then said he had pleasure in introducing a gentleman from the Far West, who would speak to the Red River interests. He called on Mr. James Ross. (Cheers.)

Mr. Ross rose and said:—Mr. Mayor, Ladies and Gentlemen,—I feel that I owe you an apology for intruding upon your time this evening; but seeing that you have so kindly received the toast of the North-West, I, as the only representative of that region, feel myself obliged to respond.

Mr. Mayor, the people of the country which I represent have been hitherto little heard of, but they must nevertheless be taken into account in the scheme of Confederation which has, for some time past, been under consideration. In all the meetings hitherto held a great deal has been said with reference to the resources, the progress, the character and standing of the various colonies represented in the Conference; but for the first time the Far West is formally recognised. The people of Red River cannot pretend to compete in point of numbers with any of the other members of the Confederation; but the extent and intrinsic value of that country must make up for want of population and the other symptoms of material progress. We have about 10,000 of a white population; 15,000 of a half caste; and 40,000 Indians. The government of the country is in the hands of the Hudson Bay Company, and is of an extremely primitive and patriarchal character. This government it is none of my duty, at the present time, to criticise; but I may say that it is anything but favorable to the progress of that country. To many in this vast assemblage it may be something new to state that the country of which I now speak is three millions of square miles in extent. Two-thirds of that may be too cold for ordinary agricultural purposes, but the southern portion, which embraces about one-third of the whole or one million of square miles, is eminently adapted for settlement, and I wish the fact to go far and wide as authentic and reliable. Being a native of that region, and a representative in an ethnological as well as a geographical sense, I beg to express my great pleasure in seeing this measure of Confederation likely to be consummated, for I believe it will benefit the North West. Apart from the extent of the country, its intrinsic value forms an important element. It is capable of sustaining a vast population, because extensive and fertile. For over 150 miles width along the boundary line there is as habitable a country as can be found on the surface of the globe. The climate has been represented by exploring expeditions sent from England and from this country as very similar to that of Canada. I know for a certainty that it is, on the whole, colder; it is also more uniform and reliable. The air may be cold, but it is bracing and healthy. In truth, it is a most salubrious climate. Apart from the fertility of the soil, a source of livelihood to immigrants would be the fish afforded by the waters of the country. There is abundance of white fish, pike, gold-eyes, perch, sturgeon, &c.—not an unimportant consideration in a new region. And the channels which contribute so much to the sustenance of an immigrant population also afford the means of internal navigation. The Red River district is thoroughly connected with all the parts of that vast region. By means of Lake Winnipeg it is connected with Nelson River, which flows into Hudson's Bay; connected with the Saskatchewan, which leads from near the Rocky Mountains; connected by the Winnipeg and Rainy rivers with Lake Winnipeg; and connected, lastly, with the interior of Minnesota near the sources of the Mississippi. There is, indeed, over the whole country a vast network of excellent water communication, well adapted for commercial purposes. And then allow me to say before this distinguished assemblage that the North-west has mineral resources of great value. Between Lake Superior and Red River there are extensive copper mines, and still more extensive ones are to be found along the Arthabasca and the Mackenzie Rivers. Coal mines, moreover, abound on the Saskatchewan, and on the branches which flow into the Assiniboine. Gold, too, has been found in the Saskatchewan region, and in such quantities elsewhere also, that there cannot be the least doubt of the auriferous character of that country. From $5 to $15 per day are being made, and every successive discovery only satisfies me more and more that the whole country abounds in gold, and that time alone is requisite to develope its resources in respect of minerals. In conclusion, allow me, a native of the Red River country, and its sole representative here—to express the deep gratification I feel in having that part of the country so prominently brought before the attention of the delegates from the Lower Provinces; and allow me to express the hope that in the scheme now being devised, the vast extent, the resources, the capabilities and the value of the North-west may be fully remembered. There is a country there to which the over-crowded populations of European countries may resort and find a comfortable home. (Cheers.)

The CHAIRMAN then proposed "Her Majesty's Ministers." The toast was drank with every demonstration of enthusiasm.

Hon. GEORGE BROWN, on rising to respond, was received with enthusiastic cheering. He said—Mr. Mayor and Gentlemen, I desire to return you the hearty thanks of my colleagues and myself for the manner in which you have received this toast. It is an old saying, that England loves not coalitions — and I am sure if the adage is true of England, it is doubly true of Canada. And I am free to say now as I have always said, that, except under the pressure of a most grave and urgent necessity, the combining of public men of opposite political sentiments to form a Government, under the British Parliamentary system, is very strongly to be deprecated. (Hear, hear.) But if ever there was a coalition that had a sufficient object to justify its formation, I do think it is that Administration which I represent here to-day. (Cheers.) The present Administration was formed for a special purpose—for a great public end—it was formed in the light of day—its whole object and end was fully and openly proclaimed to the world—and no charge of intrigue or desire for personal aggrandisement could with justice be laid at the door of any party to the compact. (Hear, hear.) But, Mr. Mayor, if any defence were required, if it were necessary to offer any justification for the formation of the coalition— I think we offer it to you abundantly here to-day, in the remarkable scene now before you, as the practical result of our three months' labors. (Great cheering.) Formed though the coalition was of very incongruous materials— this much can most truly be said of it, that so far it has realized and more than realized all the results that at its creation were anticipated from it. (Cheers.) It will be recollected that Parliament adjourned immediately after the coalition was formed, and very soon after the adjournment the Government opened communications with the Lower Provinces. It is well known that the political party with which I have the honor to be associated did not view a federation of all the Provinces with that degree of confidence with which it was regarded by a portion of our opponents. Not that any of us deemed it an objectionable thing that all the British American Provinces should be united. On the contrary, I think no public man in Canada, aspiring to the position of a statesman, could have looked at the position of these great and increasing colonies without descrying in the future their association together for purposes of defence and commerce, as an inevitable and desirable event destined at some day to be accomplished. (Cheers.) But while we all saw and acknowledged this, some of us felt at the same time that we had practical difficulties, which there was an urgent necessity should be promptly and efficiently met— and we were ill content to have our hands tied up from dealing with those great evils while waiting for a scheme, dependent on so many different Provinces, and that might be postponed for many years to come. When, therefore, the Government was formed, it was upon the express understanding that the constitutional difficulties of Canada should be met immediately—that a measure for that purpose should be submitted to Parliament at its first session —and that in the meantime we should strive with all our energies to ascertain whether or not a just and satisfactory arrangement for the union of all the British American Provinces could be effected, so that we might present it at the coming session of Parliament in lieu of the lesser scheme. And, sir, the best proof that could be given of the zeal with which we have executed our work is to be found in the assemblage before you to-day of gentlemen from all sections of the British American Provinces—gentlemen representing all the different political parties of their several sections. I had proposed to enter at some length into the details of the great scheme of union which has been elaborated by the Conference, but time is passing swiftly, and it is obvious that to our friends from the Maritime Provinces belongs the speaking on such an occasion as this. My colleague, Mr. Galt, and myself, you have all the time with you, but our friends from the Lower Provinces you may not have another opportunity of hearing until the union has been consummated — an event which, let us fondly hope, is not far distant. (Cheers.) However, as briefly as I can I shall endeavor to glance at our proceedings of the last few weeks, so as to convey at least a general idea of the scheme which has been unani-

mously adopted by the Conference. Every on
that at the very time the present Government
a conference of delegates from the Maritime Pr
about to be held, for the purpose of considerin
priety of uniting Nova Scotia, New Brunswick,
Edward Island under one Government. In
opened communications with the Government
Provinces, asking to be permitted to send rep
to their Conference—and in the kindest and m
manner they sent us a hearty welcome to the
We arrived at Charlottetown on the 1st Sept
most kindly and hospitably were we received.
invited to take seats in the Conference and to
members, and we at once proceeded to open
the object of our mission. What we said to
this—"We in Canada have had serious secti
ences; but at last we have agreed to a settlem
troubles on a basis just and equitable to all
our country; we are about to frame a new c
which will be acceptable to the great mass of
and it has occurred to us, on hearing that y
considering a change of your constitution, wheth
not be well for us all to sit down together, a
how far it would be for the welfare and good
of our Provinces were we to unite them all und
tem of government." Well, Sir, we did sit dov
—we discussed the whole subject in all its bea
looked at it from every point of view—and af
ten days' deliberation we came to the unanim
sion that if the details could be settled upon a
to all, it would be for the advantage of the wh
Provinces that we should be united. (Loud ch
haps I should state that we from Canada were
with mere argument in coming to this conclusi
passed through a large portion of the Lower
and saw with our own eyes the fairness of the l
first visit was to the beautiful Island of Princ
and I think my friend Mr. Palmer did no more
tice in what he said of his Island home—
delightful spot, a spot more likely to become
the Isle of Wight of the American continent,
possible to find. (Cheers.) And assuredly these

will not be long united before the health and pleasure-seeking portion of our people will be finding their way in thousands annually to her shores. (Cheers.) From Charlottetown we proceeded by steamer to Pictou — the chief shipping-port of the great Nova Scotia coal-beds. We examined the works of one company, conducted on a very extensive scale. Under the able management of Mr. Scott, the products of that one mine had, we were assured, in the short space of five years, been increased from 150 tons per day to the vast quantity of 2,000 tons per day. (Hear, hear.) We found lying at the wharves of Pictou not fewer than from 60 to 80 vessels taking in coal; and we were told that frequently not fewer than 100 coal vessels were waiting for cargoes in the harbor. Let it be remembered that this is a trade which has only begun to be efficiently developed, and that from Pictou is shipped off the products of but a small portion of the vast coal district of Nova Scotia. From Pictou we passed on for about forty miles through a picturesque agricultural country to the town of Truro. There we found iron claimed to be equal to the best Swedish iron, and works established by an English company for the manufacture of steel, turning out, as we were assured, not less than 15,000 tons per annum of excellent steel. We were told that this valuable iron ore extends over a very large section of the country, and I believe that the geological surveys that have been made prove the accuracy of the statement. From Truro a rapid ride over the rail brought us to the gold country, and we were afforded ample opportunity of examining the working of the gold mines. The general impression of this branch of industry is that it is a species of gambling — that the gold-seekers dig up sand, pass it through a sieve, get little or nothing for their labor for many days together, but some lucky day make a hit and realize a fortune. But very different from this are the gold mines of Nova Scotia. The precious ore is obtained regularly and certainly by patient and persistent labor. We found 200 persons employed at the mines we visited, getting at that time $8 a week, the whole weekly expenses being $1,600, and in 14 successive weeks the product of the works had been not less than $3000 a week, and sometimes considerably more. We were assured by the intelligent superintendent that the gold bearing region extends over an immense tract of country—that he had been to many of the other gold works, and while some of them might be more and others less productive than his own, still he was satisfied that, properly worked, the whole of them might be made to give an ample return for the capital and labor invested. We thus found Nova Scotia to be a land of coal, of iron, and of gold. We saw these great sources of wealth in practical development, all within the brief space of twenty-four hours—and when we couple with these the exhaustless fishing resources of that country, and its ship-building industry, I think my friend Mr. McCully was not far astray in suggesting that if Nova Scotia comes into the union she will not by any means come in empty-handed. (Cheers.) We proceeded next to Halifax, a most thriving city, and one of the first harbors of the world, but on our doings there I need not enlarge, for who does not know the enterprise and the hospitality of the good citizens of Halifax? From Nova Scotia we proceeded to the Province of New Brunswick, and there we saw St. John, a city of which, as British Americans, we may all well be proud; a city showing marked evidences of vitality—extensive commerce, large ship-building interests, lucrative timber-trade—and a harbor filled with ships from all parts of the world. (Cheers.) From St. John we passed by the beautiful St. John River to Fredericton, the political capital of New Brunswick, and we were one and all highly delighted with what we saw of the resources of the country through which we passed. Want of time forbade our visiting the Island of Newfoundland, but I am satisfied that no one who has read anything as to the resources of that Island will say that my friend Mr. Carter has over-stated its capabilities. The fishing and the mineral resources are very great — a vast fleet of ships is constantly employed in the traffic—and the revenues of the Island are very large. But even beyond these, as arguments in favor of its coming into the proposed union is this consideration: that Newfoundland is the key to the St. Lawrence, and in the event of war would be absolutely necessary to us for purposes of offence and defence (Hear, hear.) You will therefore understand, Sir, that the members of the Canadian Government all returned to this country with a most earnest desire to carry out the union of Canada with the Maritime Provinces, if it could possibly be accomplished. In this spirit we at once sought the aid of his Excellency the Governor General, in summoning a formal conference for the mature consideration of articles of union; and I cannot mention his Excellency's name without expressing my sense of the debt the country owes him for the earnestness with which he has sought to promote this measure and the hearty desire he has ever shown to give effect to the wishes of the people of this Province. (Cheers.) His Excellency, without delay, summoned a Conference of representatives from the several Governments, and the late sittings at Quebec were the result of that summons. For sixteen days we were earnestly engaged in considering all the details of the scheme; and though, of course, it was impossible that such a body of men could be without differences of opinion, looking at matters as we did from different points of view, and with different interests to protect — still it is highly questionable whether any body of thirty-three gentlemen, even if composed of men of the same country and the same party, could have sat together for so long a period discussing matters of such grave importance, with more entire harmony and more thorough good-will and respect than prevailed throughout the whole of our deliberations. (Cheers.) The various details of the Confederation scheme were brought up for consideration by the Conference in the form of resolutions. These resolutions were separately discussed, amended, and adopted; and as finally adopted by the unanimous consent of the whole Conference they now stand on record. (Cheers.) The precise course hereafter to be adopted has not yet been finally settled, but the first step in any case is to submit the results of our official deliberations to the Imperial Government. The next step that will probably be taken is to submit the scheme to the Legislatures of the different Provinces for their approval, and in the interim to address Her Majesty and the two Houses of Parliament, praying for an Act of the Imperial Legislature to give effect to the resolutions of the Conference, which Act will be and remain the foundation of our political system—the Constitution under which the new Confederation will be brought into existence. Sir, it ought ever to be borne in mind, that when we came together to consider the details of the new constitution we were about to frame there were very many interests to be considered. In the first place, we had to consider that this country is of immense extent, presenting a vast variety of interests, great and small, for which it would be exceedingly difficult for any one body of men to legislate. And in the second place, even had it been desirable to govern so vast a country by one Executive and Legislature, it would have been impossible to carry it, as our Lower Canadian fellow-subjects would never have consented to it. As the only practicable scheme, therefore, and as in my humble opinion the best scheme, we adopted the plan of constituting a general Administration and general Legislature, to which should be committed matters common to all the Provinces, and local Governments and Legislatures for the several sections, to which should be committed matters peculiar to their several localities. I know there are those who say—"Oh! we do not like a federal union, we want a legislative union which will bring us all under one legislature and executive." But setting aside the fact that this could not have been carried had it been ever so desirable, I do think the sectional jealousies and discords that have so long distracted Canada should stand out as a warning to us, and that we should diligently steer clear in the larger federation of whatever has tended to mar the harmony of our present union. And in this view I am persuaded that, by committing all purely local matters to local control, we will secure the peace and permanence of the new Confederation much more effectually than could possibly have been hoped for from a Legislative Union. I am sure it is unnecessary to say that the Governor-General of the United Provinces is to be appointed, as heretofore, by the Crown. The duration of Parliament will be limited to five years, and of course it will be composed of two branches—a Legislative Council appointed by the Government of the day on the principle of equality of the sections, and a House of Commons, in which we are to obtain that so long desired, so long earnestly contended for reform—Representation by Population. (Great cheering.) Objections will no doubt be urged against the manner in which the Upper House is to be constituted, especially by those who would prefer that the members of that body should be elected rather than appointed. But I do confess, Sir, that in my opinion an appointed Upper House and an elected Lower House would be much more in harmony with the spirit of the British Parliamentary system than two elected bodies. (Cheers.) I was one of those who, at the time the change was made from an appointed House to an elected House, resisted the innovation. Not because I was at all afraid of popular influence, but because I felt that while the Lower House controlled the Government of the day, and the Government of the day appointed the members of the Upper House, the people had full and efficient control over the public affairs of the country. But I am free to admit this, and I say it with the greatest pleasure—that the apprehension I and others entertained of a collision between the two elective bodies, and a dead-lock ensuing, has not been realised. I am bound to say that under the operation of the elective principle, we have had a body of men sent to the Upper House who would do honor to any Legislature in the world, and who have worked with a degree of harmony and a desire to benefit the country which have been really admirable. But we cannot forget that when a new power first passes into the hands of the people, great sensitiveness and care are exhibited in acting upon it—much more than when the new power has lost its freshness, and its exercise sinks down into a thing of every day wont. The Elective Upper House has not long existed in Canada. Besides, when the elected Councillors first took their seats, they found already in the Chamber a large number of old, appointed members, who, no doubt, exerted a certain degree of influence over their proceedings; and the question, I think, fairly presents itself whether, when the elective system had gone on for a number of years, and the appointed members had all disappeared, two elective chambers, both representing the people, and both claiming to have control over the public finances, would act together with the harmony necessary to the right working of Parliamentary Government. (Hear, hear.) And there is still another objection to elective Councillors The electoral divisions are necessarily of **enormous** extent—some of them 100 miles long by 60

15

wide—so large that the candidates have great difficulty in obtaining personal access to the electors, and the expense of election is so great as to banish from the House all who are not able to pay very large sums for the possession of a seat. From all these considerations, it did appear to me when our friends of Lower Canada, who were most interested in the constitution of the Upper Chamber, desired to have the members appointed by the Crown, that acting in the interest of Upper Canada it was my duty to consent. The Chamber is to consist of 76 members, distributed as follows:—

Upper Canada......................................24
Lower Canada......................................24
Nova Scotia.......................................10
New Brunswick.....................................10
Newfoundland...................................... 4
Prince Edward Island.............................. 4

Total...76

I am told that there are persons who object to Lower Canada, with so much smaller a population, receiving equal representation with Upper Canada in the Upper House; but a little reflection will, I am persuaded, remove all objections on this score. I am one of those who have always stood firmly up for the rights of the Western section of the Province. But now that our rights are admitted—now that we are seeking a compromise measure for the final settlement of all our troubles—now that we are seeking to build up a new constitution that will be just to all—I for one am ready to cast aside old feelings of hostility, and to consider not only what will be abstractly just, but what will carry with it the hearty sympathy and assent of all the parties to the new compact, and lay the foundations of our new fabric deep and permanent. I could not but feel that having obtained for Upper Canada that just preponderance in the Lower Chamber for which we have so long contended, we ought to allow the gentlemen from Lower Canada, so long as no flagrant injustice was done, to frame the constitution of the other Chamber very much as they chose. In the view taken of this matter by the Lower Canadians, all our friends from the Maritime Provinces entirely agreed. The House of Commons, as I have said, is to be constituted on the basis of Representation by Population. It is to be composed at first of 194 members, distributed as follows :—

Upper Canada...82
Lower Canada...65
Nova Scotia..19
New Brunswick.......................................15
Newfoundland... 8
Prince Edward Island.............................. 5

Total....................................194

After each decennial census the sectional representation is to be re-adjusted according to population—and for this purpose Lower Canada is always to have 65 members, and the other sections are to receive the exact number of members to which they will be severally entitled in the same ratio of representation to population as Lower Canada will enjoy by having 65 members. Thus the representation will be strictly based on population—the disparity of population between the several sections will be accurately provided for every ten years—but the number of members in the House will not be much increased.

I come now, Sir, to the powers and duties proposed to be assigned to the General Government. It is to have control over all questions of trade and commerce; all questions of currency, finance and coinage; all questions of navigation and shipping, and the fisheries; all questions of defence and militia, all matters connected with the postal service, and all questions affecting the criminal law. To it will belong the imposition of customs and excise duties, and all other modes of taxation—the construction of great public works of common benefit to all the Provinces — and the incorporation of Telegraph, Steamship, and Railway Companies. It will also have control of Banks and Savings Banks, Bills of Exchange and Promissory Notes, Interest and Legal Tenders, Bankruptcy and Insolvency, Copyright and Patents of Invention, Naturalization and Aliens, Marriage and Divorce, Immigration and Quarantine, Weights and Measures, Indians and Indian Lands, the Census, and generally all matters of a general character not specially assigned to the local governments. These are the duties proposed to be assigned to the General Government.

And now one word as to the constitution and powers of the local governments. It is proposed that each Province shall be presided over by a Lieutenant Governor, who will be advised by the heads of the various public departments. As to the constitution of the local legislatures we found there was so much difference of opinion on the subject—some of the Provinces desiring to retain their present institutions while we in Canada must necessarily establish new ones, that we thought it the wisest plan to leave the constitution of the local legislatures to the existing Parliaments of the different sections. The powers and duties of the local governments have been clearly defined by the Conference. They are to have the power of imposing direct taxation—the sale and management of the public lands in their respective sections—the maintenance and management of Prisons, Hospitals, Asylums, and charitable institutions — the construction of local works—the promotion of agriculture—and the imposition of shop, saloon, tavern, and auction licenses. The control of all the National Schools and school property is to be vested in the local governments; and they are to have authority over Municipal Corporations, and all municipal matters. They are also to have power to make laws in all matters affecting property and civil rights, and for the administration of justice. And generally, while on the one hand, as we have already seen, all matters of a general character and common to all the Provinces are to be committed to the general government; so, on the other hand, all matters of a local character will be committed to the local governments. The separate powers to be exercised by each will be clearly defined in the Constitution Act to be passed by the British Parliament, so that there will be no danger of the two bodies coming into collision. In thus defining the functions of the general and local governments, it will, no doubt, be objected that we have committed certain matters of an important character to the local bodies which the people of Upper Canada would have been well content to have seen left to the general government. But if the details of the scheme are closely

examined, it will be seen that we have given nothing to
the local bodies which did not necessarily belong to the
localities, except education and the rights of property, and
the civil law, which we were compelled to leave to the local
governments, in order to afford that protection which the
Lower Canadians claim for their language and their laws,
and their peculiar institutions. I am sure we are all glad
that they should have that security. I am sure, notwithstanding all that may been said to the contrary, that
none of us have had any desire to interfere with the mere
local institutions of our fellow-subjects of Lower Canada—
and that it will be held as a sufficient answer to all objectors that the arrangement has been made in a spirit of
justice to Lower Canada, and with the view of securing
hereafter that harmony and accord which are so desirable
in the future government of the country. (Cheers.)

There is one point to which I am desirous of calling
particular attention. I refer to the fact that in framing
our constitution we have carefully avoided what has
proved a great evil in the United States, and that is the
acknowledgment of an inherent sovereign power in the
separate States, causing a collision of authority between
the general and State governments, which, in times of
trial like the present, has been found to interfere gravely
with the efficient administration of public affairs. In the
government to be formed under this new constitution, I
believe it will be found we have avoided that difficulty.
For, while we have committed to the local governments
all that necessarily and properly belongs to the localities,
we have reserved for the general government all those
powers which will enable the legislative and administrative proceedings of the central authority to be carried out
with a firm hand. With this view we have provided that
the whole of the Judges throughout the Confederation—
those of the County Courts as well as of the Superior
Courts—are to be appointed and paid by the general government. We have also provided that the general Parliament may constitute a General Appeal Court, to which an
appeal will lie from the decisions of all the Provincial
Courts. We have likewise provided that the general
government shall be specially charged with the performance of all obligations of the Provinces, as part of the

British Empire, to foreign countries. I may mention also that the Lieutenant Governors of the different sections are to be appointed by the general government, and that the power of disallowing all Bills passed by the local legislatures is to be vested in the Governor General in Council. In this way we will have a complete chain of authority, extending down from Her Majesty the Queen to the basis of our political fabric. The Queen will appoint the Governor General. The Governor General in Council will appoint the Lieutenant Governors. And the Lieutenant Governors will be advised by Heads of Departments responsible to the people. Thus we will have the general government working in harmony with the local Executives and in hearty accord with popular sentiment as expressed through the people's representatives. (Cheers.) A very important subject is that relating to the finances of the Federation; but as my hon. friend, Mr. Galt, is about to address you, I will leave this branch of the subject to him. (Cries of "Go on !") I may briefly, however, say this, that all the debts and assets of the different Provinces are to be assumed by the general government. It has been found that, with the exception of Newfoundland and Prince Edward Island, the debts of the several Provinces are much the same in proportion to their population. Newfoundland and Prince Edward Island have, however, scarcely any debt at all, and we found a difficulty in associating Provinces which were free from debt with those that owed large public obligations. But we fell upon this plan. We struck an average of the debts of the several Provinces—and we agreed that those whose debts exceeded the average should pay interest at five per cent. annually into the public exchequer, while those whose debts were below the average should receive interest in like manner from the public chest—a basis just to all. Then it was found that while some of the Provinces could maintain their local governments without money from the public chest, there were other Provinces not accustomed to direct taxation, and in order to meet their views, we were compelled to adopt a compromise. I hope the day is not far distant when we may be able to adopt direct taxation to a much greater extent than we have yet seen in Canada—but at present it was very clear that Confederation could not be carried out unless we conceded this point. We agreed to compromise. We made the Finance Minister of each section go carefully over the public expenditures of his Province, and cut down every item to the lowest point practicable, and we found that the smallest sum for which the machinery of government in the Provinces could be carried on was $2,633,000. This sum is to be distributed annually as a full and final settlement for local purposes in the Provinces, and I am happy to say it is to be distributed on the basis of population. As our population in Upper Canada is very large, of course we get a handsome share. The principle is so just that I do not see how any one can reasonably object to it ; and as the sum distributed is not to increase, a very few years of progress will make it of comparative unimportance. There is a very pleasing feature in the finance question. A Confederation of five states is about to be formed, and it is to the credit of the whole that not one of them has ever been unable to meet its obligations to the day—(cheers)—and still further, that the finances of all are now in such a satisfactory condition that every one of them has a large surplus of revenue over expenditure for the current year. (Cheers.)

I have thus, Mr. Mayor, as briefly as possible traced the outlines of the new constitution which has received the approval of the delegates from the several Provinces. But I cannot conclude without referring to some other things which have received the grave attention of the Conference. And the first point to which I desire to call attention is the fact that the delegates have unanimously resolved that the United Provinces of British America shall be placed at the earliest moment in a thorough state of defence. (Cheers.) I am not one of those who conceive that Canada stands in danger of attack from our neighbors across the lines. I cannot doubt that they have plenty of work already on their hands without rushing on fresh embroilments—and I confess that, notwithstanding the fierce ebullitions of the American press, I have faith in the good sense and good feeling of our neighbors to believe that the idea of an unprovoked aggression on the soil of Canada never seriously entered the minds of any large number of the inhabitants of the Northern States.

But come war when it may, I am sure I speak the sentiments of every man in Upper Canada when I say that the first hostile foot placed upon our shores would be the signal and the summons for every man capable of bearing arms to meet the enemy—(enthusiastic cheering)—and that the people of Canada would show, in the hour of trial, that that spirit which was manifested in 1812 has not died in 1864. (Renewed cheers.) And, while on this point of defence, I have one word to say on a matter which I know has made a deep impression throughout Canada. Sir, no man in Canada appreciates more than I do the generous consideration that has ever been shown by the mother country towards this Province. But I desire to enter a firm protest against the manner in which of late our duty has been laid down for us, chapter and verse, by gentlemen three thousand miles off, who know very little of our circumstances, and yet venture to tell us the exact number of men we are to drill and the time we are to drill them. Sir, I venture to assert that the language recently used towards this Province is neither just, nor yet calculated to promote a desirable end. This Province, like the other colonies of the British empire, was founded on a compact entered into between the Crown and the people; an assurance was virtually given to those who emigrated to this Province that they should be protected by all the strength of British arms. And nobly has Great Britain fulfilled that promise. Never has she hesitated for a moment to expend her blood and treasure in defending her Colonial Empire. (Cheers.) I hold that Great Britain is bound to fulfil on her part the conditions on which the settlement of this and other colonies took place, and to continue to aid us until we have grown to that degree of maturity and strength which will fairly demand at our hands a reconsideration of the terms of the contract. If I am asked whether Canada, united with the Lower Provinces, is able to take upon herself a larger share of the burden of defence than she has heretofore borne, I answer without hesitation—undoubtedly "yes." (Cheers.) It were utterly unreasonable to expect that to these colonies the people of England should much longer send armies and navies for their defence, whilst we continued developing the resources of our country, and accumulating wealth untaxed for the appliances of war. But what I do say is this, that when the time arrives that a colony has outgrown the conditions of her first settlement, and when she is fairly bound to assume new and higher relations to the mother country in the matter of defence, it is only right that the whole subject should be discussed in a candid and reasonable spirit. And I am free to express my opinion that had the Canadian people been invited frankly to enter on a discussion of the changed relations in matters of defence they ought to occupy to Great Britain, the demand would have been responded to readily and heartily. (Cheers.) And it is only due to the present Colonial Minister, Mr. Cardwell, to say that this is the spirit in which he seems desirous of approaching the question; and that such is the spirit in which I believe negotiations hereafter will be carried on between these colonies and the Parent State. It is not to be concealed that we in Canada are deeply interested in this whole question of Colonial defence being thoroughly discussed and settled. We all heartily desire to perpetuate our connection with Great Britain; but it is quite evident that a feeling is growing up in England which may prove dangerous to that good feeling and attachment, unless the duties and responsibilities mutually due are clearly understood. And there is another though a much inferior motive. The attacks which have been made upon us have created the impression not only in England, Ireland and Scotland, but in the United States, and in other parts of the world, that these Provinces are in a naturally weak and feeble state—that they are, in point of fact, almost indefensible. Such an impression interferes more than any one can estimate with the permanent prosperity of our country; it stops immigration to our shores, it depreciates our public securities, and prevents the investment of capital in new enterprises, however productive they may be. If, then, we would do away with this false impression, so unjustly created, and place ourselves on a firm and secure footing in the eyes of the world, our course must be to put our country in such a position of defence that we may fearlessly look our enemies in the face. (Cheers.) Holding these views, and knowing that they are the views of the great mass of the people of this country, it is a pleasure for me to be able to state, and I am sure it will be a pleasure to all present to be informed, that the Conference at Quebec did not separate before entering into a pledge to put the military and naval defences of the United Provinces in the most complete and satisfactory position. (Cheers.) Nor let me omit to say, that in coming to this decision, there is no Minister of the Crown sitting at these tables who would not be prepared to rise now and express his conviction, that notwithstanding all that has come and gone—notwithstanding all the diatribes of the newspaper press of England, the British Government is prepared now as ever to do its duty by these colonies, and to send us their armies and their navy at any moment to aid us in our defence. (Cheers.)

Mr. Mayor, I now approach a rather delicate question—delicate, that is to say, as regards the people of the West. We have agreed—I announce it frankly—to build the Intercolonial Railway. (Cheers and laughter.) I have not been in favor of that scheme *per se*, situated as we have been. But I have at the same time been quite willing to admit—and I repeat it heartily to-day—that without the Intercolonial Railway there could be no union of these Provinces—(cheers)—and after a careful consideration of the question in all its bearings, and after counting the full cost, I am prepared to advocate the building of that road, in order to accomplish the great objects we have in view in the scheme of Confederation. (Cheers.) It may, however, be some comfort for my friends to know that we have a prospect of getting the road built upon terms much more reasonable than we had ever hoped to obtain. I shall not tell you of the tempting offers that have been made, because I have had some experience that what is promised in such offers is not always realized in the end. (Laughter.) In agreeing to build the Intercolonial Railway, it should also be stated that due regard was had to the interests of the West. I am happy to be able to say that with the unanimous consent of the members of the Conference, we have resolved on the extension of our canal system. (Cheers.) Still further, I think it well to state that while we have sought Confederation with Nova Scotia, New Brunswick, Newfoundland, and Prince Edward Island, we have not been neglectful of the

Far West, but we have made it a condition of Union that the great North-west may come into the Federation on equitable terms at any time it pleases, and that British Columbia and Vancouver Island may also be incorporated with us. (Hear, hear.) We have likewise made it a condition that so soon as the state of the finances will permit communication is to be opened up from Western Canada to the North-west territory. (Hear, hear.)

There is another little announcement which will not be without its interest to you, Mr. Mayor. The decision was unanimously arrived at by the delegates that the old and respectable city of Toronto should be the future capital of the Province of Upper Canada. (Cheers.) On the whole, Sir, when we look at the probable results of this Union, I think there is no man, from one end of the Provinces to the other, who ought not to give it his most hearty approbation. (Cheers.) But I would repeat what has been so well said by Mr. McCully, that there is one danger we have yet to fear. Let not gentlemen think we are past all danger. We have still to meet the Legislatures of the different Provinces; we have to encounter the prejudices of the people of the different Provinces; and it requires the greatest harmony of action in order to obtain a favorable result. (Hear, hear.) Therefore I would say with my hon. friend, Mr. McCully, if there is one thing more than another necessary at this moment, it is that we should banish our party discords—that we should forget for the moment that we were at one time arrayed against each other; and whatever we may do after union is accomplished, let us forget until it is obtained our feuds and differences, in securing to the country the great boon which this Confederation promises to bring about. (Cheers.) Looking at the scheme in its entirety, I cannot help feeling this, in replying to the toast you have so kindly received, that if the present Administration shall succeed in completing the great work it has begun, and of bringing into operation the political system which has been foreshadowed, under the protecting rule of the mother country, we shall all have great reason to rejoice that we had the honor of being at such a time the advisers of the Crown. [Mr. Brown resumed his seat amidst loud and long continued cheering.]

Hon. A. T. GALT, on rising, was received with loud cheers. He said—Certainly the kindness with which he had been received was quite overpowering. He had not the same claims on their consideration as his respected friend and colleague, Mr. Brown, who had addressed them in his usual and forcible way. He might be said to represent in a certain degree another portion of Canada, and in that light it was exceedingly gratifying to him to be welcomed, because though this measure of Union was, as far as Upper and Lower Canada were concerned, a measure of disunion, he trusted that the good feeling which had actuated us in the past would be carried forward into the future; and that while we might have left local matters to local legislatures, we still might feel with regard to the great common interests of all that we were a united people, that it was not Canada which was to be divided but British North America which was to become united. (Cheers.) He felt, perhaps, more than any other person present, that from other lips than his own should have come the explanations with regard to Lower Canada. He would take this opportunity of saying that there was no man in the whole length and breadth of British North America who had shown a greater degree of self-sacrifice than his friend Mr. Cartier. That gentleman had shown a degree of statesmanship, a degree of self-sacrifice, which would, he [Mr. Galt] thought, hand down his name into the future with honor equal to that of his illustrious progenitor, Jacques Cartier; that while the one was known as the discoverer of Canada, the other will be known as the one who felt that the interests of all were common, and recognized the fact. There was no doubt, so far as Lower Canada was concerned, that a good deal of feeling existed with regard to the protection of their local interests, but he thought the audience by this time understood that while provision had been made in the new constitution for the protection of those interests, they would all have desired to effect a legislative union had it been possible. They would have desired to see a central government extending its ægis over all interests. But there were difficulties which rendered this impossible, and in meeting these difficulties he trusted that the measure which would be submitted to the people, to the

Imperial Parliament, and to the Provincial Parliaments, would be found to be one which protected local interests, while national interests had been reserved for one central power, which he hoped would manage them in a way to do honor to the race from which we had sprung. (Cheers.) He would have liked, had time permitted, to say a few words with reference to those subjects to which Mr. Brown had alluded, but really he went into the matter so fully that he (Mr. Galt) felt that he would be trespassing on the patience of the audience should he venture to say more than a few words in expressing his own gratitude for the way in which they had drank the toast of the Administration. He fully endorsed the words of Mr. Brown, that the announcements made here to-night quite justified the coalition which had been effected. He thought when they were able to present a constitution—not a small affair for the settlement of local difficulties, but a project for the union with communities of the wealth, resources and intelligence of the Lower Provinces, that they would be acquitted in the sight of all of anything they had done with regard to the formation of the Government. (Cheers.) He was glad to have heard Mr. Brown say that the Intercolonial Railway ought to be built, because it was an announcement which, coupled with other explanations, he trusted would give them the support of the people of Canada in regard to the future measures which might flow from this. It meant not merely connection with the mother country—the measure went hand in hand with the opening up of the North-west Territory, and the one and the other were equally admitted to be the policy of the Confederate Government. He was glad we had a policy, glad that we were growing out of the littleness of colonial politics, and that we were preparing for the responsibilities which would fall upon us, whether welcome or not—the responsibilities of a national existence. He concurred with every word Mr. Brown had said with reference to the mother country. He believed that the people of Canada were prepared to do their duty, and if he did not believe it this would be the last moment he (Mr. Galt) would venture to say that he represented them. No one who desired to do his duty could fail to recognize the fact that we were in the presence of a great power, and that we ought to unite our resources and be prepared for whatever there might be in the future in store for us. And he welcomed the declarations made by the Governments of the different Provinces, as showing their willingness to do their part in the common cause. It was cerrtainly a most remarkable circumstance that upon this occasion they had seen the Provinces of New Brunswick and Nova Scotia entrusting the advocacy of this great measure to the leaders of the Opposition. What might we not hope when personal ambition was thus laid aside, when all were ready thus to sacrifice to the common good. (Loud applause.)

The health of the Mayor having then been proposed and duly acknowledged by His Worship, three cheers were given for the Queen, and the company dispersed.

INSPECTION OF THE VOLUNTEERS.

On the evening of the 3rd of November, shortly after seven o'clock, there was a very large assemblage of the Toronto Volunteers in their new Drill Shed in that city. They assembled in honor of the Delegates, and were inspected by Mayor General Napier, K.C.B, then in Toronto. The building was brilliantly illuminated, and otherwise was well prepared for the reception of the visitors. There were, it was supposed, fully five thousand persons present on this occasion. The General and the Delegates entered the building about half-past seven o'clock, and having taken their seats on the dais erected for their accommodation, the Volunteers were commanded to "fall in," which they did in excellent military style. General Napier, accompanied by his aides-de-camp, Captain Hall and Mr. Bell, also by the Commandant, Col. G. T. Denison, Brigade Majors Denison and Dennis—marched round the force and minutely inspected the men. This duty being performed, the inspecting party returned, when the Brigade formed into open column in front, and marched past the saluting point. The Bands of the "Queen's Own" and "10th Royals" played spirit-stirring airs during the inspection; and when the order was given for the officers and colours to "come to the front to salute the General," which was done, that gallant officer expressed his great pleasure at the military appearance of the Volunteers there assembled, and at the efficient manner in which they had gone through the various evolutions in so confined a space. He said he should have liked to have inspected them in the open plains and in broad daylight, where he was sure they would have given him great satisfaction. He thanked them for their attendance, and as it was getting late he would not detain them longer, but would entrust the commanding officers to express to their men his satisfaction at their appearance.

COLONEL GRAY, Chairman of the Convention of Maritime Delegates, having expressed a wish to address a few words to the Volunteers, they were drawn up in close order, forming three sides of a square, with the General and party in the centre.

COLONEL GRAY said that, on behalf of his colleagues the Delegates, he had been desired to address a few words to them, and in doing so he must express his great pleasure at witnessing them at drill to-night. It was, he said, very common for people to decry the volunteer movement, and even the fair sex were accustomed to look down upon the volunteers, when comparing them with their more favored brethren of the regular army; but he (Col. Gray) was a volunteer, and he did not think that those who decried the volunteers were serious in thus throwing cold water upon the movement. He was convinced that the volunteers were as much to be praised and encouraged as the members of the Royal Service. He himself had at one time belonged to that service, and he never looked slightingly upon the volunteer movement. He had mingled as a civilian a great deal with the soldiers of the Royal army, and he was happy to say that no feeling of animosity or slight was entertained by them towards the volunteers. A short time since, when there was an appearance that the services of the volunteers would have been required to assist the regulars, he was proud to learn that the volunteers of Canada sprung at once to arms to defend their hearths and homes from the attacks of the invader. (Cheers.) He did not believe that any one from his heart slighted the volunteer movement, but the cry was got up by the faint-hearted and craven to cover the disgrace of their remaining in the rear whilst their more manly companions went to the front. (Cheers.) Who is at present in command of the volunteer force in England? He was a man who had nobly fought in many a field of battle, and was son-in-law to an officer—he was going to say next only to Wellington, but he was equal to that able commander. He alluded to Col. McMurdo, son-in-law of Sir Charles Napier, who had been placed in command of the volunteer force of England, and who had ere this proved that he could command and was not afraid to lead anywhere. This noble officer had now command of 170,000 volunteers, as fine soldiers as could be wished. He (Col. Gray) was not in the habit of speaking praise to the face of any one, but he could not let this opportunity pass without saying a few words about the able General now present. He was himself an old comrade of the General's, and he knew what stuff he was made of. He could assure the volunteers that if there had been any invasion or attempted invasion of the Canadian soil, General Napier—a name at which the enemies of England grow pale—would not have been satisfied to wait until the enemy had invaded our territory; he would have met them on the borders, and side by side with their brothers in arms, would have led the volunteers where imperishable honors would have awaited them. They might rest assured they had the right kind of leader should the day of trial come. Colonel Gray related a circumstance of which he was cognizant during the time he was serving in the same force with the General. A small party of Dragoons, about 80 or 90 men, with two or three companies of mounted Riflemen under General Napier, when on outpost duty, received intelligence that a strong body of the enemy, including 700 picked warriors, were crossing a plain close at hand—

was just at the dawn of day both parties were surprised. Was there any hesitation there, notwithstanding the odds ? No! In one moment "Forward" was the word, and onward they went. The result of the day's work was seen the following day when the Commander-in-Chief rode over the field, and members of his staff counted some four hundred and fifty bodies of the slain. He alluded to the Maritime Provinces, shewing what a powerful force could be found there ready to co-operate in the defence of their territories were the Militia properly armed and organized. In one Province they could muster 50,000, in another 30,000, in a third 10,000, and what a good right or left would they not form with the aid of Upper and Lower Canada? He assured the Volunteers of Toronto that they had men of the right stamp in the Maritime Provinces. He would only mention four of the sons of Nova Scotia, Williams, Inglis, Welsford and Parker, to shew them the sort of men of which these Provinces could fairly boast, and to whom could be entrusted the sacred duty of protecting the soil on which they stood as freemen proud of their birthright. (Cheers.)

Colonel GRAY next addressed a few words to the "Naval Brigade," and said there were thirty thousand hardy fellows in Newfoundland alone well worthy of the name of the first seamen in the world, and who would be proud to give the right hand of fellowship side by side with the Naval Brigade of Toronto. He concluded by hoping that one and all would ever press forward and assist each other as brothers, in the name of "our revered and glorious Queen," and do all that was possible to maintain that Kingdom to which we owed allegiance. (Loud cheers.)

Three cheers were then given for the Queen; the bands struck up the "National Anthem;" three cheers for the General and the Delegates, when the proceedings broke up.

THE PUBLIC BALL.

A Public Ball, unsurpassed for magnificence only by that which was given in honor of the visit of the Prince of Wales, closed, on the same night as that on which the

Volunteer Review took place, the festivities of the grand reception given to the Delegates from the Maritime Provinces by the people of Toronto. The Ball was held in the same place in which the *Dejeuner* was given; and it is needless to add, that it was as brilliant an entertainment as the wealth, beauty, fashion, and high social and public positions of the people of the great cities of Western Canada could possibly make it; and indeed all the cities, great and small, of this section of the Province seemed to be fully represented at this pleasant *re-union*.

DEPARTURE FROM TORONTO.

RECEPTION OF THE DELEGATES AT HAMILTON, ST. CATHERINE'S AND CLIFTON, AND VISIT TO NIAGARA FALLS.

The Manager of the Great Western Railway, Mr. SWINYARD, having kindly placed a special train at the disposal of the Delegation party, they left Toronto on the forenoon of the 4th November for an excursion to Niagara Falls. The General Manager of the Great Western, the Hon. Mr. McMaster, Chairman of the Company, and several distinguished persons, accompanied the party. A splendid run of a little less than an hour brought the party to the Hamilton Station, where the Mayor and members of the Corporation of the City, besides many leading citizens of Hamilton, were in waiting to welcome the Delegates. The Station was very tastefully decorated with evergreens and flags, and the inner apartment was amply provided with refreshments. The Mayor read an address of welcome, in which the mission of the Delegates was warmly eulogised.

The Hon. Mr. TILLEY, of New Brunswick, responded to the address. He said he was rejoiced to know that the people of Hamilton cordially endorsed the principles of the late Conference, and this sentiment he found to increase on proceeding westward from Lower Canada. The questions involved were of a grave and important nature, involving important advantages to the Lower Provinces, and he trusted the labors of the Conference would prove acceptable to all. The future was fraught with greatness and prosperity, such as these Provinces had never before seen. A closer union was necessary to the welfare of each and all the British North American Provinces. He expressed the thanks of the Delegates for the hearty response of Hamilton to the purposes of the Conference, for the present greeting, and their regret that it should be found necessary to omit from the list of formal visits one of the most beautiful cities of the West.

Hon. ISAAC BUCHANAN, President of the Hamilton Board of Trade, then presented an address on behalf of its members. He said, that in the contemplated Confederation great benefits were anticipated for Hamilton in a commercial point, the probabilities of a large trade being speedily opened with the Lower Provinces, and direct water communication with the sea-board. Our city enjoyed commercial advantages unsurpassed in its magnificent harbor, while the Great Western Railway provided an open way to the teeming west, with branches in all directions. It was hoped that the labors of so many eminent statesmen would ensure great blessings.

Hon. Mr. SHEA, of Newfoundland, replied in a brief address. The question of the defences had been previously alluded to, and the hon. gentleman believed that the Delegates would be obliged to adopt some system of defence, unless their visit to the Upper Provinces was speedily brought to a close. (Great laughter.) The Delegates had been charmed with this section of the country, and pleased with the characteristics of its people. There were striking evidences of the elements of wealth and commercial greatness, and direct communication with the ocean was the great requirement; therein lay mutual benefits to the Upper and Lower Provinces. He believed that on the establishment of the Confederation speedy measures would ensure the completion of the great public works in view.

Hamilton and neighboring places would shortly become seaports. Mr. Shea concluded by returning thanks for the greeting of the citizens of Hamilton, and he trusted that all her hopes of the benefits of Confederation would be realized.

Mayor McElroy proposed the health of Her Majesty the Queen, which was drunk with loud cheers, and "God save the Queen," was played by the band.

At St. Catherine's Station, which was also very tastefully decorated, the Delegates were welcomed by the leading members of this small but interesting community, and an address of welcome, similar in tone and spirit to that of the Hamilton address, was read by W. McGiverin, Esq., M.P.P. for Lincoln County.

After reading the address Mr. McGiverin said he regretted to state that time and circumstances had prevented the town and district of St. Catherine's from making that display which they would like, in order to show their appreciation of the question which the gentlemen from the Lower Provinces, with our Government, had been considering. But the time of the Delegates, he knew, was short, and he must, therefore, accept that as an excuse. He regretted that the Mayor was unavoidably absent, in court, at Niagara, with several of their leading townsmen, who would have been delighted to have made the acquaintance of the Delegates. He begged to convey to the Delegates the congratulations of the municipality upon the harmony which had characterized their deliberations at Quebec, and the result they have arrived at respecting one of the most important questions which had ever been discussed on this side of the Atlantic. He tendered his hearty congratulations to them at the manner in which that result had been arrived at, believing, as he did, that the successful accomplishment of the scheme would place the United Provinces in a position of prosperity that they could never otherwise hope for. He regretted that their short stay would not enable them to view one of the prettiest towns in this Province, nor that great work, the Welland Canal, (cheers,) connecting the

Western lakes with the sea, by an enlargement of which the ships of the Lower Provinces would have free access to the extreme western boundary of Canada, and be the source of further extending and enlarging the prosperity of the United Empire, even beyond their most sanguine wishes. On the part of the municipality and citizens of St. Catherine's he begged to tender the Delegates a hearty welcome, and their best wishes for the consummation of the project in hand, and hoped they might have a pleasant journey home.

Hon. Mr. POPE, of P. E. Island, who was received with much applause, said he had been deputed to return thanks on behalf of the Delegates from the Lower Provinces, for the kind manner in which they had been received, and the very hearty welcome they had met with. The circumstances under which the Convention had assembled at Quebec — the great subject of a Confederation of the British North American Provinces which had engaged their attention, and the arguments in support of the conclusions at which the Delegates had arrived, had all been very fully stated and discussed in speeches recently delivered by the able statesmen of Canada and of the other Provinces. Thanks to the noble press of Canada, those speeches had been placed in the hands of the people throughout the country almost as soon as delivered; and had been read simultaneously in Quebec and in Sarnia. It was, therefore, not his intention to attempt a recapitulation of them. He stated that the Maritime Provinces had sent their Representatives to the Convention at the request of Canada. The people of the Maritime Provinces do not seek, by entering the Confederation, to lighten their own burdens by placing a portion of them upon the people of Canada. A scale of taxation lower than that existing in Canada supplied a revenue equal to their necessities. But he believed the people of the Maritime Provinces desired those advantages which result from Union. Many among them are the descendants of American Loyalists, and are acquainted to some extent with the progress made by the old Colonies on this continent. At the time when their grandfathers were born, the British Colonies in America were insignificant; their commerce was utterly unknown. When they left the country its export trade was greater than was that of England when they were born, in the days of Queen Ann. It should not be forgotten that the men, to whom I allude, left that country and the homes in which their children were born, and emigrated to the ports of the Lower Provinces, because they desired to live under Monarchial Institutions and the protection of the flag of old England. The hon. gentleman then referred to the great trade of the British Provinces before the separation from the mother country, and contrasted the different circumstances under which the Convention just concluded at Quebec had pursued their labors with those under which the British Provinces, which formed the nucleus of the great neighbouring Republic, discussed Confederation.

The hon. gentleman's speech was frequently cheered, and at its conclusion three hearty cheers were given for the Delegates.

After the interchange of other courtesies, the train moved off, and the party again delayed at the Clifton Station, which was decorated in a style similar to that of the others. Mr. Swinyard had here prepared a sumptuous dinner for his guests, at which speech-making was indulged as far as time permitted.

The Hon. Mr. DICKEY, of Nova Scotia, proposed the health of the General Manager of the Great Western. In the course of his brief but eloquent remarks, he said, (speaking for the Delegates)—Everywhere they had been most hospitably received, which they thought, had culminated in the noble reception they had yesterday met with at Toronto. The regret they felt at leaving that city had, however, been very greatly lessened by the kind arrangements for their comfort and accommodation which they had that day experienced at the hands of Mr. Swinyard and the Great Western Railway. He felt that since they had entered the Province of Canada the Managers of Railways had contributed in a very great degree to their pleasure, comfort and accommodation. He heartily thanked Mr. Swinyard for the kindness and forethought which had dictated the placing of a special train at the disposal of the Delegates and the ladies of their party to visit the Niagara Falls, a sight of which they would doubtless suppose would not be the faintest remembrance they would carry away with them of their visit. They had been delighted with all that they had witnessed, and their only regret was that time would not permit of a closer acquaintance with the cities of this part of the Province and the beauties of the country.

Mr. SWINYARD, on rising to respond, was received with loud cheers. He said he was truly obliged to them for the kindness they had shown in drinking to his health, and the hearty manner in which that toast had been received, for the little service the Company had been able to render to them in enabling them to visit the great wonder of the world, the Niagara Falls. He was in hopes that they would have been able to pass with him over the whole of the Great Western line, as well as the railways of their neighbours, the Michigan Central or the Detroit and Milwaukie, in order to have seen the great signs of prosperity evident everywhere in this vast western country. He assured them that they would have been greatly delighted with such a trip, but as their time would not permit of it, the people would gladly excuse them. In seeing Toronto and Hamilton he said they had only seen the results of the products and industry of Western Canada. These places have been raised to the importance they have now attained, not as they might suppose by a small section of country immediately surrounding them, but by a vast and expansive territory beyond them, extending back to the Detroit river. They would have seen that these two cities are only the emporiums of the great Peninsula of Western Canada, which had made and is now making the most rapid strides in commercial prosperity. He knew that it would not then become him to detain them with any lengthy remarks, as their anxiety was no doubt to visit the Falls. He would only say that the object for which the Conference had met seemed to be heartily and unanimously approved by the people and press of this section of Canada, and he hoped that their labours to promote a union, which should make each and all the Provinces an integral portion of one great country—all bound together by ties of commercial and personal relationship—would be crowned with success.

The Delegation party, having been provided with carriages, then visited the Falls; and although the rain fell heavily, they spent several hours in wandering about the grounds of Mr. Street, a gentleman of large property and high standing in that section of the country, and from which they had a splendid view of the Falls in all their dread magnificence.

At nearly night-fall the party returned to the Railway Station, where a few of them separated from the main body, taking their departure homeward *via* the United States. The others reached Toronto the same evening in perfect safety.

On the evening of the 5th November the Delegation party left Toronto for Montreal in a special train of the Grand Trunk Railway, again obligingly provided by Mr. Brydges, the Managing Director; and they arrived at Montreal on the following morning at 10 o'clock.

An informal meeting of all the Delegates then in Montreal was held at the St. Lawrence Hall, where the Minutes and Resolutions of the Quebec Conference were, for the last time, carefully read over; and the parchment copy of the Resolutions was afterwards signed by all the Delegates present.

The party left Montreal on the same evening, on their return to their several homes in the Eastern Provinces.

Nothing more remains for the Compiler of these unpretending pages than to introduce the Report of the Quebec Conference, which was the result of the deliberations so frequently referred to herein, and whose outlines were dimly shadowed forth in several of the speeches delivered on important public occasions after the Conference had brought its labors to a close. The Report has been extensively published throughout the British Provinces, and every intelligent person is, no doubt, familiar with its details; but the Compiler feels that this little work would be unpardonably imperfect if it did not contain a copy of it. The Report of the Convention, in all its features, may not just now be deemed practicable as the basis of a constitution for a Confederacy of the British American Provinces, as a whole—owing to sectional differences which are at present apparently irreconcilable; but as the fruit of long and patient deliberation, it may, in many points, be taken as a guide for future and more successful statesmanship.

The festivities which the Canadian people so lavishly poured upon the Delegates, and the offer of which it was found necessary to decline more frequently than to accept—were not allowed to interefere with the business of the Conference, when, preliminary matters being adjusted, the details of the proposed constitution commenced to develope themselves. Early and late hours were devoted to their discussion and consideration; and if the work of the Quebec Conference Chamber is not perfect—(what human work ever was?)—it will not be, however, without its advantages, inasmuch as it may serve to throw some light on the path of more skilful and sagacious adventurers, who—fearless of prejudice and suspicion—may be required to moil through the dark labyrinths of that most perplexing of all sciences—the framing of a Nation's Constitution.

APPENDIX.

REPORT

Of Resolutions adopted at a Conference of Delegates from the Provinces of Canada, Nova Scotia and New Brunswick, and the Colonies of Newfoundland and Prince Edward Island, held at the City of Quebec, 10th October, 1864, as the Basis of a proposed Confederation of those Provinces and Colonies.

1. The best interests and present and future prosperity of British North America will be promoted by a Federal Union under the Crown of Great Britain, provided such Union can be effected on principles just to the several Provinces.

2. In the Federation of the British North American Provinces the system of Government best adapted under existing circumstances to protect the diversified interests of the several Provinces and secure efficiency, harmony and permanency in the working of the Union, would be a general Government charged with matters of common interest to the whole Country, and Local Governments for each of the Canadas and for the Provinces of Nova Scotia, New Brunswick and Prince Edward Island, charged with the control of local matters in their respective sections—provision being made for the admission into the Union on equitable terms of Newfoundland, the North-West Territory, British Columbia and Vancouver.

3. In framing a Constitution for the General Government, the Conference, with a view to the perpetuation of our connection with the Mother Country, and to the promotion of the best interests of the people of these Provinces, desire to follow the model of the British Constitution, so far as our circumstances will permit.

4. The Executive Authority or Government shall be vested in the Sovereign of the United Kingdom of Great Britain and Ireland, and be administered according to the

well understood principles of the Britisł
the Sovereign personally, or by the Rep
Sovereign duly authorized.

5. The Sovereign or Representative
shall be Commander in Chief of the
Militia Forces.

6. There shall be a General Legislat
for the Federated Provinces, composed
Council and a House of Commons.

7. For the purpose of forming the L
the Federated Provinces shall be cons
ing of three divisions, 1st. Upper Can
Canada; 3rd. Nova Scotia, New Brun
Edward Island, each division with an eq
in the Legislative Council.

8. Upper Canada shall be represented
Council by 24 Members, Lower Canada
and the three Maritime Provinces by 24 N
Nova Scotia shall have Ten, New Bru
Prince Edward Island, Four Members.

9. The Colony of Newfoundland sha
enter the proposed Union with a repr
Legislative Council of Four Members.

10. The North-West Territory, Briti
Vancouver shall be admitted into the
terms and conditions as the Parliament
Provinces shall deem equitable, and as
assent of Her Majesty; and in the case o
British Columbia or Vancouver, as shall
the Legislature of such Province.

11. The Members of the Legislative
appointed by the Crown under the G
General Government, and shall hold C
If any Legislative Councillor shall, for
sessions of Parliament, fail to give his
said Council, his seat shall thereby becor

12. The Members of the Legislative
British Subjects by Birth or Naturalizati
of Thirty years, shall possess a continue
qualification of four thousand dollars o
incumbrances, and shall be and continue
over and above their debts and liabiliti

APPENDIX. 221

Newfoundland and Prince Edward Island the property *N-d and P.E.I. real* may be either real or personal.

13. If any question shall arise as to the qualification of a *personal qualifica* Legislative Councillor the same shall be determined by the Council.

14. The first selection of the Members of the Legislative Council shall be made, except as regards Prince Edward Island, from the Legislative Councils of the various Provinces, so far as a sufficient number be found qualified and willing to serve; such Members shall be appointed by the *first selection of L.* Crown at the recommendation of the General Executive Government, upon the nomination of the respective Local Governments; and in such nomination due regard shall be had to the claims of the Members of the Legislative Council of the Opposition in each Province, so that all political parties may as nearly as possible be fairly represented.

15. The Speaker of the Legislative Council (unless *Speaker* otherwise provided by Parliament,) shall be appointed by *app? by* the Crown from among the members of the Legislative *Crown.* Council; and shall hold office during pleasure; and shall only be entitled to a casting vote on an equality of votes.

16. Each of the twenty-four Legislative Councillors representing Lower Canada in the Legislative Council of the General Legislature shall be appointed to represent one of the twenty-four Electoral Divisions mentioned in Schedule A of Chapter first of the Consolidated Statutes of Canada, and such Councillor shall reside or possess his qualification in the Division he is appointed to represent.

17. The basis of Representation in the House of Com- *Representa-* mons shall be population, as determined by the Official *tion is* Census every ten years; and the number of Members at *H. Commons* first shall be 194, distributed as folllows: *to be by popu: =lation. 194 in all*

Upper Canada	82
Lower Canada	65
Nova Scotia	19
New Brunswick	15
Newfoundland	8
and Prince Edward Island	5

18. Until the Official Census of 1871 has been made up

there shall be no change in the number of Representatives from the several sections.

19. Immediately after the completion of the Census of 1871, and immediately after every Decennial Census thereafter, the Representation from each section in the House of Commons shall be re-adjusted on the basis of population.

20. For the purpose of such re-adjustments, Lower Canada shall always be assigned sixty-five members, and each of the other sections shall at each re-adjustment receive, for the ten years then next succeeding, the number of members to which it will be entitled on the same ratio of representation to population as Lower Canada will enjoy according to the Census last taken by having sixty-five members.

21. No reduction shall be made in the number of Members returned by any section, unless its population shall have decreased relatively to the population of the whole Union, to the extent of five per centum.

22. In computing at each decennial period the num- of Members to which each section is entitled, no fractional parts shall be considered, unless when exceeding one half the number entitling to a Member, in which case a Member shall be given for each such fractional part.

23. The Legislature of each Province shall divide such Province into the proper number of constituencies, and define the boundaries of each of them.

24. The Local Legislature of each Province may, from time to time, alter the Electoral Districts for the purposes of Representation in such local Legislature, and distribute the representatives to which the Province is entitled in any manner such Legislature may think fit.

25. The number of Members may at any time be increased by the General Parliament—regard being had to the proportionate rights then existing.

26. Until provisions are made by the General Parliament, all the Laws which, at the date of the Proclamation constituting the Union, are in force in the Provinces respectively, relating to the qualification and disqualification of any person to be elected or to sit or vote as a member of the Assembly in the said Provinces respectively —and relating to the qualification or disqualification of

voters, and to the oaths to be taken by voters, and to Returning Officers and their powers and duties,—and relating to the proceedings at Elections,—and to the period during which such Elections may be continued,—and relating to the trial of Controverted Elections,—and the proceedings incident thereto,—and relating to the vacating of seats of Members, and to the issuing and execution of new Writs in case of any seat being vacated otherwise than by a dissolution,—shall respectively apply to Elections of Members to serve in the House of Commons for places situate in those Provinces respectively.

27. Every House of Commons shall continue for five years from the day of the return of the Writs choosing the same, and no longer, subject, nevertheless, to be sooner prorogued or dissolved by the Governor.

28. There shall be a Session of the General Parliament once at least in every year, so that a period of twelve calendar months shall not intervene between the last sitting of the General Parliament in one Session and the first sitting thereof in the next session.

29. The General Parliament shall have power to make Laws for the peace, welfare and good Government of the Federated Provinces (saving the Sovereignty of England), and especially Laws respecting the following subjects:—

1. The Public Debt and Property.
2. The Regulation of Trade and Commerce.
3. The imposition or regulation of Duties of Customs on Imports and Exports, except on Exports of Timber, Logs, Masts, Spars, Deals, and Sawn Lumber, and of Coal and other Minerals.
4. The imposition or regulation of Excise Duties.
5. The raising of money by all or any other modes or systems of Taxation.
6. The borrowing of Money on the Public Credit.
7. Postal Service.
8. Lines of Steam or other Ships, Railways, Canals, and other works, connecting any two or more of the Provinces together, or extending beyond the limits of any Province.
9. Lines of Steamships between the Federated Provinces and Countries.

10. Telegraphic Communication, and the incorporation of Telegraphic Companies.
11. All such works as shall, although lying wholly within any Province, be specially declared by the Acts authorizing them to be for the general advantage.
12. The Census.
13. Militia—Military and Naval Service and Defence.
14. Beacons, Buoys and Light Houses.
15. Navigation and Shipping.
16. Quarantine.
17. Sea Coast and Inland Fisheries.
18. Ferries between any Province and a Foreign Country, or between any two Provinces.
19. Currency and Coinage.
20. Banking, Incorporation of Banks, and the issue of paper money.
21. Savings Banks.
22. Weights and Measures.
23. Bills of Exchange and Promissory Notes.
24. Interest.
25. Legal Tender.
26. Bankruptcy and Insolvency.
27. Patents of Invention and Discovery.
28. Copy Rights.
29. Indians and Lands reserved for the Indians.
30. Naturalization and Aliens.
31. Marriage and Divorce.
32. The Criminal Law, excepting the Constitution of the Courts of Criminal Jurisdiction, but including the procedure in criminal matters.
33. Rendering uniform all or any of the laws relative to property and civil rights in Upper Canada, Nova Scotia, New Brunswick, Newfoundland and Prince Edward Island, and rendering uniform the procedure of all or any of the Courts in these Provinces; but any Statute for this purpose shall have no force or authority in any Province until sanctioned by the Legislature thereof.
34. The Establishment of a General Court of Appeal for the Federated Provinces.

35. Immigration.
36. Agriculture.
37. And generally respecting all matters of a general character, not specially and exclusively reserved for the Local Governments and Legislatures.

30. The General Government and Parliament shall have all powers necessary or proper for performing the obligations of the Federated Provinces, as part of the British Empire, to Foreign Countries, arising under Treaties between Great Britain and such Countries.

31. The General Parliament may also, from time to time, establish additional Courts, and the General Government may appoint Judges and Officers thereof, when the same shall appear necessary, or for the public advantage, in order to the due execution of the laws of Parliament.

32. All Courts, Judges and Officers of the several Provinces shall aid, assist and obey the General Government in the exercise of its rights and powers, and for such purposes shall be held to be Courts, Judges and Officers of the General Government.

33. The General Government shall appoint and pay the Judges of the Superior Courts in each Province, and of the County Courts of Upper Canada, and Parliament shall fix their salaries.

34. Until the Consolidation of the Laws of Upper Canada, New Brunswick, Nova Scotia, Newfoundland and Prince Edward Island, the Judges of these Provinces appointed by the General Government shall be selected from their respective Bars.

35. The Judges of the Courts of Lower Canada shall be selected from the Bar of Lower Canada.

36. The Judges of the Court of Admiralty now receiving salaries shall be paid by the General Government.

37. The Judges of the Superior Courts shall hold their offices during good behaviour, and shall be removable only on the Address of both Houses of Parliament.

LOCAL GOVERNMENT.

38. For each of the Provinces there shall be an Executive Officer, styled the Lieutenant Governor, who shall be appointed by the Governor General in Council, under the Great Seal of the Federated Provinces, during pleasure;

226　APPENDIX.

such pleasure not to be exercised before the expiration of the first five years, except for cause: such cause to be communicated in writing to the Lieutenant Governor immediately after the exercise of the pleasure as aforesaid, and also by message to both Houses of Parliament, within the first week of the first Session afterwards.

39. The Lieutenant Governor of each Province shall be paid by the General Government.

40. In undertaking to pay the salaries of the Lieutenant Governors, the Conference does not desire to prejudice the claim of Prince Edward Island upon the Imperial Government for the amount now paid for the salary of the Lieutenant Governor thereof.

41. The Local Government and Legislature of each Province shall be constructed in such manner as the existing Legislature of such Province shall provide.

42. The Local Legislatures shall have power to alter or amend their constitution from time to time.

43. The Local Legislatures shall have power to make Laws respecting the following subjects:

1. Direct Taxation and the imposition of Duties on the export of Timber, Logs, Masts, Spars, Deals and Sawn Lumber, and of Coals and other Minerals.
2. Borrowing Money on the credit of the Province.
3. The establishment and tenure of local Offices, and the appointment and payment of local Officers.
4. Agriculture.
5. Immigration.
6. Education; saving the rights and privileges which the Protestant or Catholic minority in both Canadas may possess as to their Denominational Schools, at the time when the Union goes into operation.
7. The sale and management of Public Lands, excepting Lands belonging to the General Government.
8. Sea coast and Inland Fisheries.
9. The establishment, maintenance and management of Penitentiaries, and of Public and Reformatory Prisons.

10. The establishment, maintenance and management of Hospitals, Asylums, Charities and Eleemosynary Institutions.
11. Municipal Institutions.
12. Shop, Saloon, Tavern, Auctioneer and other Licenses.
13. Local Works.
14. The Incorporation of private and local Companies, except such as relate to matters assigned to the General Parliament.
15. Property and civil rights, excepting those portions thereof assigned to the General Parliament.
16. Inflicting punishment by fine, penalties, imprisonment, or otherwise for the breach of laws passed in relation to any subject within their jurisdiction.
17. The Administration of Justice, including the Constitution, maintenance and organization of the Courts—both of Civil and Criminal Jurisdiction, and including also the Procedure in Civil Matters.
18. And generally all matters of a private or local nature, not assigned to the General Parliament.

44. The power of respiting, reprieving and pardoning Prisoners convicted of crimes, and of commuting and remitting of sentences, in whole or in part, which belongs of right to the Crown, shall be administered by the Lieutenant Governor of each Province in Council, subject to any instructions he may from time to time receive from the General Government, and subject to any provisions that may be made in this behalf by the General Parliament.

MISCELLANEOUS.

45. In regard to all subjects over which jurisdiction belongs to both the General and Local Legislatures, the laws of the General Parliament shall control and supersede those made by the Local Legislature, and the latter shall be void so far as they are repugnant to, or inconsistent with the former.

APPENDIX.

46. Both the English and French languages may be employed in the General Parliament and in its proceedings, and in the Local Legislature of Lower Canada, and also in the Federal Courts and in the Courts of Lower Canada.

47. No lands or property belonging to the General or Local Government shall be liable to taxation.

48. All Bills for appropriating any part of the Public Revenue, or for imposing any new Tax or Impost, shall originate in the House of Commons, or in the House of Assembly, as the case may be.

49. The House of Commons or House of Assembly shall not originate or pass any Vote, Resolution, Address or Bill, for the appropriation of any part of the Public Revenue, or of any Tax or Impost to any purpose, not first recommended by Message of the Governor General, or the Lieutenant Governor, as the case may be, during the Session in which such Vote, Resolution, Address or Bill is passed.

50. Any Bill of the General Parliament may be reserved in the usual manner for Her Majesty's Assent; and any Bill of the Local Legislatures may in like manner be reserved for the consideration of the Governor General.

51. Any Bill passed by the General Parliament shall be subject to disallowance by Her Majesty within two years, as in the case of Bills passed by the Legislatures of the said Provinces hitherto; and in like manner any Bill passed by a Local Legislature shall be subject to disallowance by the Governor General within one year after the passing thereof.

52. The Seat of Government of the Federated Provinces shall be OTTAWA, subject to the Royal Prerogative.

53. Subject to any future action of the respective Local Governments, the seat of the Local Government in Upper Canada shall be Toronto; of Lower Canada, Quebec; and the Seats of the Local Governments in the other Provinces shall be as at present.

PROPERTY AND LIABILITIES.

54. All Stocks, Cash, Bankers' Balances and Securities for money belonging to each Province, at the time of the Union, except as hereinafter mentioned, shall belong to the General Government.

55. The following Public Works and Property of each Province, shall belong to the General Government—to wit:
1. Canals;
2. Public Harbours;
3. Light Houses and Piers;
4. Steamboats, Dredges and Public Vessels;
5. River and Lake Improvements;
6. Railways and Railway Stocks, Mortgages and other Debts due by Railway Companies;
7. Military Roads;
8. Custom Houses, Post Offices and other Public Buildings, except such as may be set aside by the General Government for the use of the Local Legislatures and Governments;
9. Property transferred by the Imperial Government and known as Ordnance Property;
10. Armories, Drill Sheds, Military Clothing and Munitions of War; and
11. Lands set apart for public purposes.

56. All lands, mines, minerals and royalties vested in Her Majesty in the Provinces of Upper Canada, Lower Canada, New Brunswick and Prince Edward Island, for the use of such Provinces, shall belong to the Local Government of the territory in which the same are so situate; subject to any trusts that may exist in respect to any of such lands, or to any interest of other persons in respect of the same.

57. All sums due from purchasers or lessees of such lands, mines or minerals at the time of the Union, shall also belong to the Local Governments.

58. All assets connected with such portions of the public debt of any Province as are assumed by the Local Governments shall also belong to those Governments respectively.

59. The several Provinces shall retain all other Public Property therein, subject to the right of the General Government to assume any Lands or Public Property required for Fortifications or the Defence of the Country.

60. The General Government shall assume all the Debts and Liabilities of each Province.

61. The Debt of Canada, not specially assumed by

Upper and Lower Canada respectively, shall not exceed at the time of the Union, $62,500,000; Nova Scotia shall enter the Union with a debt not exceeding $8,000,000, and New Brunswick with a debt not exceeding $7,000,000.

62. In case Nova Scotia or New Brunswick do not incur liabilities beyond those for which their Governments are now bound, and which shall make their debts at the date of Union less than $8,000,000 and $7,000,000 respectively, they shall be entitled to interest at five per cent. on the amount not so incurred, in like manner as is hereinafter provided for Newfoundland and Prince Edward Island; the foregoing resolution being in no respect intended to limit the powers given to the respective Governments of those Provinces by Legislative authority, but only to limit the maximum amount of charge to be assumed by the General Government. Provided always that the powers so conferred by the respective Legislatures shall be exercised within five years from this date or the same shall then lapse.

63. Newfoundland and Prince Edward Island, not having incurred debts equal to those of the other Provinces, shall be entitled to receive, by half yearly payments, in advance, from the General Government, the Interest at five per cent. on the difference between the actual amount of their respective Debts at the time of the Union and the average amount of indebtedness per head of the population of Canada, Nova Scotia and New Brunswick.

64. In consideration of the transfer to the General Parliament of the powers of Taxation, an annual grant in aid of each Province shall be made, equal to 80 cents per head of the Population, as established by the Census of 1861. The Population of Newfoundland being estimated at 130,000. Such aid shall be in full settlement of all future demands upon the General Government for local purposes, and shall be paid half-yearly in advance to each Province.

65. The position of New Brunswick being such as to entail large immediate charges upon her local revenues, it is agreed that for the period of ten years from the time when the Union takes effect, an additional allowance of $63,000 per annum shall be made to that Province. But that so long as the liability of that Province remains

under $7,000,000, a deduction equal to the interest on such deficiency shall be made from the $63,000.

66. In consideration of the surrender to the General Government by Newfoundland of all its rights in Mines and Minerals, and of all the ungranted and unoccupied Lands of the Crown, it is agreed that the sum of $150,000 shall each year be paid that Province, by semi-annual payments. Provided that that Colony shall retain the right of opening, constructing and controlling Roads and Bridges through any of the said Lands, subject to any Laws which the General Parliament may pass in respect of the same.

67. All engagements that may, before the Union, be entered into with the Imperial Government for the Defence of the Country, shall be assumed by the General Government.

68. The General Government shall secure, without delay, the completion of the Intercolonial Railway from Riviere-du-Loup through New Brunswick to Truro in Nova Scotia.

69. The communications with the North-Western Territory, and the improvements required for the developement of the Trade of the Great West with the Seaboard, are regarded by this Conference as subjects of the highest importance to the Federated Provinces, and shall be prosecuted at the earliest possible period that the state of the Finances will permit.

70. The sanction of the Imperial and Local Parliaments shall be sought for the Union of the Province, on the principles adopted by the Conference.

71. That Her Majesty the Queen be solicited to determine the rank and name of the Federated Provinces.

72. The proceedings of the Conference shall be authenticated by the signatures of the Delegates, and submitted by each Delegation to its own Government, and the Chairman is authorized to submit a copy to the Governor General for transmission to the Secretary of State for the Colonies.

www.ingramcontent.com/pod-product-compliance
Lightning Source LLC
Chambersburg PA
CBHW021804230426
43669CB00008B/626